THIRD WORLD POLITICS

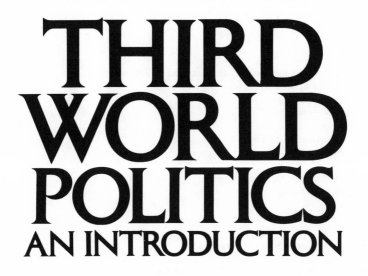

THIRD WORLD POLITICS

AN INTRODUCTION

CHRISTOPHER CLAPHAM

THE UNIVERSITY OF WISCONSIN PRESS

THIRD WORLD POLITICS / Clapham

Published in the United States of American and Canada by
The University of Wisconsin Press
114 North Murray Street
Madison, Wisconsin 53715

Published in Great Britain by
Croom Helm Ltd.

Printings 1985, 1986, 1988

Printed in the United States of America

Library of Congress Cataloging in Publication Data
Clapham, Christopher S.
  Third World politics.
  Includes index.
  1. Developing countries—Politics and government.
1. Title
D883.C48   1985   320.9172'4   84-25637
ISBN 0-299-10330-7
ISBN 0-299-10334-X (pbk.)

CONTENTS

ACKNOWLEDGEMENTS

A book which purports to discuss the politics of half the world asserts a degree of presumption on its author's part which no amount of acknowledgements can ever efface. In writing this book, I have none the less been constantly aware of my debts, first to the peoples of the third world, amongst whom I have enjoyed living, and whose politics, even at their most depressing, I have found fascinating; and secondly to all those scholars whose efforts to understand the subject, whether on a broad scale or through detailed studies, have guided my own. While my most specific obligations are acknowledged in the footnotes, my approach to third world politics has been guided in more general terms by a much wider range of literature, much of which I would be hard-pressed to specify. My own views, equally, have evolved over the last twenty years, in keeping with the subject itself, and will doubtless be seen to reflect the spirit of the particular time at which they have been written down. I have three more specific institutional obligations: to the University of Lancaster, which has paid me; to the Social Science Research Council of the United Kingdom, which has financed most of my visits to different areas of the third world; and to the European Consortium for Political Research, whose workshops provide an un-rivalled setting for the discussion of academic problems in collaboration with like-minded scholars. And lastly my acknowledgements to my two families: to the academic and secretarial staff and students of the Lancaster Politics Department on the one hand; and to Caroline, Phoebe and Tom on the other.

Christopher Clapham
Lancaster

1 POLITICS AND THE THIRD WORLD

Politics everywhere, in its essentials, is much the same. People do not greatly differ. They want security, wealth and the power through which to get them. They have particular interests and ambitions which they try to achieve, and which in some ways conflict, in others coincide, with the interests and ambitions of others. They band together with other people, either as a matter of convenience or as part of more permanent groups to which they acknowledge some kind of loyalty or obligation. Other groups, similarly formed, they regard with indifference, suspicion or downright hostility. And in seeking these interests, and forming these groups, they gain power over others and are subjected to power themselves, either directly through the imposition of physical force, or indirectly through the organisation of their surroundings in ways which reduce, and perhaps almost entirely remove, their capacity for individual choice. Any form of organisation, essential though it may be for the achievement of group and individual goals, and the management of conflict between competing interests, itself produces inequalities of power, and thus further differences of interest between those who have more power and those who have less.

Much of what is described in this book as 'third world' politics will, therefore, be familiar to anyone who is acquainted with the workings of politics in other parts of the globe. What makes the politics of the third world in some measure distinctive is not the nature of the peoples and politicians who take part in it, but the nature of the circumstances in which they find themselves; and even what is unfamiliar may thus for the most part be readily understood by anyone prepared to try to appreciate those circumstances and the kinds of action to which they are likely to lead. These common circumstances, shared in some degree by a very large proportion of the peoples of the world, in turn define what the 'third world' is, and the extent to which it may be taken as a category appropriate to some kind of comparative political analysis.

The phrase 'the third world' is generally taken, and is taken here, to include the Americas south of the United States; the whole of Africa; Asia apart from the Soviet Union, China and Japan; and the oceanic islands apart from Australia and New Zealand. Any book which presumes to distinguish and discuss the politics of this enormous area, encompassing roughly half the peoples in the world and well over half of the independent states, must first make good its implied assumption that this area can be distinguished for political purposes from other parts of the globe, and has some common characteristics which give it some unity. The term itself seems to owe its origins to one of the less useful categorisations of the world's 170-odd states: non-membership either of the 'western' bloc of capitalist, industrial and on the whole liberal democratic states led by the United States, or of the 'eastern' bloc of Marxist-Leninist states led by the Soviet Union. This categorisation does indeed provide a reasonable clustering of the states which this book is about, and has even received recognition from those states themselves under the heading of 'non-alignment', which likewise implies a tripartite division of the world in terms of bloc membership and non-membership; but I do not wish to signal acceptance of the 'us, them and the rest' view of the world which underlies it. I have chosen to use the term not because of its meaning in this respect, but rather, in a sense, because of its meaninglessness. Its alternatives all carry conceptual overtones which are even more misleading, in that they imply positive elements of commonality rather than a simply negative residual category. The most familiar examples all incorporate some usage of the term 'development', whether in the form of 'developing', 'underdeveloped' or 'less developed' countries, the last of which also appears as the acronym LDCs. The idea of development (or equally often just the word, used without much concern for what it means but none the less carrying ideological overtones) has bedevilled the analysis of third world politics, and in my view has led to a great deal of conceptual confusion and misleading generalisation. I shall use it as seldom as possible. Other categorisations draw on the simple poverty of third world societies; but while this is at least readily comprehensible (unlike 'development', which can mean many different things), and is an extremely important fact about most of them, as a guide to analysis it points us in the wrong direction. The fact that some states which seem in all other respects to be characteristically 'third worldly' are extremely rich, including Kuwait which has the highest *per capita* income in the world, helps to indicate that poverty itself is not what we are concerned with; while even in those numerous societies where it is extremely acute, it is an outcome of geophysical, economic or political conditions, rather than a guide to the common elements which make such societies what they are.

Geographical classifications are even less helpful. The term 'Afro-Asian' was once in vogue, but even if one discounts it on grounds of sheer practicality, given the number of additional hyphens needed to incorporate the Caribbean, Central and South America, and the Pacific, it still does not tell us much except where these states are. In a negative way, though, it at least helps to indicate the range and potential variety of the peoples which it includes, and thus helps to dispose of the idea that the third world might be formed as the result of the cultural characteristics of its people: no plausible similarities of indigenous culture could be held to link together the immigrant societies of the Caribbean, the nomads of the Sahara, and the densely-populated rice-growing civilisations of Asia.

The common circumstances none the less exist. What produces them, paradoxically, is the existence not of three worlds but of one. The 'third world' is one result of the process by which, since the late fifteenth century, the previously scattered peoples of the globe have been brought together into what is in many respects a single society, economy and political system. By far the major part of this process has taken place over the last century, while its political aspects with which this book is essentially concerned are the product of the emergence of third world states which, except in Latin America, have mostly become independent since the Second World War. What distinguishes the third world is its peripherality. Economic peripherality has meant separation from, and subordination to, the dominant industrial economies which have developed especially in Europe and North America. Though I do not hold the view that all third world states are thereby doomed to a permanently menial economic status, they have entered the world economy especially through the supply of primary products such as minerals and cash crops to the industrial economies, and for the most part continue to be primary export producers. What is distinctive about this productive structure is not that it necessarily creates poverty, since occasionally (as in the case of Kuwait) it can turn a minor trading port into a booming city wealthy enough to command all the benefits that modern technology can provide, but that it ties the economy to a global system of production and distribution. In a sense, of course, the dominant industrial economies are no less dependent on this system of production and distribution than are the third world primary producers; each group of states, for example, has a similar proportion of its national product committed to external trade. But it is the industrial economies which created the system, which developed the technology needed to work it, and which have the sophisticated productive capacity that holds it together. In addition, and at least in part as a result, they are able to assure their peoples a much higher standard of living than is available to any but a very small proportion of the people of the third world.

Social and cultural peripherality is scarcely less important. While third world cultures may have very little in common with one another, what they do have in common is that they are 'non-western' – another phrase, this time with implicit racial overtones, which is also sometimes used to denote the third world. Part of what matters here is that third world peoples were physically subordinated to European ones during the period, that of colonialism, during which the single world system was being created, with the result that European cultural patterns have become superimposed on (or have sometimes totally displaced) indigenous ones. This is especially evident in the field of language. In some parts of the third world, notably the Caribbean and Latin America, there is no indigenous language, and people speak the former colonial language with varying degrees of local adaptation. There are some areas, too, such as the Arabic-speaking states, where an indigenous language has a wide degree not just of domestic but equally of international currency. But in many areas, especially in Africa but also in parts of Asia, the former colonial language remains the language of government, and is equally essential for any contact – social, economic or political – with the outside world. Learning that language thus becomes the means by which one may acquire some power within one's own society, by acquiring links with similarly equipped compatriots and with the international system. Education is a terminal that connects you with the outside.

But this outside connection is not just a matter of learning a language. It also provides, or at least may provide, an entry to ways of doing things which are characteristically western, and which are essential for the control of the technology through which western superiority has been maintained. Running a machine, or more generally, running a society which is maintained to an important degree by machinery, is not just a matter of learning about a particular piece of equipment; it may also, more basically, require you to internalise attitudes towards both people and things which underlie a machine-based culture. The most successful 'westernising' states have been those, like Japan, in which indigenous cultural patterns can fairly readily be adapted to this purpose without a great deal of overt westernisation. Personal and national advancement in Japan, for example, does not require much knowledge of European languages. In many other societies a much clearer process of westernisation, and hence perhaps of alienation from one's own culture, seems to be called for. In the field of politics, a specially important aspect of western technology, and one which is very easily overlooked by those who see technology especially in terms of sophisticated machinery, is the technology of organisation. The capacity to maintain and control large organisations is the base on which any 'modern' society is built. In the economy, this is most obvious in the role of the major corporation, employing many thousands of people and extending its operations over many countries and continents. The Japanese capacity to instil loyalty to the corporation is, much more than any matter of being 'clever with machines', what has made the economic miracle. Many third world societies are by contrast hampered by the enormous difficulty, grounded in cultural patterns appropriate to small-scale subsistence societies, of maintaining institutions which are beyond the effective control of a single boss and which can readily adapt to changes in leadership. Since the largest organisation in most third world states is government, this difficulty is especially clear in the maintenance of an effective bureaucracy. The problem is presented in its starkest form when the army seizes power, and an essentially bureaucratic organisation becomes directly responsible for the political management of the state.

Since the political consequences of peripherality are the subject of this book, there is less need to discuss them here. Their most dramatic aspect, the extension of European colonial empires over by far the greater part of the inhabited world, is assessed in the next chapter. In the process Europe created political territories which were artificial, in the sense that they did not arise from the societies which they governed but were instead imposed on them, and indeed often societies that were artificial too, resulting from large-scale and sometimes involuntary movements of population. Though the external relations of third world states are treated in one particular chapter, the element of 'externality' is one that permeates the entire book. This does not mean, to anticipate a point that will be made later, that third world states and societies are simple playthings of the international system, dancing to the tune it plays. On the contrary, one of the main themes of the book is that they have a life of their own, and appreciable opportunities to manipulate the external world and adapt it to their own needs. It is none the less the external element that created the third world in the first place, and much of such freedom of action as third world states possess lies in their ability to choose different ways of reacting to it.

The resulting tension between the international setting of the third world and its domestic peoples, societies and governments not only accounts for much of what is most distinctive about the actual working of third world politics. It also underlies any theoretical attempt to understand it. In particular, the two implicitly contrasting viewpoints, that which takes the third world state as its primary level of analysis, and that which takes the international system, distinguish the two main schools in grand theorising about third world politics over the last quarter-century or so. Each of them has split into competing and often mutually contradictory views, and has contained (along with a lot of shoddy thought and ideological special pleading) a great deal also that has been of lasting value, and that has in any event so shaped our thinking about the third world that it is almost impossible to escape. The first school, which might in a broad sense be described as 'nationalist', sought regularities in the internal evolution of each state which could be expressed in terms of some conception, however reluctantly adopted or inadequately defined, of *development*. While this term gained some plausibility from common circumstances which applied across a wide range of states, it was inherently unsatisfactory, and readily lent itself to teleological nonsense of the kind expressed in Almond and Powell's famous statement that: 'The forces of techno- logical change and cultural diffusion are driving political systems in certain directions, which seem discernible and susceptible to analysis in terms of increasing levels of development.'[1] Immeasurably the greatest exponent of the school, Samuel P. Huntington, explicitly rejected the term 'political development', but yet managed in *Political Order in Changing Societies* (1968)[2] to express most of the useful things which it had to say. This book was a kind of Pilgrim's Progress, tracing the paths which societies (or more explicitly states) might tread from tradi- tional stability through the changing patterns of modernisation to the distant goal of modern stability, together with the thickets, morasses and blind turnings which met them on the way. The staff which would see the pilgrim safely through was that of political organisation, which alone could create the effective institutions which modern stability required.

This work, magnificent in its spread and extremely illuminating in many of its individual vignettes, was almost Marxian in its periodisation of history and positively Leninist in its concern for political organisa- tion. It none the less grandly ignored the two principal emphases of the much more explicitly Marxist and Leninist school that followed. This school might equally broadly be described as 'internationalist', since its starting point (like mine) was the incorporation of the third world into a global order. In contrast to the 'nationalists', who tended to draw their experience from the new states of Africa and Asia, the 'inter- nationalists' derived theirs especially from Latin America, where independence was a century and a half away, and the defects of 'development' as a guiding theme were all too obvious. Their equivalent key word was, rather, *underdevelopment*. This school gave special attention to the colonial period, which scarcely figured at all in Huntington's analysis, and in its grandest form, that of Immanuel Wallerstein's world systems approach, set this within the context of global development since the fifteenth century.[3] Its second emphasis was on the economy as the motor for political change, and especially on the process of class formation within third world or 'underdeveloped' states. Implicitly or (more often) explicitly underlying this was, normally, a charge of capitalist exploitation as positively creating the poverty of the third world, and a belief in fundamental change, usually of a revolutionary kind, as the means by which this should be reversed. Writers of this school differ appreciably in ideology, emphasis and prescription. At an analytical level, there is a spread from writers such as Wallerstein who see an absolute impoverishment of third world peoples, to ones like Cardoso who believe in the possibility of 'associated dependent development' in at least some third world states, and even to revisionists like Warren who argue that capitalist imperialism has actually promoted the economic development of the third world.[4] These differences lead to correspondingly variable policy prescriptions. The analysis of 'semi-peripheral' states, such as Brazil, which are not readily classified among either the dominant capitalist core or the exploited periphery, also raises difficulties, as does the role of the 'socialist' bloc. Where the internationalists also tend to suffer, from the viewpoint of those concerned with third world politics in itself, is in their analysis of actual political situations. Class differences, for example, are unquestionably very marked in most third world states, but class itself is rarely of direct and immediate importance in the working of their politics; and while this can doubtless be explained, the school is not so good at explaining what kind of politics takes place instead. The internationalist emphasis likewise tends to divert attention from the very active politics that is taking place internally, and to dismiss it — unless a revolution is in the offing — as of little account. An awkward explanatory gap also sometimes exists between the international causes of exploitation and underdevelopment, and the domestic revolution prescribed as the means to end them.

This book does not seek to propound any particular theory of third world politics, nor is it concerned to assess the theories advanced by others. It is none the less built about a few basic themes which I feel to be important, accounting for much that is most distinctive about the politics of the third world, and constituting perhaps the elements from which a theoretical synthesis might be built.

The first theme is that neither the nationalist nor the internationalist approach is adequate in itself, and that an understanding of third world politics depends on superimposing and integrating the two. The internationalists are right to start by emphasising the way in which the third world was created, but wrong to assume, as they too easily do, that the relationships of dominance and dependence established through colonialism continue essentially unaltered into the independent state. The external element still, of course, remains. It is usually a significant part in the make-up of third world politics, and may on occasion become an overwhelmingly dominant one, especially in the smaller states. But the internal element, built up over six generations in most of Latin America and suddenly released through the nationalist movements in the territories decolonised a generation or so ago, is usually no less important a part of politics and often much more so. The next chapter, on the colonial state and its demise, is concerned both with the creation of a global political order and with the localist third world responses which it aroused. A fuller picture would require also an assessment of the equivalent and accompanying processes of social and economic change, but that lies beyond the self-imposed limits of this book.

The second and central theme is then the nature of the third world state, which in my view provides the central synthesis of domestic and external elements through which politics is conducted. It is this state that makes third world politics a kind of activity which is in some measure distinctive, related to but none the less different from politics elsewhere. The third chapter, which examines these characteristics and relates them to the nature of politics, is thus the key chapter of the book, from which the later chapters follow. Chapters 4, 5 and 6 then look at the main problems and choices for political management, seen essentially — as the word 'management' suggests — from the viewpoint of that small governing group or elite that seeks to control the state. The first problem, discussed in Chapter 4, is that of controlling the state itself, through the imposition of central power and the manipulation of the sets of interests that constitute domestic politics. The second problem, that of controlling the economy, exemplifies the nature of the third world state through its intricate mingling of domestic and external, as well as economic and political, elements. The idea of a 'political economy', whose renaissance we owe principally though not entirely to the internationalist school, is essential to understanding the way in which both political and economic management (which are indeed often the same thing) operate in third world states. The third of these chapters then concentrates on the international element in third world politics, though in keeping with the general theme of the centrality of the state, it sees this — contrary to the usual viewpoint of the internationalist school — as a source of strength and opportunity to the third world state, quite as much as a limitation on it. The final two chapters look at two distinctive groups of people who may seek to take over the state, and at the results which they achieve. The soldiers, who form the subject of Chapter 7, operate of necessity from within the state itself, and its maintenance is their primary concern, even though they are paradoxically responsible for some of the most dramatic instances of state collapse. The revolutionaries, by contrast, usually present themselves as its enemies, and seek to overthrow it either by action at the centre or by rural guerrilla warfare. Paradoxically again, Chapter 8 suggests that they may end up by strengthening it, and that the revolutionary state may be an effective realisation of an ideal sought by rulers all over the third world.

Any introduction to a subject as broad as that covered in this book must of necessity be both simplified and generalised. For simplification I make no apology. Much of third world politics, as of politics elsewhere, *is* simple. It is a matter of seeking those basic goals outlined in the first paragraph of this chapter, within the constraints that people and governments in the third world have to work under. Sophisticated conceptual approaches and detailed local expertise are unquestionably needed for a fuller understanding of the subject, but without some sense of how it all fits together, they can easily bemuse one with abstruse theoretical jargon and confusing local detail. Third world politics, with its mass of variegated states and its lack of the signposts provided by the electoral party systems and party-state apparatuses of the 'first' or 'second' world, is quite confusing enough already. It is this sense of how things fit together, necessarily a personal and disputable one, that this book seeks to provide. Generalisation is the price which has to be paid for it. It is a real price, in that simplicity can be misleading just as detail can be confusing. One common way round the problem is to intersperse short case studies among the general material, or even to base the book as a whole on a set of individual country studies selected to display the varieties and similarities of third world experience. This is a halfway house which I find awkward, both in the constant hopping back and forth between different levels of analysis which it involves, and in the extent to which it leaves the reader to decide which aspects of a given state's experience are generalisable, and which the result of specific local circumstances. I have chosen instead simply to make brief allusion to particular countries and events where these seem to bear out the general point which I am making.

The idea of a third world politics, on which in a sense this book is based, itself provide no hard and fast set of criteria which divide states which count as being in the third world, from other states which do not. Dividing lines in the social sciences are invariably blurred, and categories imprecise; while we have to be able to divide and categorise in order to be able to understand, it defeats our purpose if we try to make these categories more precise than they really are. The dividing line adopted for this book, for example, includes Turkey within the third world, but leaves Greece out of it. But I do not thereby seek to assert that Greek politics is fundamentally different from Turkish. There is no substitute for studying both Greece and Turkey, and seeking to understand what you find there. There are likewise enormous variations within the area which I have classified as belonging to the third world: those which divide sophisticated economies and societies like Argentina or South Korea from simple ones like Kuwait and Botswana, large states like India or Brazil from small ones like Burundi or Grenada, societies based on indigenous structures like Burundi and India from ones derived from immigration like Grenada or Brazil. An introduction may provide an opening for a longer and closer acquaintance, but cannot serve as a substitute for it.

Though a short and general book is not inherently more liable to bias than a long and specialised one, its values and judgements are much less easily hidden behind a mass of facts or the paraphernalia of academic discourse. I make no claims for the possibility of a value-free political science, and a book of this kind is necessarily crammed with the personal judgements of its author. I have, however, so far as possible sought to avoid both moral judgements about third world political actors, and prescriptions as to what they ought to do: political commitment, however necessary for those who seek to change the world, is in my view much more of a hindrance than a help to those who seek merely to understand it. Much more difficult to manage is the kind of implicit bias which creeps into analysis from the way in which an author chooses to approach his subject, and in this respect I am particularly aware that, in taking as its theme the centrality of the third world state, this book has concentrated on the winners in the political process, and ignored the losers. There is little here about what politics means to many people in the third world. The urban destitute and the industrious peasant erupt onto the page only when a riot or a revolutionary guerrilla movement turns them into a threat to the great and powerful; the exile and the refugee figure scarcely at all. There is a certain logic to justify this. Politics does have winners and losers, in the third world more cruelly than in most places; and while on a universal scale of human values all may be equally worthy of our concern, the study of politics requires one to deal most with those who matter most. This is, however, something that the reader should bear in mind.

Notes

1. G.A. Almond and G.B. Powell, *Comparative Politics: A Developmental Approach* (Little, Brown, 1966), p. 301.

2. S.P. Huntington, *Political Order in Changing Societies* (Yale University Press, 1968).

3. I. Wallerstein, *The Modern World System: Capitalist Agriculture and the Origins of European World Economy in the 16th Century* (Academic Press, 1974).

4. See I. Wallerstein, *The Capitalist World-Economy* (Cambridge University Press, 1979); F.H. Cardoso, 'Associated Dependent Development' in A. Stepan, *Authoritarian Brazil* (Yale University Press, 1973); B. Warren, *Imperialism: Pioneer of Capitalism* (Verso, 1980).

2 THE COLONIAL STATE AND ITS DEMISE

European Colonialism

I have already argued that the idea of a 'third world politics' makes sense only in the context of a single world. Before the creation of a global political order, and the global economy to go with it, the infinitely varied political structures of Asia, Africa and the Americas possessed no common features which could bring them together as a single category for analysis. The importance of European colonialism is that it was, more than anything else, the means by which this global political and economic order was created. In the process, societies with their own internal structures and dynamics became linked with, and subordinated to, a set of global interactions and institutions with a dynamic of its own. By far the greater part of what is now known as the third world was, at one time or another, subjected to formal colonial rule by one or another of the states of the western European seaboard. Even those societies which retained their independence were obliged to come to terms with a world in which European influence was dominant, and to adapt their own domestic political structures and economies to meet the European prerequisites of statehood.

The Imposition of Colonial Rule

There was, however, no uniform imposition of European dominance on exotic societies. Some areas were effectively colonised by the late fifteenth century, others not until early in the twentieth. Almost the whole of what is now Latin America had been independent for well over half a century before the first District Commissioner set foot in many parts of Africa. Colonialism took different forms, depending on the colonising state itself, the reasons for which it sought to extend itself overseas and, especially, on the social organisation and response of the colonised people. A simple timescale of the process is, therefore, needed.[1]

The ultimate basis of colonialism was technological, and its principal motive was economic. The states of western Europe developed inventions and forms of organisation which enabled them, slowly at first, to control others and thereby to acquire wealth. The first, and for many centuries the most important, of their technological advantages was the ocean-going sailing ship, in which they could break out of the enclosing ring set by the Atlantic Ocean to their west and north, and the Islamic societies to their east and south. Europeans could reach other parts of the world; others, save the Turks and Arabs, could not reach Europe. Developed from the mid-fifteenth century onwards, the ocean-going ship had within well under a hundred years enabled Europeans to reach all the way round the globe. The Portuguese reached Cape Verde, only 1,700 miles from Lisbon, in 1460; Magellan's circumnavigation took place in 1519-22. But while ships enabled Europeans to reach other parts of the world, what happened when they got there depended on what, and who, they found. Their search was, initially at least, for areas rich enough to exploit and weak enough to control. On this basis, a very broad distinction can be made between three main forms of colonialism, each chiefly associated with a particular era, a particular continent and a particular set of colonial powers: the Americas, both rich and easy to control; Asia, rich but difficult to control; and Africa, for the most part poor and so scarcely worth controlling.

What was distinctive about colonialism in the Americas was the thoroughness and brutality with which it destroyed the indigenous Amerindian societies. In the islands of the Caribbean − the easiest of conquests for a seaborne colonialism − the local peoples were almost entirely wiped out within a few generations. On the mainland the Inca and Aztec empires, no matter how wealthy and sophisticated, were quite incapable of defending themselves against the smallest bands of Spanish conquistadors. The extent to which the Amerindians were physically exterminated varied from area to area. They still account for an appreciable proportion of the population of parts of north-west South America, with some 70 per cent of the population in Bolivia and 46 per cent in Peru, and form sizeable minorities in some other South and Central American states such as Ecuador (39 per cent) and Mexico (30 per cent).[2] They are virtually non-existent in southern South America and entirely absent from the islands. Even where substantial populations survive, however, they remain socially, economically and politically subordinate. Independence, as in the United States and the 'white dominions' of Canada, Australia and New Zealand, has marked the transfer of power to settler rather than indigenous communities.

The destruction of indigenous society made possible (and indeed was prompted by) the imposition of European-oriented economies, a process carried through with much greater intensity in the Americas than in any other large area of the third world. This in turn helped to determine the pattern of external settlement. The closest approximations to the European economies themselves developed in temperate areas without easily exploitable mineral wealth, notably in what are now the northern United States and Canada, though also in some degree in the extreme south of the continent, in Argentina and Chile. These areas were almost entirely confined to European settlement, slower to develop and, at least until the early nineteenth century, less wealthy than the tropical zones. Paradoxically, and following much greater levels of European immigration during the nineteenth century, the United States and Canada developed to the extent that they are now archetypical 'first world' states, while the semi-temperate Latin American states (Argentina, Chile, Mexico) are among the most industrialised of third world states, even while displaying a number of characteristically third world political patterns.

Those areas which proved suitable for the production of tropical crops for the European market had a very different experience from the temperate zones, both of immigration and of dependence. Sugar, tobacco, cotton and coffee were most effectively grown in plantations owned and managed by Europeans with a large, controlled labour force. Though this labour force could be composed of Europeans or Amerindians, the solution adopted in Brazil, the Caribbean and the southern United States was to import slaves from the west coast of Africa, a trade which continued for some three hundred years from the mid-sixteenth century and poured millions of Africans into the Americas. The corrosive political effects of that trade are still the dominant political legacy of the areas in which it occurred, even long after its original economic rationale has disappeared. In some parts of the Caribbean, notably Guyana and Trinidad, a renewed demand for plantation labour in the later nineteenth century led to the import of Indian workers, as indentured labourers rather than as slaves, whose descendants now uneasily co-exist with those of the earlier African immigration. The effects of colonialism in transporting disparate groups of people — Africans, Indians, Europeans, even Chinese — to distant parts of the world, and then leaving them to get on as best they may, are nowhere more starkly illustrated than in the West Indies.

The Americas, and especially Latin America, remain the most sharply distinguishable area within the third world. The differences between Africa and Asia are nothing like as great as those between either of them and Latin America. The principal difference in straightforwardly political terms, Latin America's much earlier achievement of national independence, means that it is effectively excluded from the rest of this chapter, which deals with the structure of colonial government and the indigenous movements formed to displace it. Another and more basic difference, the virtual absence of any 'traditional' or indigenous society, also has pervasive political consequences. In Latin America, moreover, unlike any other area of the third world save the exceptional cases of Israel and South Africa, the dominant groups are almost entirely of European origin. While American political scientists have often argued that the pattern of immigration into the United States accounted for the much lower salience of social class as a political factor there than in the European countries of origin, the effect of immigration into Latin America seems to have been paradoxically quite the opposite. Class has a salience in Latin American politics altogether at variance with its role in most other areas of the third world. Part of this salience is certainly due to the higher levels of urbanisation and industrialisation in Latin America than in Africa or much of Asia; but it is also due to the weakness or absence of those linkages which bound followers to leaders (and vice versa) in 'traditional' Afro-Asian societies, and their replacement by the much more exploitative relations derived from the elites' control, first of land and secondly of the state. So far from making Latin American states less 'third worldly', however, this pattern of class politics has produced effects which (in addition to their position in the global economy and the role of the United States as a surrogate colonial power) make them more comparable with Afro-Asian states and less like the liberal systems produced by commercial capitalism in western Europe. In particular, it has emphasised the role of the state, the entrenchment of a bureaucratic bourgeoisie as the guardians and beneficiaries of that state, and a characteristically third world set of political consequences most sharply indicated by the level of military intervention.

An 'American' pattern of colonialism can be found in some other parts of the world. Mauritius, for example, is in almost every respect a Caribbean island transported to the Indian Ocean, complete with its sugar plantations, its European creole elite, its descendants of African slaves and of Indian indentured labourers. Plantation economies, reminiscent of the Americas but without African slave labour, were established on south-east Asian islands in the Indonesian archipelago and the Philippines. What distinguished Asia from the Americas, however, was the strength of its indigenous societies. In no case could these simply be destroyed or subordinated to a preponderantly settler society, as in the Americas. Although the economic advantages of European expansion in Asia were evident even before the discovery of the New World (itself the by-product of the search for a western route to India), European colonialism was for many years largely restricted to coastal trading posts. The rivalry between European powers in the region in the seventeenth and eighteenth centuries, and their felt need to assure themselves of friendly and peaceful neighbours, gradually sucked colonial rulers into the interior; but by far the greater part of the colonial acquisition of mainland Asia was a product of the nineteenth century. It proceeded by taking over existing political systems in their entirety, often (as with the British in India) preserving not only their boundaries but also their rulers and the external trappings of a distinct political identity. Elsewhere in the region, in Burma for example or Indo-China, river valley civilisations were annexed intact by one or another colonial power, the new fixed colonial frontiers roughly coinciding with the undemarcated boundaries within which pre-colonial rulers had claimed some kind of suzerainty. A number of such pre-colonial states, including Iran, Afghanistan and Thailand, remained independent, owing partly to the shrewdness and strength of their rulers, partly to their usefulness as buffer zones between rival colonialists. In eastern Asia, Japan and China retained, despite substantial European penetration, a far more genuine independence.

In western Asia, the area now known as the Middle East experienced a peculiar combination of indigenous and external forms of government. Subject to European incursions since the time of the Crusades, almost the whole area (including northern Africa and south-east Europe) had, by the seventeenth century, come under the control of the Ottoman (Turkish) empire, which persisted until the First World War. Even before the empire's final collapse, European powers including Britain, France and Italy had carved off bits of it as colonies or protectorates of their own, while afterwards Britain and France ruled most of the remaining Arab territories in conjunction with local dynasties. The impact of western colonialism was mitigated not only by a degree of internal self-government, but also by a pronounced sense of regional identity expressed in political form through Pan-Arabism and in religious form through Islam. Unlike the state-centred nationalisms of Iran or Thailand, Arab nationalism cut across the boundaries established by the administering powers, in a way which — more than in any other area of the third world — has challenged the pre-eminence of the post-colonial state as the framework for political activity.

The African pattern was different again. A continent with little evident wealth (except in the form of its people, exported as slaves), and with an interior difficult to penetrate, it attracted little more than a few colonial coastal settlements until the very end of the nineteenth century. Outside Arab north Africa, where Algeria was colonised by France in 1830, only what is now South Africa attracted any substantial degree of permanent European occupation. Other settlements, like Dakar and Saint-Louis in Senegal, Freetown in Sierra Leone or the Republic of Liberia founded in 1822 for free people of colour from America, clung closely to the coast. Colonial occupation of the interior came late, from the later 1880s onwards, and extremely rapidly. It involved neither the extermination of indigenous people, as in the Americas, nor the creation of colonies broadly coinciding with existing cultures and political systems, as in Asia. Instead, colonial boundaries were laid down with an arbitrariness which took no account of indigenous societies or geographical zones, frequently by the simple expedient of drawing a line on a map several thousand miles away. Only one existing African state, the Empire of Ethiopia, succeeded in retaining its independence, though in the process it expanded its own frontiers until it was ethnically no less heterogeneous than any other African territory. Here and there, an indigenous kingdom such as Swaziland, Lesotho, Rwanda or Burundi, maintained its separate identity as a microcolony of a European state. Elsewhere, colonial boundaries marched across the ground with a casual disregard for the people whom they thus allocated to one or another colony. Along the Gulf of Guinea, colonial boundaries from Ivory Coast to Nigeria stretched at right angles to the coast, separating Akans, Ewes and Yorubas between different colonies, each of which included socially and politically disparate zones of coastal strip, forest and sub-Saharan savannah. Seventy or eighty years later, these arbitrary lines became the frontiers between independent states.

The Structure of Colonial Government

Much of the discussion of colonialism, especially in Africa, has concentrated on the differences between colonial powers and, in particular, on their various theories or philosophies of colonial rule — a legacy of the days when colonialism as such was largely taken for granted, and the colonisers argued among themselves about the best way to justify and implement it. Many of these differences were not unimportant, and many of the variations in the political structures and experience of post-colonial states can be traced back to them, but they only became significant within the context of the common features imposed by colonialism on the colonised territories and societies as a whole. It is these common features which define the post-colonial state: the differences only go to indicate some of the forms which it can take.

First, then, colonialism established territories and territorial boundaries where none had existed before. As has been shown, the degree to which these coincided with the boundaries of indigenous societies and political systems varied markedly from one area to another; but even where, as in south-east Asia, they coincided to a fair degree with indigenous cultural units, a fixed line was imposed in place of previously fluid frontier zones whose allegiance or degree of independence might vary with the strengths of its neighbours on either side. Any indigenous process of state formation, like the rise of the Zulu empire in southern Africa, was brought to an abrupt halt, and the authorities which it had created, if they were allowed to survive, were corralled within the grid laid down in agreements between colonial powers. Amended here and there, but basically unchanged, this grid now defines the existence of independent states.

Secondly, colonialism established within each territory a political order and the administrative hierarchy to run it. The ultimate basis of this political order was, invariably, force: there is no other way in which a small group of alien rulers can establish control over a people not their own. The extent to which force needed to be continuously and directly applied, however, varied very greatly, in keeping with the level of effective military challenge which the colonised peoples and their leaders could sustain at the moment of conquest, and the degree of exploitation and repression imposed by the conquerors thereafter. It tended to be greater, therefore, in colonies of settlement, and greatest of all in colonies of settlement accompanied by intensive production. In many areas, notably in Africa, colonial rule was maintained, after the initial conquest, with astonishingly small amounts of force, many of the forces themselves being locally recruited. Failure to resist, obviously enough, does not refute the view that colonial rule was basically forcible in nature: it merely shows that many of the colonised appreciated that resistance was not worthwhile. The small colonial forces on the spot could and would, when occasion required, be reinforced from other colonies and the metropolitan country. But over and above that, force backed by manifest technological superiority acquired a peculiar legitimacy of its own. It was not simply not worth fighting: such power, and the people who exercised it, embodied a mystique, expressed not simply in guns but in books, uniforms, social behaviour and a mass of manufactured products. Only by accepting these things and those who brought them would it be possible to penetrate this mystique and grasp the power which lay behind it. The hold which colonial rule maintained over its subjects thus came to be psychological rather than crudely military, a point which helps to explain its continued relevance long after the colonial forces, and the colonisers themselves, had been withdrawn.

The administrative structure established to run the colonial territory was necessarily both centralised and authoritarian. Authority came from overseas, from governments and ministries in London or Paris, and was channelled at local level through the governor, then distributed all the way down through the provincial commissioner to the district commissioner or *commandant de cercle*, and thence to the local auxiliaries of the administration, the chief or village headman. Since independence this structure has been indigenised, adapted and much extended. It runs back only to the new state's capital city and the direct link overseas has been broken. Many of the assumptions and values which guided the old colonial services have been abandoned. But the structure itself is still recognisably the same, and with the decay in many cases of the political institutions generated at the time of independence, it has often emerged with increasing starkness as the frame on which the state is built. With it, again adapted but still recognisable, go the attitudes towards it, and thus towards the business of government in general, which colonialism induced – or perhaps in some cases simply strengthened. From the rulers, a sense of superiority over those whom they ruled, a sense of power emanating from above, rather than growing from below; for the ruled, a sense of the state as an alien imposition, to be accepted, certainly, and to be feared, cajoled and where possible exploited, but existing on a plane above the people whom it governed, and beyond any chance of control.

Two further aspects of colonisation, going beyond the simple imposition of a colonial administration but enormously affected by it, fall outside the necessarily limited political focus of this book. One is the introduction of the colonial economy, the other that of new social attitudes, institutions and forms of communication between the colonised peoples themselves. These both reinforced external penetration and internal dependence, but at the same time, when added to the more straightforwardly political effects of colonialism, they did much to differentiate people within the new colonial territory from people outside, even if those outside were relatives, those inside traditional enemies. The colonial economy was channelled through mechanisms which duplicated the colonial administration, along roads and railways which penetrated the hinterland from the colonial administrative centres and the principal port cities. Deliberate colonial measures to create and control a cash economy, for instance by the imposition of a head tax and the introduction of produce marketing boards, reinforced the connection. The use of a common colonial language, and its spread through education, trade and government, both enabled the colonised to communicate with one another, and frequently cut them off from peoples controlled by a different coloniser beyond the frontier. There is still no more striking, even shocking, reminder of the impact of colonialism in Africa than to cross an entirely artificial frontier and witness the instant change of language — and with it a myriad number of associated manifestations of culture and government — that results.

All this meant that the colonial state became the principal unit of political activity, accepted as such by indigenous peoples and leaders quite as much as by the colonial officials themselves. Politics and administration, at anything more than the very local level, meant dealing with colonial officialdom, and hence accepting — even, often, while opposing — the institutions which it had established. Liberation from colonial rule came to be seen as a matter of taking over these institutions rather than destroying them. In the process, the colonial state acquired a legitimacy as the framework for the creation of a nation, sometimes reinforcing pre-colonial identities — as in Burma, Kampuchea and Vietnam — but more often, especially in Africa, quite at variance with them, to such a degree that the cultures and institutions of local peoples themselves came to be branded by the new nationalist leaders as the manifestations of an illegitimate and divisive tribalism.

The differences between forms of colonialism can only be appreciated within an understanding of these basic similarities. These derived from three main sources: the nature and impact of economic change, the structure of indigenous societies, and the policies and practices of the different colonial powers. Since the first two of these are touched on elsewhere, only the last will be examined here. Some selection is needed. Almost all of the states of western Europe, and several of their extracontinental offshoots, had colonies to a greater or lesser degree in the present-day third world: Portugal, Spain, France, Britain, Belgium, The Netherlands, Denmark, Germany, Italy and, among non-European countries, Australia, South Africa and the United States. Apart from the early Spanish and Portuguese empires, most of which were lost to metropolitan control by the early nineteenth century, only Britain and France had substantial empires spread over several continents. Germany lost her colonies after the First World War, Italy after the Second, while several of the others had only one colony of any significance, notably the Congo (Belgium), Indonesia (The Netherlands) and the Philippines (United States). Of the remainder, Portugal with its African possessions was substantially the most important. There is thus a lot to be said for the traditional comparison between Britain and France, since only there is it possible to distinguish broad outlines of policy from immediate local circumstances. In addition, they present such contrasting conceptual approaches to colonialism that most other states fall broadly into the range that they define, while similarities between them show the practical limitations on generally formulated policies.

The means by which a colonial power justifies and exercises its power over those whom it has conquered tell one more perhaps about the colonisers than about the colonised. There is, first of all, a premise of inequality inherent in the colonisers' conception of their own superiority, and their consequent arrogation to themselves of the right to determine the fate of the governed. This is in turn offset by the need to find some legitimising formula, for domestic, colonial and external consumption, which must necessarily be cast in universalistic terms. Though this inevitably calls on some conception of 'civilisation', by which values of a supposedly universal superiority are transferred from the coloniser to the colonised, the nature of the values and their transfer can have a lasting effect on those who find themselves on the receiving end.

For the French, the key ideas were those of centralisation and assimilation, derived from the experience of nation-building in metropolitan France, coupled with an appeal to the egalitarian principles of the revolution of 1789. Indigenous social and cultural systems were, in principle, dismissed as worthless, but indigenous peoples were, in accordance with the Rights of Man, to be offered the chance of assimilation to the ideals of France herself, by acquiring French language, culture and nationality, and hence in time becoming indistinguishable from other Frenchmen. It was an ideal which was implicitly non-racialist, in that it regarded the inferiority of the colonised as being cultural rather than genetic, but the practical obstacles to its achievement were none the less overwhelming. Its full implementation would have called for human and financial resources which were entirely out of the question, for an intensive programme of education and acculturation, the improvement of living standards at least to a point at which comparison with metropolitan France would not be farcical, and doubtless also the forcible conversion of those who – especially in Indo-China and the Islamic parts of West Africa – had no desire to abandon their cultures, religions and identities for those of France.

Nor is there any indication that France would have been willing to see her metropolitan citizens outvoted, in the National Assembly, by newly created and enfranchised Frenchmen from overseas.

None the less these ideals, watered down after the Second World War to the more practicable level of 'association' rather than full assimilation, shaped the nature of French colonial government. In the field of local administration, they resulted where possible in the weakening of traditional rulers, by breaking up existing political units and, in West Africa, appointing *chefs de canton*, who generally had little status and whose authority was further diminished by charging them with unpopular tasks such as tax collection and forced labour. Even so, 'traditional' leaders, such as the Mossi emperor in Upper Volta or the Muslim brotherhoods of Senegal, sometimes possessed such authority over their people that for the sake of easy government the administration had little option but to recognise and work with them. At the centre, the policy created a highly sophisticated indigenous elite who were indeed, in many respects, almost indistinguishable from Frenchmen, and whose privileged position was recognised both legally and politically. French colonies, starting with Senegal in 1851 but not fully until 1945, elected representatives to the National Assembly in Paris. Assimilated citizens could reach high rank in the administration, the best known being Felix Eboue, the black West Indian who declared for the Free French as Governor of Chad in 1940. Even among this tiny band some reaction to assimilation arose, characteristically expressed in the cultural 'negritude' of the West Indian Cesaire and the Senegalese Senghor in the 1930s; but the implicit clash between assimilation and the elite's place in its own society was most intensively raised in northern Vietnam, where the large Catholic population with its ties to French colonialism and the existing administration was forced to take refuge in the south (or in France) after the Communist takeover in 1954.

For the British, the idea of assimilation was unthinkable, as a result perhaps partly of a view (derived from Burke rather than from the French revolution) which sees political culture in particularist rather than universalist terms, and partly of a racial exclusiveness which implicitly denied that any of the indigenous peoples of the Empire could ever become really English. The highly Europeanised Asian or African, in a sense the supreme achievement of French imperialism, was the subject of suspicion and stereotyped contempt to the British. The model implicitly followed was that of the British dominions of settlement, Australia, Canada and New Zealand. The ultimate though distant goal, when the colonies were 'ready' for it, was independence. One result of this was that the British system was far less centralised than the French. Rather than being directed to a single goal, the colonies were seen as having distinctive characteristics of their own, and as moving at their own pace towards different destinies. The latitude given to the colonial governor was reflected at lower levels, where the British resident or district commissioner was expected to adapt himself to the local culture rather than impose his own. Most distinctive of all was the reliance on indigenous authorities which has come to be known by the general title of 'indirect rule'. Where traditional polities presented any substantial threat to British control they were dismantled, as in Burma. Where they did not, they were retained, protected, even on occasion created where none had existed before, or painstakingly recreated on ancient models. This system was at its most extreme in India, an administrative patchwork of direct British colonial possessions on the one hand, and 'native states' under varying degrees of British tutelage on the other, with their own administrations and such perquisites as the right to issue postage stamps. Some of the same facilities were enjoyed by the rulers of Malay states, while Sarawak was administered as a personal possession by a British Rajah until after the Second World War. In Africa, more rapidly and systematically colonised, there were no such anomalies, but 'native administrations' had considerable local powers, and their rulers were important figures in the national politics of, especially, Nigeria and Uganda.

This system satisfied many interests. From the viewpoint of the British Treasury, it was cheap; there were far fewer European administrators per head of population in British than in French colonies — one for every 15,000 inhabitants in British Nigeria in the 1930s, for example, against one for every 4,000 in neighbouring French West Africa,[3] though even there the 'white line' of the administration was extremely thin. It appealed to the strong deferential element in British political culture. It naturally pleased the native rulers themselves. And in some degree, it moderated the impact of alien rule upon their people. The people to whom it had least to offer were the city dwellers and especially the educated elite — those 'rootless elements' which colonial administration regarded so warily — and from this viewpoint it is scarcely surprising that anticolonial agitation generally arose much earlier in British than in French colonies. The indirect rule system did not operate everywhere. In the Caribbean there was no traditional authority to maintain (save perhaps the slaveowning plantocracy, whose local legislatures were mostly replaced by crown colony government at about the time of emancipation), while in parts of Africa such as

Tanganyika or South-east Nigeria the local political traditions were scarcely conducive to indirect rule, despite the administration's attempts to introduce it. Even where it did exist, moreover, the indirect ruler was in a very different position from the independent ruler he succeeded. He could be deposed by government, sometimes after petitions by his own people (in Sierra Leone, cannibalism was discovered to be a particularly efficacious charge to bring against unpopular rulers); more often, sustained in power as an instrument of colonial government, he could escape from traditional constraints on his government and rule less acountably than before. In either case, he had degenerated into a middleman between his subjects and his superiors.

The Non-colonial States

The territories in Africa and Asia which escaped direct colonial rule (there were none in the Americas) took on much of the colouring of a colonial state with an indigenous ruling elite. They negotiated fixed boundaries with their colonial neighbours, set up western-style institutions (which often perpetuated traditional patterns of government beneath a European façade), and started to establish both the communications systems and the economic structures characteristic of colonial rule. Since these states (as in Thailand, Iran or Ethiopia) were usually the heirs of ancient political entities, they carried forward a conscious sense of national identity which was strengthened by the incalculable moral advantage of running their own government, of not being dispossessed by an alien regime. And since their rulers relied on the support they could raise within their own society, rather than on force derived from overseas, they were generally (save for peripheral peoples sometimes ruthlessly incorporated in the process of state consolidation) less disruptive than colonialism of existing social values and institutions. These rulers, however, soon emerged as modernising autocrats rather than traditional monarchs. Strong central leadership was the essential requirement both for staving off an external colonialism and for internal state-building. Very often a traditional monarchical form disguised a thrusting autocrat who had risen from the ranks like the first Pahlevi Shah of Iran in 1925, or from the provincial aristocracy like Menilek of Ethiopia in 1889 and his successor Haile Selassie in 1916. Saudi Arabia was in effect newly created by a single man, Ibn Saud, in the 1920s. Central monarchical power was then strengthened by privileged access to external technology, especially armaments. Often very effective at handling the process of state consolidation, these monarchical regimes were (save perhaps in Thailand where the king was removed from direct political power as early as 1932) very much less capable of handling the later demands for political participation which arose there, as in the colonial territories. It is not then entirely surprising that some of the most violent upheavals in Africa and Asia have taken place in non-colonial states such as Ethiopia, Iran and Afghanistan.

An intermediate pattern occurred in monarchies which modernised beneath the control (under one guise or another) of a European colonial power. There were a surprising number of these semi-colonial monarchies, including Morocco, Libya and Egypt in North Africa; Rwanda, Burundi, Zanzibar (now part of Tanzania), Basutoland (Lesotho) and Swaziland in tropical Africa; Jordan, Iraq and the emirates of the Arabian peninsula in western Asia; Nepal and Brunei in central and eastern Asia; and even Tonga in the Pacific. While in a sense these were all colonies operating under a glorified form of indirect rule, the fact that the ruler's territory was coterminous with that of the colonial administration gave him a central political position far removed from the essentially local autonomy enjoyed by indigenous rulers in territories such as India or Malaya. The monarch symbolised the unity of the territory, and where he was the authentic representative of an indigenous political tradition (not the case, say, in Egypt, Iraq or Zanzibar) he could himself lead a form of nationalist movement and eventually emerge as the king of an independent state. How such kings have fared since independence has, however, depended as much on their own skills and local circumstances as on the institution of monarchy in itself.

Nationalism and Decolonisation

The Decline of Western European Colonialism

The collapse of western European colonialism has been rapid and — in a sense — complete. The main colonial empires were almost entirely dismantled within the twenty years following the end of the Second World War, starting in Asia and carrying over from there to Africa and the Caribbean. By the mid-1960s only a few anomalous colonial territories remained, and by the early 1980s these had been further reduced to a group of microcolonies, almost all of them islands, which were either incorporated into the metropolitan state like Reunion or Martinique, or else — like Gibraltar or the Falklands — presented peculiar difficulties of disposal. To the metropolitan powers themselves, colonialism was always, in principle at least, a temporary and transitional form of government, leading either to independence or to full assimilation, but the collapse none the less came vastly more quickly than they had expected, and often led to outcomes quite different from those they had envisaged.

At a global level, the Second World War produced and reflected a drastic shift in international power and status away from the states of the western European littoral and towards continental powers with a tradition of overland expansion, which were generally opposed to seaborne colonialism. This did not result in any *direct* threat to the European empires: neither the Soviet Union nor the United States ever used force to compel colonial withdrawal, while China has been prepared to tolerate even the defenceless British foothold on the Chinese mainland at Hong Kong. But by the same token the United States made clear that it was not prepared to help defend the colonies – the geographical scope of the NATO alliance was explicitly limited with this point in mind – and at a number of critical moments in the postwar period American disapproval was made clear. The most striking example, American disavowal of the Anglo-French intervention at Suez in 1956, did not arise in a specifically colonial context, but none the less made the new military and economic dependence of Britain and France on the United States brutally obvious, and helped to affect the anti-colonial ethos of the postwar world. From the viewpoint of crude *realpolitik*, moreover, the new superpowers could expect to extend their influence as the European powers withdrew. The Soviet Union saw in the end of empire an opportunity to expand from being an essentially regional power into a global one, while the United States took on something of the world-policing role which the Europeans had abandoned – with consequences of tragic irony in Vietnam.

At the second level, it is possible to relate the decline of colonialism to the fading determination of the colonial powers themselves. Most of them were economically shattered by the war, many of them subjected to several years of enemy occupation, and in contrast to the expansionist years of the late nineteenth and early twentieth centuries, when European rivalries were extended into a scramble for overseas possessions, they now looked for security principally to a much closer association among western European states themselves, together with the American alliance. Though the European Community was to maintain its economic links with many of the former colonies through the Yaounde and Lomé Conventions, its immediate effect was to mark a reduction in the interest and importance of colonial possessions as such.

There was in addition an implicit contradiction between the political ideals of democracy and equality which guided domestic politics, especially under the predominantly centre-left regimes of postwar western Europe, and the necessarily authoritarian and inegalitarian, and often racialist, bases of empire overseas. Again the direct connections should not be exaggerated; but they were certainly present in such important decisions as the extension of the franchise in the French colonies in 1945-6, and the granting of independence to India and Pakistan by the British Labour government in 1947. These were both in their ways reflections of the problem that for a democratic country empire must be justified in ways which can be turned against it; it is vulnerable to the rhetoric of self-determination which only in exceptional circumstances will lead to any permanent identification of the colonised with the colonial power.

The sharpest clash of all between democracy and empire arises when the maintenance of control over the colonies requires unpopular measures at home, especially when these take the form of compulsory military service and a large number of casualties. For Britain, this clash never really arose. Minor confrontations, such as the Malayan emergency and the Mau-Mau movement in Kenya in the 1950s, could be dealt with, in each case because they were largely confined to local minorities and alarmed other influential groups who allied with the colonial power to suppress them. Once it became clear that anticolonial movements enjoyed substantial support, British governments committed to ending conscription at home proved quite ready to pull out, while making arrangements for the transfer of power — which will be considered later. The French were less lucky, or less wise. The principles on which their empire was constructed did not so readily allow the easy option of cutting their losses and leaving, and both in Indo-China and in Algeria they found themselves committed to large-scale and long-term military action which had a seriously — in the Algerian case decisively — weakening effect on the institutions of the Fourth Republic, leading to de Gaulle's assumption of power in 1958. It is scarcely too much to say that de Gaulle's successful solution of the decolonisation problem was the base on which the stability of the Fifth Republic was founded. Portugal was the exception which proved the rule. The Salazar and Caetano regimes, undemocratic at home, clung onto Portugal's African colonies for a decade after the other colonial powers had withdrawn, in part because they were under no pressure to introduce any measures for African participation in politics (quite the opposite, in fact — any recognition of democratic forces in Africa would have strengthened demands for their recognition in Portugal), but much more importantly because they could maintain the conscription necessary to fight wars in the colonies. As in France but in heightened form, the colonial wars triggered the collapse of the regime, and the 1974 revolution both led to rapid decolonisation, and required decolonisation as the essential precondition for the establishment of democratic government in Portugal.

At a third level, the postwar period produced important changes within the colonies themselves. These were most direct and dramatic in Southeast Asia, the only major part of the colonial world to come under enemy occupation during the Second World War. Colonialism, as we have seen, depended in large part on a myth of imperial invincibility: the belief among the indigenous peoples that the metropolitan state was so powerful that resistance to it was simply not worthwhile. The astonishingly rapid Japanese victories of 1941-2 shattered this myth for ever. In French Indo-China and Dutch Indonesia the colonial power never fully succeeded in re-establishing control after 1945. British Burma and the American Philippines became independent shortly after the war, and only in British Malaya was the colonial system fully restored. The effects of the Second World War spread much more widely. Indian co-operation with the British to resist the Japanese was secured only on the promise of postwar independence, and forces raised in British Africa (which mostly fought in Southeast Asia) carried the lessons of the war back home. The links between France, Belgium and The Netherlands and their colonies were broken by German occupation of the home country, while Italy's colonies were placed under United Nations trusteeship with the guarantee of eventual independence.

The Nationalist Movements

Whatever the general reasons for the decline of western colonialism, the most immediate and important precipitant of its downfall was the opposition to it of the colonised peoples, expressed in the nationalist movements. These movements were very different in nature from the initial opposition or 'primary resistance' of third world peoples to the imposition of European rule. Opposition certainly remained, but this was combined with an acceptance of many of the changes which colonialism had introduced to produce a characteristic synthesis of indigenous and imported elements. The nationalist movements looked forward to a postcolonial future, not back to a precolonial past, though a suitably edited version of the past often found a place in their rhetoric. Most importantly, they almost always accepted the colonial state, with its boundaries and its administrative structure, as the frame on which the new nation was to be built; and with this went an acceptance, usually indeed an enthusiastic espousal, of ideals of progress or development conceived implicitly in western terms.

The synthetic nature of nationalism, and in turn therefore of the new states which arose from it, is most evident in the background of its leaders, who were almost invariably those Asians and Africans who had been most deeply affected by the economic and educational impact of colonialism. The point is most strikingly made by looking at leaders who at first sight might seem to be exceptions. Gandhi, most familiar as a wrinkled old man in a loincloth preaching traditional Indian values, was a barrister-at-law of the Inner Temple in London, who gained his first political experience as an opponent of racial discrimination in South Africa. His colleague and successor Nehru, educated at Harrow School and Cambridge University, was one of the most westernised of all third world leaders. Ho Chi Minh, leader of the Vietnamese struggle against the French and subsequently the United States, was not only the founder of the Vietnamese Communist Party, but had also, in the course of a long stay in France, been a founding member of the French Communist Party in Paris in 1920. It is hard to find a single one of the African nationalist leaders, whether radical or conservative, who was not a graduate of a western university or else had some other prolonged exposure to western life.

The creation of this westernised leadership, though a vital element in the growth of nationalism, was by no means enough. The earliest gener-ation of westernised Africans, men like Blaise Diagne and Africanus Horton in late nineteenth and early twentieth century West Africa, saw colonialism with some justice as a progressive force, and pressed for equal rights with Europeans, and restrictions on traditional institutions such as chieftancy. A second phase, dating from the 1880s in India and the interwar years in British West Africa, saw the growth of political organisations which pressed for self-government but which, largely confined to a small urban elite, attained little effective power; they often remained in being only because of the rather artificial opportun-ities, such as service on legislative councils, which colonialism created for them. It was only when the elite turned from this sort of activity to the mobilisation of discontents among the masses, that they were able to provide themselves with a popular base from which to mount a genuine challenge to the colonial regimes, and to reach for the prize of political power which in the earlier periods had been beyond their grasp.

This stage was reached at different periods in different parts of the colonial world. In India, the Indian National Congress expanded from

an elite to a mass movement in the 1920s, as a result of the civil dis-
obedience compaigns organised by Gandhi and Nehru. In the West
Indies, the European economic depression of the 1930s had disastrous
repercussions for the highly dependent local economies, and prompted
riots which were exploited by leaders such as Grantley Adams in
Barbados and Alexander Bustamante in Jamaica. In West Africa it was a
phenomenon of the late 1940s, growing from the emergence of politically conscious urban groups of demobilised soldiers and primary
school leavers, while in much of East and Central Africa the equivalent
stage occurred in the 1950s or even, in the Portuguese possessions, the
early 1960s. What prompted the growth of a mass political awareness
was, as often as not, some quite specific local grievance, which placed
the colonial regime at odds with the aspirations or interests of
important sections of the people. In the Gold Coast (Ghana), there was
the issue of 'swollen shoot', a disease of cocoa trees which the government dealt with by cutting down and burning the affected plants. In
Northern Rhodesia (Zambia) and Nyasaland (Malawi) mobilisation was
prompted by the formation in 1952 of the Central African Federation,
which had the effect of placing these territories under the control of a
government dominated by the white settlers of Southern Rhodesia
(Zimbabwe). In British Somaliland (Somalia), the return to Ethiopia
in 1954-5 of Somali-inhabited territories administered by Britain since
the Second World War brought a similar reaction.

Where some such widely shared grievance coincided with an articulate nationalist leadership, the results could be immediate and explosive. The classic situation, perhaps, was one in which the leader returned
home from a long sojourn in one of the western industrial states. This
sojourn could sometimes be a very long one – Dr Hastings Banda had
been out of Nyasaland for over forty years before he came back to lead
the Malawi Congress Party, while Nkrumah in the Gold Coast and
Kenyatta in Kenya were away for between ten and twenty years. The
leader then gathered around him a group of lieutenants or disciples,
usually younger and less educated men who had not been abroad, and
started to preach the gospel of independence. This religious imagery is
scarcely inappropriate, particularly in countries where Christian
missions were responsible for most primary education, and with it for a
pulpit style of public rhetoric. Nkrumah's famous slogan, 'Seek ye first
the political kingdom, and all things will be added unto you', perfectly
expresses both the language of nationalism and the range of aspirations
– all things – which were predicated on the achievement of independence. And where this rhetoric called forth an echo, from a whole

variety of specific grievances and frustrations, and from a simple gut reaction to alien domination, the nationalist movements spread like the proverbial bush fire in an exhilarating moment of optimism and enthusiasm such as few territories have achieved before, or, sadly, since.

On inspection, of course, any 'mass' disaggregates itself into separate particles with varying and often conflicting interests and attitudes, and the mass to which the nationalist parties appealed was no exception. Those who took up their symbols and slogans, and organised the new party branches, were very rarely the poor, the peasants, or even the proletariat and lumpenproletariat of the new colonial towns. They were, in so far as a single class label can be tied to such a disparate group of people, the petty bourgeoisie: people with a little education but not much; people who had got their feet onto the bottom of the ladder which led to fame and fortune in the modern sector but found their way up it blocked, and blocked especially by colonial rule; village schoolmasters, small town clerks and storekeepers, produce buyers, tax collectors, local court officials. They brought with them into the new movements the most diverse collection of hopes and grievances, from the extraordinarily specific to the impossibly diffuse. They had a great deal of enthusiasm, a variable amount of organisational efficiency, and very little by way of hard ideology. They constituted no Leninist vanguard party, despite a love of socialist or even Marxist rhetoric which colonial rulers sometimes found alarming, but rather a grand conglomerate, an omnium gatherum, in which everything was predicated on the great moment of independence.

The nationalist movements, moreover, were more variegated even than this suggests, for in many colonies, especially in those parts of Africa where the hand of colonialism had been fairly light, there were substantial areas which had not acquired sufficient development to create an anticolonial petty bourgeoisie or give its demands a popular following. There, for a party to spread, it was obliged to make deals with local leaders for the support of their unmobilised populations, in which votes were traded for promises of local or personal favours. Even a radical nationalist party such as Kwame Nkrumah's CPP was obliged to do this to some extent, teasing out support from the tangled local rivalries which crisscrossed the politics of the rural Gold Coast. But in some countries the entire nationalist movement remained in the hands of men whose basic alliances were with rural ruling groups, and whose anticolonialism was moderate or even non-existent. Such countries included Sierra Leone, where the ruling party at independence (misleadingly named the Sierra Leone People's Party) had no grassroots organisation beyond that supplied for it by the paramount chiefs; Senegal, where a similar role was taken by the Islamic priesthood; and most famous of all, northern Nigeria, where the Northern People's Congress rested firmly on the Fulani aristocracy.

Furthermore, though our discussion so far has referred simply to 'the nationalist movement', as though there was only one, territories varied enormously in the degree of unity or division within the movements that nationalism gave rise to. The process of political mobilisation which preceded independence − graphically referred to in West Africa as 'the time when politics came' − was not just an anticolonial one. It also raised critical issues of local political control, which had lain dormant under the common rule of colonialism. The closer independence came, the clearer it became that the rewards of victory were going to be very great, and the more intense became the competition between individuals, factions and (most dangerously) ethnic, regional or religious groups over who was going to enjoy them. In practice, different territories varied all the way along a continuum between movements in which there was virtually no internal conflict at one end, and ones in which divisions were too intense to be contained within a single state at the other. In a few territories, one party entirely monopolised indigenous political activity, either because of the skill of its leader in preventing breakaways (as was perhaps the case with the PDCI in Ivory Coast), or because there was little basis for differentiation in the society (as with TANU in Tanganyika), or because one single issue overwhelmingly dominated the decolonisation process like the question of the Central African Federation in Nyasaland (Malawi). Elsewhere, it was not uncommon for one party to dominate the political scene, as the party of nationalism and independence, while a variety of minor parties, more right wing or left wing, regional or religious, gathered around it; the Congress in India, or the CPP in Gold Coast (Ghana) would serve as examples. In places, a genuine two-party system developed, in which parties were differentiated to some degree on policy lines, to a greater extent by factional and clientelist rivalries, but were none the less capable of alternating in power in classic 'Westminster' fashion; this pattern was most characteristic of the West Indian islands, notably with the JLP and PNP in Jamaica, but Ceylon (Sri Lanka) with the UNP and SLSSP was in many ways similar. It depended critically on the existence of a coherent elite group spanning both parties (the two founding party leaders in Jamaica, Alexander Bustamante and Norman Manley, were cousins), and their ability to mobilise support across ethnic divisions where these existed; for these reasons it was almost unknown in Africa, the closest approximation being perhaps the SLPP and APC in Sierra Leone. More commonly in Africa, and in some degree elsewhere, rival parties based themselves on ethnic or regional followings, with potentially explosive consequences. In Nigeria, it soon became clear that the monopolisation of the early nationalist parties by the more educated peoples of the south presented a threat to the northern part of the country, and especially to the entrenched social hierarchy of the Muslim north; the party formed in response was called the *Northern* People's Congress, and its motto, 'One North, One People', made explicit its total lack of concern for any national or Nigerian identity. In British Guiana (Guyana), a colony almost equally divided between peoples of Indian and African descent, the first nationalist party, the PPP, was led by an Indian, Cheddi Jagan; his deputy, the Afro-Guyanese Forbes Burnham, took advantage of the ethnic division and the external suspicions aroused by Jagan's avowed Marxism, to split off and form, with tacit American support, the heavily African PNM — and with help from changes in the electoral system, to assume power at independence. Finally, the Muslim League in British India opted for independence as a separate state of Pakistan, rather than remain within an India dominated by the Congress.

This mobilisation of internal divisions was often capricious in its causes, but almost always lasting in its effects. Territories with single-party monopolies like Nyasaland (Malawi) or Ivory Coast, were in no way inherently more united in ethnic or economic terms than ones with substantial inter-party competition, like Northern Rhodesia (Zambia), Kenya or Senegal. But even though the initial mobilisation might have been the result of accidents of circumstance or leadership, it often pro-duced loyalties and identities which persisted through decades of polit-ical disruption and surfaced whenever conditions allowed. When in 1979 Nigeria held elections for a return to civilian rule, following thirteen years of military government including a bitter civil war, all five of the party leaders were old nationalist politicians who had come to prominence some twenty-five years earlier, and three of them headed revamped versions of the parties they had led in the pre-independence elections of 1959. As an episode in the political history of ex-colonial states, the nationalist period was transient and peculiar, but its consequences were to persist.

The Colonial Response and the Transfer of Power

While the nationalist movements can certainly be seen, in large measure, as a natural gut reaction to the alienness and injustice of colonialism, they were also concerned with the immediate and instrumental goal of gaining political power, and this forced them into a working relationship with the regimes which they aimed to displace. The nationalist leaders were middlemen, and their accession to power required them to strike just that balance between internal and external elements which was subsequently to characterise the postcolonial state. They depended on the support which they could raise from within the colonised society – in the form of votes or if need be of demonstrations, economic action or, ultimately, military force – to confront the colonial power; but at the same time their goal was, if at all possible, to take over control peacefully of the state which colonialism had established, and thus within a framework which the colonial power laid down. If, at one extreme, they moved too close to outright collaboration with the colonial government, they might find themselves outflanked by rival nationalists employing a more radical rhetoric and more actively mobilising the population; this was the fate of the United Gold Coast Convention in the Gold Coast (Ghana), a staid constitutionalist party of lawyers and businessmen which was left standing at the starting post by Nkrumah's vastly more dynamic CPP. If, at the other, their opposition to colonialism was too violent and virulent, the regime might, if some suitable ally was available, give tacit support to a more moderate grouping; this was especially the case with those very few nationalist movements which took a Marxist stance, such as Jagan's PPP in British Guiana (Guyana) or the UPC in French Cameroun, while an analogous pattern occurred in the Philippines, where the United States favoured the Liberal Party, and helped to suppress the Huk rebellion, which sprang from the defeated Democratic Alliance.

In reaching this balance between nationalism and compliance, a great deal depended on the attitude of the colonial power, and especially on its readiness to concede peaceful decolonisation within a fairly limited period. Some of the domestic considerations affecting this attitude have already been briefly noted. For Britain, the experience of withdrawal from the white dominions (Canada, Australia, New Zealand, South Africa) provided a precedent and a mechanism which could be applied elsewhere, first in southern Asia and later in Africa, the Caribbean and the Pacific. The first step in the process was to test the credentials of would-be successors, on the one hand by holding elections for assemblies with limited powers, on the other by attempting to suppress movements regarded as too radical or 'irresponsible'. If suppression failed and no credible alternative was available, the colonial government could still seek to save its position by offering collaboration: Nkrumah moved within twenty-four hours from jail to Leader of Government Business within a newly elected legislative council. There followed a period of 'dyarchy' in which powers were gradually devolved from the colonial government to the elected politicians, though before independence two further important steps had to be taken: first the negotiation of the new independence constitution, and secondly the holding of elections to determine who would take power under it. Though the British did not generally seek to fix the elections, or to impede the progress of the most successful party to power, they did frequently get caught by the implications of their indirect rule policies, and by their attempts to negotiate constitutions which would safeguard the interests of entrenched minority groups. At times, as in Uganda and Nigeria, this led to the imposition of constitutions which proved to be quite unworkable; and since the ex-colonial government was powerless to sustain such constitutions once independence had been achieved, all that the new government had to do was to wait and then adapt them to its own purposes. The only substantial failures of British decolonisation were in Southern Rhodesia (Zimbabwe) and South Africa, where an early transfer of power to a white settler minority (with South African independence in 1910, Rhodesian internal self-government in 1923) removed from Britain the power to supervise and hand over power to an indigenous nationalist party.

Even though France did not seriously consider independence as an option for most of her colonies until 1958, the assimilation policy in practice usually produced both the elites and the political structures which peaceful decolonisation required. The two great failures here, already noted, were Indo-China and Algeria. After the Second World War, the colonies started to elect representatives to the National Assembly in Paris. This led to the formation of political parties to organise the electorate, which essentially operated at the level of the individual colonial territory, while banding together to increase their bargaining power in Paris. The leaders of these parties became the local political bosses of their territories, and thus in effect potential nationalist leaders, even though they sat in the French parliament and did not press for immediate independence. The possibility of independence was not indeed raised until 1958, when de Gaulle after coming to power offered all French colonies (though not areas such as Algeria, which was formally an integral part of France) a carefully slanted referendum choice between immediate independence and continued association with France. Only Guinea opted for independence on the very disadvantageous terms presented, yet within two years all of the other French black African colonies, save only the French Somali Coast (Djibouti), had become independent in close association with France. Once Ghana and Guinea could present themselves as sovereign independent states, the lure of independence for other African territories became too strong to be resisted; and both French and Africans, learning from the Guinean episode, ensured that this took place in close association with France, including the maintenance of aid, currency and military links.

Two other patterns of decolonisation, even though they applied only to a small number of territories, are of interest in revealing the parameters within which the process took place. The Belgians ruled the Congo (Zaire) in many ways with an enlightened paternalism, reflected for example in the high proportion of the population which received primary education; but regarding independence only as a very distant goal, they took no steps to create an indigenous political leadership such as followed from the postwar extension of the franchise in British and French colonies – though formation of territorial political organisations in such a vast and diverse area as the Congo would have been difficult in any case. When in the very late 1950s, the Belgians accepted the possibility of early independence, there existed neither the parties nor the leaders capable of running the newly independent state, merely a set of inexperienced rivals each with a separate local power base. The collapse of public order after independence was extraordinarily rapid. Within a few days the army had mutinied, the Prime Minister (Lumumba) had lost control, one of the main regional bosses (Tshombe in Katanga) had declared a secessionist independence, and United Nations forces had been called in to prop up the disintegrating structure of the state. The whole episode provided the clearest lesson of the link between peaceful decolonisation and the creation of a successor political elite.

The opposite occurred in the Portuguese colonies where, instead of leaving almost overnight, the colonial power detemined to stay. The same pattern could be seen in the failure to decolonise in Indo-China or Algeria, or in the settler colony of Southern Rhodesia. Here an indigenous political leadership emerged but, denied any peaceful and legitimate channel for decolonisation, turned instead to the creation of a nationalist guerrilla army. The route to independence by this means was long and bitter, but in all the cases noted above it eventually succeeded – though it has not yet done so in a number of territories which are in some respects analogous: Sahara, Eritrea, Namibia, South

Africa. The governments which eventually emerged lacked the close connections with the colonial power which often followed from peaceful decolonisation, and invariably developed a radical, often Marxist, ideology and organisation. These cases demonstrate that the demand for independence was, ultimately, enforceable against the colonial powers: that when these 'granted' independence, they were giving with an appearance of willingness something which they would ultimately have had to hand over anyway. They equally show that by allowing a peaceful decolonisation, the colonial powers were able to retain vital connections with the new governments which they would otherwise have lost, and that peaceful decolonisation served their interests as well as those of the successor elites. But the guerrilla path to independence did not necessarily lead either to a united nationalist movement or to a revolutionary postcolonial state. Divisions within the movement carried over, in Angola and Rhodesia (Zimbabwe), to the formation of rival armies led by opposing leaders, sometimes capable of allying against the colonial power but equally liable to fight one another; the same has happened in Eritrea. And while some guerrilla leaders tried after independence to launch a revolutionary state on Marxist-Leninist lines, others were concerned to capture and govern through the existing state apparatus. The ultimate outcome of violent decolonisation thus did not always differ from that of the peaceful path to statehood.

Independence, for most of those third world states which gained it after the Second World War, now lies over twenty years into the past. It none the less laid a foundation which, no matter how overlain by later experiences, continues to shape the pattern of politics both in the area of domestic conflict and in the relationships between the state and the outside world. In particular, it contained within it ambivalences and uncertainties which in most cases have yet to be worked out: between the unifying influence of anticolonial nationalism, and the fragmenting effect of domestic competition for power; between the populist fervour of the nationalist parties, and the fact that power at independence passed to an elite; between the liberal democratic norms of the independence constitutions, and the authoritarianism both of many of the new leaders, and of the colonial state apparatus which they inherited; between the anticolonialism of the nationalist movements, and the fact that most of them came peacefully to power under the tutelage of the colonial government itself; perhaps most of all, between the formal transfer of power at independence, and the continuation of dependence in almost every other sphere of life.

Notes

1. The outstanding short general history of colonialism is D.K. Fieldhouse, *The Colonial Empires: A Comparative Survey from the Eighteenth Century*, 2nd edn (Macmillan, 1982).

2. Figures taken from C. Veliz (ed.), *Latin America and the Caribbean: A Handbook* (Blond, 1968).

3. See A.H.M. Kirk-Greene, 'The Thin White Line: The Size of the British Colonial Service in Africa', *African Affairs*, vol. 79, no. 314 (1980), pp. 25-44; the figures cited are from R. Delavignette, *Freedom and Authority in French West Africa* (Cass, 1968).

3 THE THIRD WORLD STATE

The Nature of the Third World State

What actually happened at independence? There was a ceremony and a celebration, a lowering of the old flag and a raising of the new, a formal handover by some representative of the colonial administration of the 'instruments of government' to the designated successor. This symbolic action was also extremely exact. What the new rulers actually received was the right, usually conferred by elections before independence and confirmed by the outgoing colonial regime, to control the instruments of government – in the sense of the actual institutions – created by that regime for its own use. These institutions then constituted 'the state', and it is this state which has emerged as the key to the structure of third world politics. The state has gained a similar centrality in those few third world countries which were not subject to formal colonialism through the process of monarchical modernisation which has already been touched on, and this centrality has been maintained in regions such as Latin America in which the experience of colonialism now lies well in the past.

What distinguishes the third world state from its equivalents in other parts of the world is the combination of its power and its fragility. Of these two elements, the power is by far the more evident. What the state consists of in its most basic sense is a structure of control. Arising from the colonial setting in which the first imperative was to secure the obedience of an alien people – or in its indigenous monarchical setting to reduce the autonomy of regional potentates – it is usually strongly hierarchical. The grid of power radiates from the capital, through a set of territorial subdivisions which only rarely (in India, Nigeria, Brazil, for instance) gain the limited autonomy provided by federalism. The primary responsibility of this grid is the maintenance of order, and the servants of the state whose concern this is – the regional prefect or governor, the police force and the courts and, lying in reserve, the army – are the dominant elements in the whole structure. Close beneath them and closely associated with them, however, are the agencies concerned with the economic management of the state. Appearances to the contrary, these are not primarily interested in economic 'development'. Like the colonial state from which it is descended, the third world state has to maintain itself by extracting resources from the domestic economy, and especially from the trade generated by the economy's incorporation into a global structure of exchange. Whereas the developmental functions of the state are often patchy and inadequate, sometimes almost non-existent, its extractive ones are omnipresent. Lastly come those elements of the state which are immediately concerned with providing benefits for its citizens, rather than for the state itself: education, health and other social services. Along with the state come the people who own it. These are drawn overwhelmingly from the most educated and articulate sections of the population, and associated in most cases with those groups within society which already enjoy the greatest social status, wealth and power. The state becomes in their hands not only a source of benefits in itself, but also a means to defend themselves against domestic discontent, and in some measure also against external penetration.

Yet the state is not the all-powerful monolith which this sketch may suggest. For one thing, its power is attractive, and competition to control that power saps and subverts the state itself. In any country, control over the state is one of the central things — indeed *the* main thing — which politics is about; but where the state provides a source of power and wealth entirely disproportionate to that available from any other organised force within society, the quest for state power takes on a pathological dimension. Whereas in established Marxist-Leninist states, access to this power is rigidly channelled by the state itself and its associated party (though even then not without its characteristic traumas), few if any third world states have managed to turn themselves into self-sufficient bureaucratic apparatuses. Control over the state is a prize which can be fought for, and therefore is. In the period before independence and immediately after it, the fight takes place between formally organised political parties, with their leaders, their programmes and their support drawn from one or another section of the population in the form of votes or sometimes more direct and violent political action. Occasionally, this system survives. Much more often, it proves incapable of withstanding a situation in which the power of the state is allied with that of the most successful political party, which is then ideally placed either to attract or to repress its rivals. Even then, however, essentially the same conflict takes place, perhaps violently on the streets as the opposition groupings seek to mobilise their forces, perhaps secretly as they conspire to overthrow the government in power, or through factional manoeuvres within the government itself; one way or another, the prize of state control is too appealing to be abandoned. Exactly the same is true for the government in power, whose determination to cling on is likely to be strengthened by a growing dependence on the comforts of office, and the fear of retaliation should their opponents get in. On the state as a simple agency for extraction and control, must then be superimposed the state as a prize in political competition, and as a means by which those who win that competition can serve their amibitions and suppress their opponents. A third element is introduced when competition for control over the state is extended to include parts of the state itself among the competitors. A ruler who has very little to fear from popular opposition may easily be toppled by military coup. Where the state is by far the strongest source of organised political power, government of the state, by the state and for the state becomes extremely likely, and even rulers not directly projected into power from the ranks of the state's own servants may well fall back on it as the easiest and least risky way of running the government. This in turn, however, raises problems of political management both within the state bureaucracy, civil and military, and in the relationships between the state and the wider society — which are most conveniently examined in the chapter on military regimes.

If the state cannot be controlled, it may at least be subverted. One of the features of the third world state which prevents it from developing into a totalitarian structure of hierarchical control is the fact that it is so readily permeated by the society in which it exists. The colonial state was not so permeable. It did very largely operate as a self-contained bureaucratic institution, responsible to its own rules and its own superiors, and open to infiltration by the society which it governed only at the lowest level, through the influence of indigenous local rulers or of locally recruited clerks, interpreters or policemen. That was possible because it was alien. Even its indigenous employees were responsible to a chain of command which led directly overseas, and had to abide by its standards on pain of losing the most privileged positions which colonialism had to offer. After independence it was different, though some sections of the bureaucracy in countries such as India or Ghana continued to cling to colonial standards — in which by this time they had acquired an interest, since these helped to protect them from the demands of their political masters. On the whole, however, civil servants became part of the indigenous political process, identifiable with the class, caste or regional group from which they came, readily suspected of serving their own particularist interests on the one hand, while subject to influence and inducement on the other. At times, indeed, civil servants turned themselves into spokesmen for political interests, especially during periods of military government when the ordinary channels of political articulation were withdrawn, and even the army could become divided between 'politicals' and 'professionals'. In the process, the boundary between state and society became blurred, as the state itself became less coherent.

What did *not* take place, however – and this again is central to the character and role of the third world state – was any merging of state and society as common expressions of a set of shared values. In part, this too was a legacy of colonial imposition. Where, as in Africa or Asia, the state was imported along with the people who ran it, the division between indigenous society and external political structure was not eradicated by the replacement of colonial by local officials. The new state was now capable of being influenced, even subverted, by political action, but it was rarely something to which loyalty was owed in itself. Something of the same effect could be found in states in the Caribbean and parts of Latin America, where the people were imported as well as the political structure, and everything was artificial, except for the national boundaries which in the island territories at least were set by the sea. In some states, such as Jamaica and Barbados, this artificial society does appear to have been welded into a national community with its own set of political institutions (copied though these are from a metropolitan model). None the less, the state in its origins was the preserve of the dominant immigrant group (characteristically the white slave owners) and used as an agency of control. Where racial divisions persist, either between dominant immigrants and subordinate indigenous groups, as in Bolivia and Peru, or between rival groups of immigrants, as in Guyana or to some degree in Trinidad, the state is still readily associated with those who control it. The most extreme example of this process is South Africa. Even in those states such as Thailand or Ethiopia which escaped colonialism, the state is often associated with a core national community, which imposes its role on peripheral areas inhabited by other peoples.

The lack of organic unity or shared values between state and society, compounded though it is by the myriad effects of social change and incorporation into the global economy and political structure, is the single most basic reason for the fragility of the third world state. Political fragility is something very different from a simple lack of state capacity. Third world states differ sharply in the amount that they can actually do. Some, such as Singapore and South Korea, are as efficiently controlled as any in the world, whereas others, such as

Burma or Ethiopia, cannot even control much of their own territory. Other indicators of state capacity, such as government share of gross national product or the proportion of the population employed in internal security duties, likewise rank third world states among both the highest and lowest in the world. Fragility in the sense in which I am concerned with here, rather, is most immediately expressed in the weakness of 'legitimacy', seen as a sustained and widespread public commitment to particular forms of governmental institution which will select and sustain political leaders. The absence of such legitimacy in turn fuels governmental insecurity amounting sometimes to paranoia. Personal and political corruption likewise reflects the lack of accepted and enforceable public values. Both of these aspects of the lack of shared values accept the state as the basic framework for public action: autocrats and coup leaders seek to control the state, just as corrupt officials seek to profit by it. Neither would get anywhere once it ceased to exercise its coercive and extractive functions. The lack of value consensus none the less ultimately carries a threat to the state's own survival — the ultimate débâcle for a third world (or for that matter any) political system. Sometimes, as in Uganda, a state which (despite internal divisions) is apparently quite viable may be brought to its knees by the combined brutality and incompetence of a single leader. Some states, such as Chad, were from the start highly artificial amalgamations of disparate political factions whose divisions could easily destroy the prize for which they were contending. In Lebanon, a fragile though up to a point quite successful domestic political balance was shattered by the incursion of rival Palestinian, Israeli and Syrian armies whose conflicts were ultimately not about Lebanon at all. Other states have been forcibly split in two, like Pakistan and Bangladesh, or amalgamated, like North and South Vietnam. On the whole, the great majority of third world states have survived, due to an alliance of domestic and external interests which favours their preservation, and which will be examined further in Chapter 6; but that survival is certainly not something to be taken for granted.

This combination of power and fragility, with its accompanying disjunction between the state and any shared set of social values, in turn accounts for almost every distinctive aspect of third world politics, and the rest of this book is in a sense simply the exploration of its implications. The first question that arises is that if the state does not work according to the classic (and clearly western) model of the nation-state, in which the constitutional structure is ultimately upheld by a sense of national self-identify, then how *does* it work? It does not usually operate simply by force, yet nor is it usually ineffective; and in so far as any single general theme can be used to illuminate the diverse politics of widely scattered states, this is the theme of 'neo-patrimonialism', which is examined in the next section. A second question is, how *might* it work? This is a matter, not of the theories used by social scientists to make sense of third world politics, but of the theories devised by the leaders of third world states in order to guide or justify their own activities. Such theories, or 'ideologies' if that seems a better word for them, naturally enough reflect the structural situation and personal self-interest of those who devise them; that indeed is part of their importance. But as with theories or ideologies of colonial administration, the way in which politicians seek to make sense of the position they are in and the options which they face is always instructive, and provides at least one guide to what they actually do. What they actually do — the problem of political management — then forms the core of the subsequent chapters: the consolidation of leadership, the management or mismanagement of domestic political relationships, the economy and contacts with the outside world.

Neo-patrimonialism and its Consequences

Forms of Authority

Both the organisation and the legitimacy of the modern state rest, in principle at least, on what Weber described as rational-legal authority. The basis of that authority is that individuals in public positions, possessing power over their fellow citizens, exercise that power in accordance with a legally defined structure directed towards a publicly acknowledged goal. What provides the element of 'authority' or morally accepted or justified power, is that goals themselves are widely accepted, and that the structures are likewise accepted as the most efficient means of achieving these goals. What is then necessary to make the structures work is a strict division between an individual's public and private roles, encapsulated in the notion of an 'office'. In office, the official acts simply as an official, exercising the powers which his office gives him and accepting the restraints which it likewise places on him, while treating other individuals impersonally according to the criteria which the office lays down, whether they be his superiors, his subordinates or the 'public' with which he deals. If he is shifted to another office, he will instantly start to behave in the way which the new office requires, while the individual who replaces him in his old office will behave as he did before. Outside the office, he reverts to the status of a private individual, having private ambitions and obligations, but unable to use his public position to achieve them.

This ideal type, obviously enough, is nowhere fully achieved. The most basic reason for the failure to achieve it is that it goes against our natural instincts as human beings, calling on us to divide into rigidly demarcated public and private compartments aspects of our lives which we would otherwise put together. It is the modern state which is artificial, together with the modern economy which underlies it, and it calls for a corresponding artificiality in the behaviour of the people who run it. In this sense it is public rather than private behaviour which is the 'problem', and it is for this reason that no state has ever fully succeeded in maintaining itself as an entirely public entity, divorced from the personal interests of its constituent individuals. Even in so far as a rational bureaucratic organisation is maintained, moreover, it may be directed to the bureaucracy or its masters rather than to public goals shared by the mass of the population. The rational-legal idea none the less retains a central importance, since it is only through this ideal that the enormous powers of the modern state can be exercised in a way which is both efficient and legitimate. From this viewpoint, perhaps the basic problem of the third world state — and hence more generally of third world politics — is its failure in most cases even to approximate to a rational-legal mode of operation.

One level at which this is evident is the formal constitution of the state itself, which should in principle provide the ultimate legal framework through which rational-legal behaviour is defined. The failure to maintain a constitution is thus the simplest measure of the failure to maintain an agreed set of state objectives and of institutions through which to achieve them. In the former colonial states, the constitutions inherited at independence have rarely lasted for long, though there are exceptions, notably in the Caribbean, where constitutional longevity has reflected some sense of political order. More often, and especially in Africa, they have been brusquely changed to suit the needs of incumbent governments, and equally easily replaced or simply abolished by their successors. In some respects, independence constitutions reflected a balance of power which became anachronistic with the act of independence itself, since the major role in formulating them was played by the departing colonial power which (especially in the case of British colonies) often showed a sensitivity to opposition and minority demands which the new regime quickly reversed. Newly drawn up indigenous constitutions, which might be expected to reflect the realities of the domestic power structure, none the less rarely fared much better, while constitutional upheavals have continued at a rapid rate even in states which have never experienced direct colonialism, or have now put it far behind them. In only three of the twenty Latin American states has a single constitution remained continuously in effect since 1960, while established non-colonial states such as Thailand or Turkey have changed or suspended their constitutions at intervals of ten years or less over most of the last forty years. Where a single constitution has remained in force over a substantial period, as in South Africa or in Liberia before 1980, this has as often as not been because it served as a vehicle for regulating the internal competition of a small elite group to which power has been effectively confined.

Another test of rational-legal authority lies in the behaviour of public officials, and especially the courts and the bureaucracy. This test is less stringent than that of constitutional continuity, since it concerns the internal organisation of the government rather than the overall structure of the political system. 'Going by the book' is also in some ways in the interests of bureaucrats themselves, protecting them against external pressure. However, cases can certainly be cited of both individual bureaucrats and bureaucratic structures as a whole which operate honestly and efficiently according to their rules, while judges especially sometimes show astonishing courage in resisting political pressures. The overall conclusion reached by the great majority of studies of third world bureaucracy is none the less that formal rational-legal criteria are a very inadequate guide to their behaviour.[1] And having made every qualification for the tendency of scholars investigating this behaviour to set it against a rigid ideal type which is realised nowhere in the world (and certainly not in the United States, for instance), it is still not all that surprising to find that western industrial forms of administrative institution cannot be parachuted into third world states and expected to work in the same way as they do in societies with very different values, economies and patterns of historical development.

Some of the earliest attempts to analyse authority structures in third world states, from the 1950s onwards, drew on Weber's alternative ideal type of charismatic authority. Charisma, most familiar from the example of messianic religious leaders, was a form of authority inherent in an individual, who through his own virtue and example crystallised a new concept of authority, even though this would have consistent elements drawn from previous experience, and would ultimately, if successful, be routinised in a new institutional form. It was a concept tailor-made for the nationalist leaders, then at the height of their reputations, and perhaps over-enthusiastically applied to them by scholars anxious to identify with postcolonial aspirations. Certainly, new leaders did embody the heady feelings of 'the time when politics came', and some of them did settle down to impart to their states after independence lasting aspects of their own ideologies and attitudes. None the less, charisma was always much too feeble a base on which to build any general analysis of political authority, even in those states where an appropriate leader could be identified – and some staggeringly inappropriate leaders, such as Marcos in the Philippines, were also accorded the accolade. The idea effectively died with the overthrow of Kwame Nkrumah in Ghana, one of the classic 'charismatic' leaders, in February 1966, and was buried by photographs of joyful Ghanaians destroying the outsize statue of the man once hailed as their redeemer.

In retrospect, the idea of charisma may best be regarded as an attempt to grapple with the distinctive forms of politics which occur when new social groups are rapidly being incorporated into the political process. It was the peculiar situation in which they were working, rather than any personal quality inherent in themselves, that distinguished the nationalist leaders from 'routinised' politicians engaged in managing an existing system – even though the mobilisation of new groups often required a level of personal leadership which was reflected in the prestige accruing to the leader himself. Precisely this same process of mobilisation is evident in other situations which give rise to 'charismatic' leadership, one of the clearest examples being Juan Perón in Argentina between 1943 and 1955 – a rare case of a military leader forming his own mass urban following. Gamel Abdel Nasser in Egypt after 1952 is another example, while the relationship between 'charisma' and mobilisation is most striking of all in revolutionary leaders such as Castro in Cuba or Mao Tse-Tung in China. As a general approach to the structure of authority in third world states, however, charismatic leadership is too evidently inadequate to be worth reviving.

We can however get further through the third of Weber's authority types, that of patrimonialism. The distinctive features of patrimonialism are that, in contrast to rational-legal relationships, authority is ascribed to a person rather than an office-holder, while in contrast to charisma, that person is firmly anchored in a social and political order. As the word implies, the concept of authority which underlies it is that of a father over his children – a concept which constantly recurred in the rhetoric of such a traditionalist patrimonial ruler as Haile Selassie of Ethiopia – and the classic setting in which it is found may broadly be described as feudal. In a system held together by a patrimonial logic, those lower down the political hierarchy are not subordinates, in the sense of officials with defined powers and functions of their own, but rather vassals or retainers whose position depends on the leader to whom they owe allegiance. Neither leader nor followers have defined powers, since what matters about power is not the amount of it that you have, but rather on whose behalf you exercise it. The system as a whole is held together by the oath of loyalty, or by kinship ties (often symbolic and fictitious) rather than by a hierarchy of administrative grades and functions. When, for example, the leader of an Ethiopian army died in battle, like the Emperor Yohannes fighting the Mahdists at Metemma in 1889, the command did not automatically devolve on his immediate subordinate; instead the whole army disintegrated, there and then, into its component sections. The logic which held it together had gone, and a new army could only be formed by another individual establishing his own separate authority.

Third world states, of course, are not feudal systems, even in so far as that description can be applied to the old Ethiopian Empire, though here and there touches of pure patrimonialism survive, for example in the way that each new Saudi king builds his own palace, leaving that of his predecessor as an abandoned shell. What characterises them, rather, is *neo-patrimonialism*, a form of organisation in which relationships of a broadly patrimonial type pervade a political and administrative system which is formally constructed on rational-legal lines.[2] Officials hold positions in bureaucratic organisations with powers which are formally defined, but exercise those powers, so far as they can, as a form not of public service but of private property. Relationships with others likewise fall into the patrimonial pattern of vassal and lord, rather than the rational-legal one of subordinate and superior, and behaviour is correspondingly devised to display a personal status, rather than to perform an official function. The postal clerk who shuts down his counter half an hour early, for apparently no better reason than to spite the patient queue of people waiting to buy stamps, and the head of state who insists that all his ministers and leading officials turn up at the airport to bid him farewell on a visit abroad, are both doing essentially the same thing: demonstrating that the relationship between themselves and their clients or underlings is one of personal subordination. The implications of the same approach plague the ordinary business of government administration. It is not just that officials, treating their posts as personal fiefdoms, use them to extract bribes or to appoint relatives, though that will shortly be considered under the heading of corruption. There are characteristic problems, too, about delegation. A superior will consider that he has the right to intervene personally in any matter which comes within his jurisdiction, and will do so regardless of the chaos it may cause, before going on to intervene elsewhere. A subordinate who takes decisions without referring them upwards may be regarded as slighting the authority of his boss — since to act independently of him is implicitly to challenge him. When the boss is away, especially in the case of the head of state, the decision-making process waits on his return. If he is reluctant to make decisions, the entire system sinks into a torpor from which it may only be rescued by his overthrow and replacement by a new boss who rapidly gets things under way. Within the context of a patrimonial system, all of these features serve the valuable function of maintaining a single legitimate source of authority. Imposed upon the structure of a bureaucratic state, they can rapidly gum up the works.

Neo-patrimonialism, like charisma or rational-legality, is an ideal type, realised to a varying degree both in third world states and elsewhere. There are, however, a number of reasons why it is most often the salient type in third world societies. First, the natural human disinclination to distinguish between one's private and official self equally corresponds to the normal forms of social organisation in precolonial societies. Neo-patrimonialism is far more than just a feudal hangover. It also characterises tribal societies in which loyalty to one's kin group is the primary social value, and plural societies like the immigrant states of the new world in which status and identity were determined by ethnic group affiliation or position on a caste-like social hierarchy; that is one of the reasons why it survives in the ethnic politics of the United States. Beneath the facade of the modern state, the same principles continue to operate. They are particularly obvious in the behaviour of the non-elite mass of the population, both in the speed with which a following of claimants gathers round a successful bureaucrat or politician, and in the readiness with which the abuse of office by public officials (as it would be reckoned, at any rate, by western industrial standards) is accepted as normal behaviour, condemned only in so far as it benefits someone else rather than oneself. Further, both the artificiality of national communities, and the incorporation of the society into the global economy, help to corrode a sense of common values, and hence indirectly to encourage neo-patrimonialism, which can be readily adapted to an instrumental form, in which straightforward considerations of personal benefit and the exchange of favours come to replace the reciprocal obligations which characterise patrimonialism in its original or traditional form. Two closely linked areas in which this is particularly evident are those of corruption and patron-client relations.

Corruption

Corruption is the use of public powers in order to achieve private goals. The very concept of corruption itself thus turns on the distinction between the public and the private which underlies Weber's ideal type of rational-legal authority. In a truly patrimonial system, the idea of corruption in itself makes no sense because that distinction does not arise: there is no embezzlement because the ruler's personal income is the same as the government revenue, no nepotism because there is no criterion for appointment to office apart from the ruler's favour. In a neo-patrimonial system, on the other hand, corruption does arise because the system itself is formally constructed on the principle of rational-legality. Nor is this just a form: corruption cannot, as it were, be abolished by declaring the state to be a patrimonial one after all, and thereby appropriating the revenues for one's own personal use, as was done in effect by President Bokassa of the Central African Republic when in 1976 he declared himself to be an Emperor and sucked the national economy dry to pay for his coronation. The modern state depends on forms of organisation, and insists on exercising powers, which must ultimately rest — if they are to be rendered legitimate at all — on rational-legality. In all states, those powers are in some degree corruptly exercised, because of the inherent artificiality of the public/private distinction already noted, and the difficulty of controlling officials in even the most highly accountable system. But the dangers of corruption are at their greatest when the distinction itself is scarcely recognised, and when public office consequently becomes accepted as a route to personal wealth and power. As always in dealing with ideal types, one must beware of treating a formal model as empirical fact applicable in this case to all third world states. They both differ from one another and change over time, while in the case of a state such as Great Britain the public/private distinction was established over a period of some three hundred years, from the early seventeenth to the late nineteenth centuries, through a succession of measures which progressively established the limits of acceptable public behaviour. There is no doubt, however, that corruption is a very considerable problem almost throughout the third world, amounting in extreme cases to a system of government for purposes of personal enrichment, which has been described as 'kleptocracy' or rule by theft. This cannot plausibly be ascribed just to the moral failings of individual officials — even though moral criteria may quite properly distinguish between people who, within a given system, behave with particular honesty or graft. A general phenomenon calls for a general explanation, which the idea of neo-patrimonialism most conveniently encapsulates.

Among the reasons most often given for the salience of third world corruption is the carry-over into present-day political behaviour of cultural values inherited from a patrimonial past. In some ways, this is convincing enough. The practice of gift-giving, for example, is almost universal in patrimonial societies. When a chief or some other person of authority visited the village, or when a dispute was taken before a judge, it was normal and accepted to make a gift, usually of food, to the person concerned. This gift expressed, within a tributary system, a recognition of the authority of the person who received it; *not* to make it would be taken as expressing insubordination or contempt. Even in patrimonial societies, this may readily be viewed in Marxist terms as a means by which the dominant class extracted a surplus from producers; in the context of the modern state, it is easily converted into bribery on one side, or extortion on the other. The same goes for the deeply entrenched principle of mutual support among fellow members of the extended family, village, clan, or other communal group. A highly functional response to the economic and political insecurity of subsistence agriculture, it readily converts into nepotism, or into a form of extortion from below in which a member of the community who has made good in the modern world is placed under the most intense social pressure to use his position for the benefit of those who feel that they have a valid moral claim on his services.

Yet these traditionalist explanations for corruption readily degenerate into self-justifying excuses if they do not recognise the key role played by the structure of the third world state. It is unreasonable to expect a set of rational-legal values to develop among public officials without any effective mechanism for their enforcement, and the basic problem here is the weakness of accountability by the governors to the governed. Some of the constitutional aspects of this, notably the inability in most countries to establish liberal democratic forms of government which (for all their faults) provide the best means for ensuring accountability, will be discussed in the next chapter; but these rest on more general points related to the state itself, and its relations with the international system. First, there is the sheer social distance established as members of what has become an elite acquire western education and move into well-paid modern sector jobs, accompanied very often by physical distance as they move into towns where they can enjoy an appropriate life style and, even within the towns, enclose themselves in separate residential areas. While the immigrant societies of the new world lack the distinction between a 'traditional' and a 'modern' sector, they more than make up for it by the fact that income inequalities are greater in Latin America than anywhere else on earth.[3] Accountability must, therefore, largely be achieved by members of the elite among themselves. Secondly, the state provides an enormous and institutionalised inequality of power. Not only is it in itself highly hierarchical, but it is unchecked by countervailing powers such as those produced by capitalism and private property in the development of the western liberal states. Similar problems are of course found in the party-state *apparats* of the Soviet bloc. In so far as officials are unchecked by their own superiors, even petty employees of government — the traffic policeman, for instance — can use their little bits of state power as a means to increase their income. Low-level government officials are often not paid much anyway, and their salaries may come irregularly owing to inefficiency or extortion higher up, or just because there is no money in the treasury; they make up the difference by collecting it from their subjects. At a higher level, senior politicans often feel that their status and role demand an ostentatious life style which falls well beyond their salary, requiring either bribery, or else perhaps opportunities for legitimate private profit made possible by their official position. India is rare in having an indigenous ascetic ethic which enables powerful men to gain status through poverty; more often, and especially in Africa, wealth is flaunted rather than concealed.

Effective control over corruption is difficult to maintain. Occasionally a head of state such as Dr Banda in Malawi, an autocrat with the rigid morality of an elder of the Kirk of Scotland, is able to enforce his own standards on his subordinates. More often, although the head of state's speeches are peppered with exhortations, these are part of the official rhetoric which no one takes very seriously. The common stereotype in which the leader is regarded as honest while his ministers are regarded as corrupt, provides the leader not just with extra moral authority, but with a threat which he can use to keep the rest in line; when he wishes to dispense with someone anyway, corruption provides a pretext for doing so. The chance of being brought to book in the wake of a military coup provides no more than an uncertain threat to a few prominent individuals; insecurity may indeed be an incentive to salt away money while the going is good. Military regimes characteristically come into power with a strong rhetorical appeal to honesty and efficiency, but even if they believe this at the time – as they may well do – it can rarely survive for long in government. Militaries, after all, form part of the same state apparatus as civilian bureaucrats and politicians; they govern through it, and benefit from the structural inequalities implicit in it. One of the most sharply depressing scenes in African literature comes in Ayi Kewei Armah's *The Beautyful Ones Are not Yet Born*, when a policeman, manning a road block immediately after the army and police overthrow of the corrupt Nkrumah regime, points his finger to his mouth in a gesture to indicate that a bribe would be acceptable; deep-seated structural conditions are not to be altered by a simple change in government.

A further reason for the salience of corruption lies in the external connections of the third world state. At one level, many of the benefits which corruption provides are external ones, such as imported luxury consumer goods or overseas travel and education; without access to the world market in one form or another, there is usually not very much that you can do with the money, apart from passing it down the line to build up political support. At another, contacts between third world governments and the international economy provide lucrative opportunities for corruption which (though the domestic society pays for them in the end) are less immediately visible and politically unpopular than direct exactions from one's own people: government contracts, concession agreements, suppliers' credits, import licences all provide links between the domestic and international economy, controlled by state officials who may charge their own personal management fee. Finally, a regime with a shaky domestic political base may survive through the support of external powers, either indirectly through aid or directly by military intervention on its behalf, and as a result is better able to exploit its own people. While both western and Soviet blocs have supported some extremely unpleasant regimes, it is on the whole true to say that the western ones have been more corrupt in financial terms, the Soviet ones more brutal in terms of physical extermination. The external connections of the third world state are examined in a later chapter.

Several distinctions have been made between different kinds of corruption, most of which come down to the difference between parochial or distributive corruption on the one hand, and market or extractive corruption on the other. Parochial corruption is generally small in scale, fits into an existing set of values and obligations, and leads to the redistribution and exchange of benefits within a community, rather than the siphoning of resources from it. Extractive corruption is often on a large scale, rests on the manipulation of state power, and maintains the life style of a privileged class of state employees and their confederates. Although a low level of petty corruption may be ascribed to indigenous values which are harmless and even helpful in maintaining social solidarity, the weight of corruption falls into the second category, and can be crudely described as the means by which those with power get money. No purpose is served by the abusive moral condemnation of those who succumb to this temptation by those who have not had the chance to; but viewed as a social phenomenon, it has corrosive effects on trust in public authorities, and hence on their capacity to direct communal action towards the achievement of common goals, as well as wasting resources both through inefficiency and by directing them abroad. Even though it is a symptom quite as much as a cause, it provides the most striking indication of the failure to link society and government in a shared sense of values.

Patrons and Clients

The power and fragility of the state, and the social, economic and political gap between those who run it and the great majority of those who are ruled by it, raise an acute problem in the relationship between political power on the one hand and popular support and participation on the other. The key political difficulty facing third world rulers is to extend their support beyond the immediate group of courtiers who have a personal stake in their survival. It is a problem which many do not solve, and which some do not seriously try to. At a minimum, survival may depend simply on their ability to maintain a force more effective than any directed against them, like Amin of Uganda's bodyguard, sustained by a weekly airlift of luxuries from the United Kingdom, before the Tanzanian invasion of 1978-9. A successful coup d'état, launched at times by forces of trivial size, often serves to show that there is no one outside the leader's entourage who is prepared to take any action to try to preserve the regime.

But if a regime is to seek support, how can it do it? The initial boost provided by anticolonial nationalism or by some equivalent triumph cannot be sustained for long. The class divisions which maintain the principal parties of western European states rarely serve the purpose in the third world, not because there are no such divisions — far from it — but because the ruling class is usually so well established that class solidarity is a pointless appeal. It is only in highly developed states, such as Chile, that there is a threat to the economically dominant classes sufficient to bring them together in support of the Pinochet regime, and previously to sustain the pre-Allende Christian Democratic governments. An ideological political base in itself generally depends on the support of a class whose interests are served by the ideology, and equally on a competitive party structure through which the relevance of alternative ideologies can be made clear. This is not impossible — Jamaica provides at least a partial example — but it is unusual.

The solution characteristically attempted in third world states is through some form of clientelism or patron-client relationship.[4] Clientelism is indeed the application of the principles of neo-patrimonialism to relationships between superiors and inferiors. It is, fundamentally, a relationship of exchange in which a superior (or patron) provides security for an inferior (or client), and the client in turn provides support for the patron. The form taken by this security and support may vary widely: on the one hand physical or legal protection, land or a job, some kind of economic development assistance, even religious intercession; on the other, military service, voting, economic labour power, information. Very often several of these are joined together, and the bond strengthened by some moral sanction which obliges each side to support the other. It is a kind of relationship which characterises any society in which there are sharp divisions (usually on class lines) between superiors and inferiors, but in which neither superiors nor inferiors form politically coherent class units acting together; instead, individual superiors or inferiors need the security and support which is provided by members of the other class. The most familiar arena for patron-client ties is an agrarian economy of a broadly 'feudal' type in which control of land is vested in a landowning class whose members are in constant competition with one another; each landowner needs to attract peasants to work his land, providing him both with produce and with a political-military following, while each peasant, if he is to survive, needs to find a landlord who will provide him with land and protect his right to work it. It is an inherently unequal exchange, hence liable to exploitation, but none the less meeting essential interests on both sides.

The neo-patrimonial state — indeed the modern state as a whole — provides an equally fertile breeding ground for exactly the same kind of relationship. It likewise embodies inherent inequalities, between those who control the state (or more generally, those who have the technical qualifications to do so if they get the chance) and those who do not, and also between those higher and lower within the state hierarchy. Control of the state carries with it the power to provide (or with-

hold) security, and to allocate benefits in the form of jobs, development projects and so forth; and where the government is under no
compulsion to furnish these benefits according to public or universal
criteria such as justice, efficiency and need, it may do so at its own dis-
cretion to encourage political support. By the same token, those who
control the state do generally need political support, unless they can
rely on a repressive apparatus which is both loyal and efficient enough
to deal with any opposition. In one situation, they need it very badly:
when there is an effective electoral system which gives votes to all of
the adult citizens, and which awards control of the state to the party
which (allowing for the workings of particular electoral systems) wins
most votes. Clientelist organisation is, therefore, especially characteristic of competitive party systems, and often, therefore, of the period
immediately before independence when rival parties were struggling to
win control of the state; the same kind of organisation, and the attitudes
to politics which go with it, then usually survive into the post-independence period.

One common way in which it works is this: political party leaders at
the national level look around for local leaders who command appreciable support within their own areas. They offer the local leader (or
perhaps one of his close relatives or associates) a place in the party,
perhaps as a candidate in his home constituency. The local leader gets
out the vote, essentially through his own contacts and authority, and
delivers it to the national party. The national party in turn − assuming
that it wins power − delivers benefits to its local representative, in the
form either of economic allocations from the centre to the constituency, such as a road or a piped water supply, or of a purely personal
pay-off, or of central government support in local political conflicts.
Local politics is often extremely factionalised and it is common for
one village, or one chief or magnate and his following, to support one
party, while their rivals go for the other one. After the election comes
the settling of the scores: the successful village gets its piped water
supply, the unsuccessful chief is deposed. In the process, the local
leader becomes a broker between his own community and central
government, passing benefits in each direction and (if he is lucky and
successful) taking his share of them. Even when the period of competitive elections passes, and the central government no longer really needs
the electoral support which the broker provided, he may still retain his
status as a local political boss, someone who is kept on in government
because he is still taken as 'representing' an area with which the regime
wishes to remain associated. He may then become effectively the repre-

sentative of government in that area, holding his own local court, the target of supplicants who beg him for government favours. Come a military coup and he will be out, perhaps imprisoned, condemned for corruption; his local rivals will be enthroned in his place, favouring their own villages, installing their own chiefs, praising the new government, in a general reversal of fortunes. But given new elections, or a counter-coup, the original boss may well be back again, unless he has died (or been executed) in the meantime, or so abused his position in the years of triumph that his people refuse to support him. Local level politics in third world states must constantly adapt itself to the realities of central power, but usually survives remarkably unscathed by the vicissitudes of politics at the centre.

In societies without strong local identities, clientelism may work in different ways. In Jamaica, a fairly homogenous and heavily urbanised society, the trade unions affiliated to each of the major political parties may be seen as essentially clientelist organisations formed to maintain support and provide jobs for party stalwarts. In Senegal, where the principal brokers have been the Muslim brotherhoods, these extend from the countryside into the towns, where they collect cash subscriptions from their members and adapt the benefits they provide to the urban setting. Indeed immigrants into towns are often so vulnerable that the protection provided by a patron is well worth paying for. These in turn become brokers whom political parties will seek to recruit, and who in the Latin American context, say, can be used to organise demonstrations of support for, or opposition to, the governing party or junta's policies.[5] In Brazil, the military government in power since 1964 has been able to form and manipulate political parties in this way, especially the ARENA party, and thus provide itself with at least some appearance of popular support.[6] The much greater difficulties of Argentine military regimes, reflected in their resort both to domestic political repression and to external military adventure, have to some degree been due to the fact that these resources had already been mobilised by rival (and in their way equally clientelist) civilian political movements, especially Peronism.

One of the strongest, most alluring, and at the same time most dangerous forms of clientelism is the mobilisation of ethnic identities. We have already seen how the artificiality of the colonial state, the unevenness of social and economic change and the competition for power among indigenous parties during the nationalist period, all tended to intensify ethnic awareness. From a political viewpoint, ethnicity may be seen as a means for giving a moral bond or cement to a clientelist network. The party leadership is placed under an obligation to look after the interests of its constituent race, tribe, caste or religious group; equally to the point, the leadership acquires a kind of legitimacy as the authentic representative of that group, regardless of the enormous differences of class and wealth, and in some respects of political interest, between it and its followers. Clientelism, which depends for its existence on a hierarchically ordered society in which class differences are often intense, both serves as a mechanism for maintaining ruling class interests and, at the same time, systematically inhibits the articulation of class as a source of overt political conflict.

Even when patron-client bonds are not reinforced by the dubious morality of ethnic consciousness, their strength should never be underestimated. They have a resilience, a flexibility, and a degree of rationality for the interests of both patron and client which enable them to survive even the most drastic attempts at their suppression — a point most strikingly illustrated by the role of clientelism within the elephantine *apparats* of the Soviet party and state.[7] They bear a high degree of responsibility for the astonishing rarity of revolutionary upheavals, or even of effective revolutionary movements, anywhere in the third world. For so long as people are vulnerable to political and economic circumstances, and for so long as clientelist networks offer some plausible hope at least for alleviating (though never for fully overcoming) that vulnerability, then the network offers a far less risky option than the untried dangers of revolution. At the same time, clientelism provides some kind of political structure, some mechanism for representation and participation in politics by and on behalf of people outside the central elite. It has many of the advantages, and also the defects, of the oligopolistic economic structure which in so many ways it resembles: where there is a market, in that the producers of government benefits have something to supply to consumers, and something that they want from them in return, then entrepreneurs will spring up unbidden to manage that market.

The fact that clientelism has something to offer both the patrons and the clients should not mislead one into supposing, however, that it is an inherently desirable and beneficial system. There are two main reasons why this is not so. First, it is founded on a premiss of inequality between patrons and clients, and the benefits accruing to each of them from the exchange may be very uneven indeed. Clients only benefit in so far as they have anything to offer which the patrons feel a need to pay for (and cannot just exact by force). Unless there is an effective electoral system which gives real choice to clients, this may not be very much; it is much more likely to be a small sweetener to give them some kind of stake in the system, while its main benefits go elsewhere. Secondly, the particularistic or neo-patrimonial nature of the exchange carries serious defects of its own. It may serve to intensify ethnic conflicts, though it is equally capable of adaptation so that each group gets a slice of the cake. It leads to allocations often very different from those which would be produced by 'universal' criteria of efficiency and need: the road goes to the 'wrong' place, the 'wrong' person gets the job. Itself a form of corruption, it encourages corruption in other ways: what one is looking for from government is the satisfaction of a private benefit, not of a public need. It is oriented towards the consumption of government services, but does nothing whatever to supply the means for their production: it lends itself to a form of government by hand-out, in which the government itself becomes dependent on the sources of funds through which it is effectively obliged to buy support, whether these be foreign aid receipts or royalties from multinational corporations. Most of all, it supplies no way by which governments can develop the efficiency and accountability which are needed to render legitimate the enormous powers of the modern state.

Clientelism is a form of political organisation which characterises several different kinds of system, of which the underdeveloped state is one of the most important. It depends ultimately on the vulnerability of clients, and may give way to other forms of organisation either though a decline in that vulnerability, such that the services of patrons are no longer needed, or through an increase in it, such that there is not the slightest prospect of their being effective. In the first case, which has been described from a number of both European and non-European studies,[8] a process of economic development reduces vulnerability and makes it rational for clients to pursue their goals through other, more objectively efficient, mechanisms. In the second, a progressive descent into immiserisation and despair from which no other mechanism offers any prospect of relief may lead clients to follow, at whatever cost, some new and revolutionary path, which will also be based on universalistic rather than particularistic values. The great majority of third world peoples are still subsisting in the middle ground between these two extremes.

Notes

1. See, for example, F. Riggs, *Administration in Developing Countries: The*

Theory of Prismatic Society (Houghton Mifflin, 1964).

2. See J.F. Medard, 'The Underdeveloped State in Tropical Africa: Political Clientelism or Neo-patrimonialism?' in C. Clapham (ed.), *Private Patronage and Public Power: Political Clientelism in the Modern State* (Pinter, 1982).

3. See World Bank, *World Development Report 1981* (Oxford University Press, 1981), Table 25.

4. See C. Clapham, 'Clientelism and the State' in Clapham, *Private Patronage and Public Power*.

5. See for example the contributions by Foltz, Cornelius, Chalmers and Guasti in S.W. Schmidt *et al.* (eds.), *Friends, Followers and Factions: A Reader in Political Clientelism* (University of California Press, 1977).

6. P. Cammack, 'Clientelism and Military Government in Brazil' in Clapham, *Private Patronage and Public Power*.

7. R.H. Baker, 'Clientelism in the Post-Revolutionary State: The Soviet Union' in Clapham, ibid.

8. See the contributions by Silverman and Cornelius in Schmidt *et al.*, *Friends, Followers and Factions*.

4 MANAGING THE STATE

The Process of State Consolidation

A very great deal of politics is concerned with the activities of a very small number of people. True of almost any form of politics, this is especially so in third world states where institutions linking the mass of the population with political action are weak or non-existent and where the fragile but powerful state, linked to indigenous social formations by contracts of convenience rather than ties of loyalty, is itself monopolised by an elite. At the most basic level, the problem facing this elite is to increase the effectiveness of the state and diminish its fragility, ideally by creating a moral sense of its value and associating other social formations with it. This objective can be pursued at two levels, both of which are particularly clearly demonstrated in the common experience of new states in the years immediately after independence. At the ideological level, dominant elites develop patterns of thought and rhetoric which, expressing their own interests, glorify and justify the organisation on which their power depends. At the level of practical politics, they seek the same end by suppressing other organisations which constitute potential challengers to it − in the process, paradoxically, often destroying the very institutions on which a more effective linkage of state to society would eventually have to depend. The two levels combine to form a characteristic process of postcolonial state consolidation.

The Ideologies of Independence

An ideology is the set of beliefs which we use to make sense of the world about us. Almost every human being has an ideology − the only alternatives are mental breakdown or vegetable passivity − though some people, especially politicians who need to project their views on a public stage, articulate it more than others. Even though, as a set of beliefs, it is inherently subjective (and thus incapable of being either 'true' or 'false'), it must bear some working relationship to the individual's own experience and inevitably comes to be shaped by that individual's position in society − in which class is an important ingredient but not the only one. Its primary function is to mediate between this experience and the actions which the individual then takes in order to shape

61

his environment in accordance with his goals.

Looked at in this light, the most important determinant of nationalist leaders' ideologies is likely to be their immediate past experience
of ousting the colonial regime, and the principal ingredient in this is
often a strong sense of identity between the leader and the people
whom he leads. This may be expressed in the leader's self-perception as
the founding father of his nation, as in the new Ghanaian coins
inscribed round the rim (in Latin, of all languages) 'Kwame Nkrumah
Ghanaensis Conditor', or the new honorific titles bestowed upon him.
But the identification has more than personal implications. It also
defines the boundaries of legitimate and illegitimate political action.
Legitimacy is ascribed to the leader, the nation and the party or movement which links the two, *unity* with which then becomes the core
value of the ideology as a whole. This emphasis on unity, which is the
leitmotiv of almost every post-independence leadership ideology,
serves several related functions. One of them, of course, is that it bridges
over the characteristic class division between a leadership group drawn
heavily from the more privileged strata and the mass of their ordinary
followers; any nationalist ideology inherently plays down internal class
divisions, though this only acquires much relevance for political action
once the government starts to implement measures which reflect its
particular class interests. Equally significant is the role of 'unity' in
dealing with internal ethnic divisions, either by including different
groups within the nation, in which case the differences between them
become of no account, or by excluding them – a fate most often
reserved for immigrant merchant groups such as the Lebanese in West
Africa, Indians in East Africa, and Southeast Asian Chinese. In each
case, though the formal basis for unity is that of leader, party and
nation, the actual basis is that of the state. Nationhood is defined by
reference to state boundaries, rather (except in rare cases) than ethnic
ones. The often artificial territorial entity created by colonialism becomes the legitimate framework for political action, while the basis for
indigenous and precolonial identity is set aside.

Illegitimacy is then ascribed to any political activity outside the
protected union of ruler, 'nation' and state. Opposition parties are
particularly vulnerable in that they necessarily deny the ruler's claimed
or perceived identity between himself and the nation. There is no lack
of grounds on which this vulnerability can be exploited. Where the
opposition is based on ethnic or regional divisions, these are themselves
regarded as the manifestations of an illegitimate racism or tribalism,
and are accordingly liable to suppression. Any class-based opposition

may likewise be defined out of account, especially when — as is usually the case — it derives from a privileged stratum of the population which has been cut off from political support by the victorious party's greater success in appealing to the popular vote. Where the difference between parties is neither ethnic nor class oriented, but is factional in nature, they are open to Nyerere's graphic critique of rival parties as being like football teams, engaged in sterile conflict with one another when they would be better employed in joining together to promote national goals. What goes for opposition parties in this respect is equally applicable to any other form of political activity which falls outside the supervision of the state, including for example the press or the trade unions. What is basic to the whole conception of legitimacy is the idea of a single national interest, which should be expressed in the form of a single national will — a conception very close to Rousseau's idea of the general will and, like it, very easily adopted by any government which can identify itself with the nation. The 'problem' of legitimacy is then that an ideology which is all too obviously statist in inspiration can rarely elicit the moral consent of those who do not evidently stand to gain from it.

This portrait of an ideology is itself an ideal type. It depicts the set of ideas most easily, in a sense 'rationally', derived from the situation and interests of the leader of a newly independent state. Elements of this type recur much too frequently to be dismissed, but variations equally occur in keeping with the personality, experience and current situation of particular leaders. Two such variables are the degree of anticolonial radicalism in the nationalist movement and the degree of opposition to it, a peak of paranoia being reached when a radical nationalist movement gains power over, as it sees it, a neocolonialist opposition backed by the imperial regime. A quotation from the party newspaper in Mali will make the point:[1]

> We have enemies. They are on the outside. They are within. Those outside are more numerous.
> Those within, small in number, are only puppets, political merchants whose stores in Mali have long since been closed.
> They are the egoists, the envious, the poachers, the traitors in the pay of the imperialists, colonialists and neocolonialists.

By contrast, the less anticolonial a nationalist movement, the more secure its leaders and the more these are drawn from an established elite (three criteria which often go together), the more likely it is to tolerate a measure of opposition and the more muted will be its overt ideological rhetoric. Only when government and opposition leaders are drawn from the same stratum of society, in both class and ethnic terms, is this likely to lead, however, to any alternation of parties in power on the classic liberal democratic model. Right-wing leaders have generally been no less determined to stay in power than left-wing ones, and some of them — Dr Hastings Kamuzu Banda of Malawi being a case in point — have developed a rhetoric quite as shrill as anything to be heard on the left.

Governments the world over have difficulty in distinguishing between their own interests and those of the people whom they rule. Third world governments often add to this natural authoritarian tendency the awareness that — in countries where education is generally limited — they have a special intellectual right to decide what should be done. Government is the haunt of the educated; the governed, correspondingly, are overwhelmingly the ignorant. In this, the nationalist leaders easily take over the attitudes characteristic of colonial administration, and add to them a sense of their own special status as the elect of the people. In the process, the pre-independence relationship between leaders and people is reversed. It is no longer the leaders who seek support from the mass of the population, but the population which must adapt itself to the dictates of the leaders. Not that these dictates are necessarily oppressive or uncaring, but even the most committed of leaders — a Nyerere of Tanzania, for example — feels far more confident of his own ability to determine what is best for his people than of their own ability to determine it for themselves. In this sense, a belief in democracy is very rarely part of the ideology of nationalist politicians.

This account of ideology has so far touched only incidentally on a criterion which is often taken as virtually coterminous with ideology itself: its degree of 'rightness' or 'leftness'. This is deliberate. In my view, the ideology of government overrides such distinctions, and incidentally goes far to explain why regimes in power behave so similarly, regardless of their position on a right/left spectrum. There *is* such a spectrum, though, and three main clusters can be distinguished on it: third world marxist, populist socialist and third world capitalist;[2] the geographical qualification is added to the first and last of these by way of a warning that they should not be identified with the socio-economic and political systems either of the Soviet Union and its allies, or of the western industrial states. All of them are most easily identified as ideologies of economic development, and are discussed as such in a later chapter, while the Marxist option also characterises the revolutionary state, examined in Chapter 8. But they have more general implications. There are only a small number of Marxist third world states, characteristically the result of a domestic social revolution which may also accompany a violent decolonisation struggle or the ousting of an entrenched protecting power. Vietnam, Cuba and Ethiopia provide examples. They involve an attempt to create a new social order based on the abolition of private control over the means of production and (usually) on a Communist Party and a close alliance with the Soviet bloc. The populist socialist cluster is most easily distinguished from these by the absence of a social revolution, and by an attempt to use the state to control the dominant sector of the economy, combined with a non-aligned foreign policy stance. This is the characteristic stance of the nationalist ideologue, exemplified by men such as Sukarno or Sihanouk in Asia, Nasser, Nkrumah or Nyerere in Africa, Manley in the Caribbean and those Latin American leaders who have sought national control over expatriate corporations without violently disrupting the domestic social structure. Capitalism in a sense represents the maintenance of the *status quo*, including an economy with a high level of private ownership and strong connections with the western industrial states, but should not be taken as necessarily indicating either a pro-western foreign policy or favourable conditions for western multinationals. The creation of an indigenous capitalist class may well call for restrictions on foreign businesses and an assertive foreign policy, Nigeria being a good example.

These examples extend the use of the term 'ideology' from essentially personal sets of beliefs into regime types which draw not simply on the leader's convictions but on a much wider set of historical circumstances. No single leader can make a revolution unless he is at the very least strongly assisted by social conditions, and even the choice between capitalist and populist socialist paths will be affected by the existing social structure — especially the groups from which the successful nationalist movement draws its main support. For all that, the priorities set by the first independent leader have often left a legacy which must be ascribed in part at least to individual choice rather than socio-economic causation. The contrast between Houphouet-Boigny's capitalist Ivory Coast and its two socialist neighbours, Nkrumah's Ghana and Sékou Touré's Guinea, is one well-known example. So, at the other end of Africa, is the difference between Nyerere's Tanzania and Banda's Malawi; had either of these leaders chosen to opt the other way, Banda for socialism or Nyerere for capitalism, there is nothing very evident in the structure of their countries or parties which would have prevented them from doing so. These were (and in some cases still are) the founding fathers of their states, and the way in which they chose to approach the problems of government which suddenly faced them at independence has had a lasting effect.

The Consolidation of State Control

The power of nationalist leaders at independence rested on two institutions: the parties which they themselves (in most cases) had formed in order to generate popular support, and the administrations which they took over from the colonial regimes. In almost every case, their main source of power shifted rapidly in the years immediately after independence from the party to the state, leaving the party — like a first-stage rocket which has put its payload into orbit — to fall away behind them.

The first stage in this process — guided by the statist ideologies just examined — was the dismantling, where possible, of rival centres of power. This was not of course directed against the governing party: indeed its immediate outcome was to raise the party to a pinnacle of pre-eminence, formally at least, as the single or overwhelmingly dominant political organisation within the state. But the suppression of the opposition was achieved, not by the use of the governing party as such, but by using the power of the state. In most cases, this was not difficult. Even though opposition leaders had a vested interest in a liberal ideology, corresponding exactly to the interest which governments had in a statist one, this rarely attracted any substantial commitment even from the opposition itself, the principal exception being in states where — as in India or the West Indies, or in a more limited degree Ghana or Sierra Leone — it was backed by a substantial professional class. Oppositions, like governing parties, had formed to compete for state power. Without it, they were left exposed, even where an ethnic base for party identity gave them a fairly stable support base amongst a section of the population. The weapons at the government's disposal ranged from simple and forcible suppression to the subtler use of the state's regulative and financial powers. The manipulation of benefits was the easiest to manage. When the piped water supply or the tarmac road went to the ruling party's constituency, and stopped sharply at the boundary with the opposition one, it did not take the people across that boundary long to perceive the virtues of loyalty. Opposition politicians were sometimes — as in Ghana, say — forced into exile or imprisoned under a variety of pretexts, but might equally — as in Kenya — be induced to move over (to 'cross-carpet' was the phrase used in Sierra Leone) to the government side. Joining the ruling party was a move which could be sanctioned in ideological terms, as aiding the essential task of creating national unity, but which equally held practical benefits for party leaders and members who saw no future in the permanent wasteland of opposition. Where opposition parties remained in being, harassment and electoral manipulation generally ensured that they had no chance of taking over control of government. The postcolonial third world states in which an opposition party has, after winning a contested election, peacefully taken control of central government, fall comfortably into single figures: India (1977, 1980), Sri Lanka (1977), Jamaica (1972, 1980), Barbados (1976), Mauritius (1982, 1983). It has yet to happen in Africa, though both in Lesotho (1970) and in Sierra Leone (1967) the opposition has won an election but been prevented from assuming power. Opposition has held little save the hope that a turn of fortune's wheel (in the form of a military coup, say) might overthrow the government and so lead eventually to a new civilian regime. It is, there-fore, not altogether surprising that some opposition leaders have been tempted to give the wheel a push themselves – most remarkably in Burma in 1947, when the leader of the opposition arranged for the entire cabinet to be assassinated, in the belief that the conventions of Westminster democracy would lead to his being invited to form the next administration. He was hanged.

In some states, a federal system enabled opposition parties to entrench themseles behind the feeble barricades provided by their own small regional quota of state power, but these were rarely enough to keep out a determined central government. For one thing, the central government retained control over both financial allocations and military force, and usually the police as well. With these, it could manipulate and undermine regional autonomy, with the threat of forcible interven-tion held in reserve. In India, the constitution allowed (and allows) individual states to be brought under direct presidential rule, a measure which it might be unwise to apply to a state under firm opposition control (like Tamil Nadu under the DMK after 1967), but which was easily applied when local factionalism (often fomented from the centre) made the state difficult to govern in any case. In the Western Region of Nigeria in 1962, a state of emergency was engineered in order to remove the opposition Action Group administration, which was itself divided by a breakaway of those who favoured collaboration with the central government. Constitutions which sought to divide power within central government, characteristically between a prime minister and a head of state, rapidly led to a showdown between the two: between Obote and the Kabaka of Buganda in Uganda, Lumumba and Kasavubu in Congo (Zaire), and Senghor and Mamadou Dia in Senegal; only in countries such as India, where the president is clearly subordinate to the prime minister, has a dual executive been able to survive.

Other potential sources of organised opposition may equally be absorbed by government or subordinated to it. Trade unions, often under colonial rule a haphazard collection of craft, industrial and company unions, are an obvious target for rationalisation into a single structure supervised by the government or ruling party, and limited by strict controls on strike action. Sometimes they too are divided into rival congresses on ideological or ethnic lines which offer scope for state manipulation; in Jamaica the two rival unions are each organised by the rival political parties. The principal newspaper, often owned in colonial times by an overseas publishing group, is likewise taken over as a government organ, and constraints placed on the remainder. 'Traditional' rulers rarely present much of a problem, since they are subject to the controls which the new government has taken over from the colonial regime, and while individual rulers associated with opposition parties have frequently been deposed, even populist socialist governments rarely abolish the institution itself: it serves, in the right hands, as too convenient an agency for controlling the rural areas. Two exceptions are the abolition of chieftaincy in Guinea, where it was an unpopular creation of colonial rule with no traditional deference attached to it, and the abolition in India of the patchwork of princely states, at odds with any systematic nationwide administration, left over from the haphazard history of British colonisation.

Much of this process of state consolidation can be seen as a return to the authoritarianism of colonial rule, after that brief and highly uncharacteristic period during which the colonial administration had first liberalised its own ways by allowing nationalist parties to operate, and then left behind (on its departure) liberal constitutions which imposed restrictions on government which it had never tolerated itself. If decolonisation is seen as the displacement of alien rulers by indigenous ones, and liberal democracy as the means by which this transition is achieved, then there is no reason why such democracy should outlive this limited function. The new district officer can move into the old district officer's bungalow, hoist his new flag outside it, and continue governing in the way to which his subjects have long been accustomed. Yet in three ways things are different. One is that the very alienness of the colonial administrators, together with the political values of the societies from which they came, enabled them to establish an institutionalised bureaucracy which could operate by formal rules placing them at a distance from the people whom they governed. The new rulers are, regardless of their own values and training, instantly locatable within the society, as members of this or that regional or ethnic group, religion, class or caste. This formed, certainly, one element in the development of the clientelist patterns of politics which were considered in the last chapter. Second, the new governments had a much wider conception of their role than had their predecessors, with a sharply increased emphasis on 'development', conceived not simply in economic terms but also including education and social welfare, and political development through one or another kind of nation-building exercise. The main instrument to hand for achieving these goals was, again, the state. Foreign companies could be and often were encouraged to invest, but populist socialist regimes especially regarded them with suspicion, and some of these launched rapid expansions in the state-controlled sector of the economy. Foreign religious missions were even less acceptable as agencies for the expansion of an educational system which was intended not simply to instruct but to inculcate new values, and have often, as in Papua New Guinea, aroused the resentment of indigenous politicians. The result was an increase in government employment, fuelled by the third new element, the growing number of trained indigenous people for whom the public service continued to be the major source of jobs. Some indication of the increase in the size and hence the cost of the public service is given by figures for public consumption as a percentage of gross domestic product, which between 1960 and 1979 rose from 11 per cent to 27 per cent in Zambia, 7 per cent to 20 per cent in Jamaica, and 11 per cent to 20 per cent in Kenya.[3] Some of this may have resulted from the cost of new and beneficial services, or from the transfer into government hands of functions previously undertaken privately, but it is also true that the state and its agents have been extracting a steadily increasing 'fee' for their management of the societies which they rule.

It would be a mistake, of course, to equate the increase in state power and functions with an increase in those of the government of the day. It is first necessary for the government to control its own servants. In some cases, where the victorious political party drew its main support from populist groups opposed to the elites entrenched in the bureaucracy, the two fought a running battle from the start. In Ghana, this conflict was especially intense, and Nkrumah's CPP government constantly created parallel organisations, staffed by political appointees, through which it could operate behind the backs of the official bureaucracy.[4] There was a parallel foreign ministry, a parallel regional administration, even eventually (and fatally) a parallel army, the President's Own Guard Regiment, all of them adding to the costs of government. Most governments controlled their bureaucracies better than this, while at the same time dismantling constitutional provisions intended to safeguard the independence of the civil service and judiciary which stood in their way. None the less these too came to depend on the instrument which they had created. The military coup is often, as we shall see, the bureaucracy's revenge on its own masters.

Meanwhile, what of the nationalist movement itself? The key to the survival of nationalist political parties after independence lies partly in the kinds of organisation they were in the first place, partly in the functions which they were subsequently expected to perform. If, as I have suggested, the nationalist movements were not — or were very rarely — ideologically coherent and dedicated groups, but rather collections of disparate people brought together by disparate goals all predicated on the achievement of national independence, then they could not be expected to transform themselves into single parties based (however loosely) on the Soviet model. Attempts to give them, after independence, the ideological stiffening which they had lacked before it rarely got anywhere. Nkrumaism in Ghana, with its Ideological Institute and its Little Black Book of the Thoughts of Kwame Nkrumah (Freedom Fighters' Edition) was little more than a joke.[5] Ujamaa in Tanzania was very much more serious; the Arusha Declaration of 1967 provided it with principles and President Nyerere with dedicated backing, but even this involved a constant struggle against the interests of those who constituted the party.[6] In most cases, as Wallerstein has pointed out with reference to Africa, the single-party state declined in effect into a no-party state.[7] As the momentum of achieving independence died away, the better qualified party workers moved across into government, and the state took over the party's functions in formulating policy, competing with political rivals, and even the time-consuming day-to-day activities of fund-raising and local organisation. The opening of a new palatial party headquarters, built with government funds, in place of its previous scruffy offices, marked, if not the total disappearance of the party as an effective institution, then at any rate the last stage in its transformation into an institution of a very different kind: an organ for the dispersal of government patronage. The result, especially as central bureaucrats took an increasing share of government resources and left less for distribution to the countryside and to local

party activists, was a 'shrinking political arena', in which the number
and range of people with the ability to participate effectively in politics
declined along with the party itself.[8]

Those countries in which political parties remained active and effective were, overwhelmingly, those in which they continued to perform
their original liberal function of providing a legitimate framework for
the competition for power. Where liberal constitutions were retained, in
practice rather than just on paper, the prospect of achieving power at
the next election sustained opposition parties and compelled governing
ones — despite a marked tendency to lean on the state for support —
to organise against them. Likewise, whenever departing military regimes
held reasonably fair elections to choose their successors, there was no
lack of parties available to contest them. The logic of party competition
outlined by Schumpeter[9] applies just as well to third world as to industrial states.

The decolonisation period and its immediate aftermath were a
peculiar episode in the political evolution of the formerly colonial
states. A new form of politics, a new set of political identities, emerged,
blossomed rapidly and, in most cases, equally quickly died away: a
moment of great hope, swiftly deflated. This was, however, the process
by which the colonial states fitted themselves into a pattern of third
world politics which goes beyond the simple colonial experience, and
what emerged at the end of it was a large group of states not essentially
different in most respects from those (especially in the central and
southern Americas) which had been decolonised long before, and those
which for some reason had escaped formal colonisation. From that
point, it becomes less and less useful to talk about 'new states' or ex-
colonial ones, and increasingly useful to talk about third world politics
as a whole.

The Management of the Core

The consolidation of state control intensifies rather than resolves the
problem of managing the state itself. The leader, elevated to a supreme
position and pandered to by a fulsome press, cannot escape at least
ultimate responsibility for the results which his government achieves,
and in the short term has to avoid the dangers of a palace coup. The
state gains a similar supremacy and runs an equivalent risk: that if over
a period and despite the efforts of successive rulers, it fails to meet the
minimum expectations of its people, it may be overthrown by some

new form of state which at least claims to be able to do so. While the leader is at risk from a coup, the state (or at any rate the elite who manage it) is at risk from a revolution, or from a degree of mismanagement which leads to its collapse from within even if there is not much organised threat to it from alternative wielders of power.

The Ruler and the Court

Top leadership is always personal. The very few individuals who reach the highest position in any state place their own stamp on the way they run their governments, and have a vastly greater opportunity than other individuals to shape policies and politics in the way they choose. If the leaders of third world states are personal rulers, then so in a sense are Reagan and Mitterand, Thatcher and Chernenko. The institutional weakness of third world states, and their consequent reliance on neo-patrimonial relationships in order to maintain their political structure, mean, however, that their leaders have far fewer immediate constraints on the way in which they exercise power, with, as the other side of the coin, far less institutionalised support which they can rely upon to guide and sustain them. This lack of immediate institutional constraints on rulers, combined with the intense constraints under which they operate as a result of their states' position in the global political structure and economy, accounts for many of the most paradoxical aspects of third world politics – especially visible in the arena of foreign policy.

Regimes differ, certainly, in the degree to which they provide institutional constraints on, and hence support for, rulers. Characteristically, military regimes tend to be appreciably more institutionalised in this respect than political party ones. It is consequently much more common for military than for civilian regimes to provide a genuinely collective leadership, and to be able to replace leaders peacefully from within their own ranks – though it is also quite common for military rulers to rise up from initially collective leadership until they enjoy a position of personal dominance which can be challenged only by a coup d'état such as that which brought them to power in the first place. It is equally characteristic of personal leadership, though, that after a short while the particular means by which a leader came to power becomes secondary to the way in which he exercises it. What matters here, essentially, is individual skill. It is a world familiar from Machiavelli's *Prince*, a world in which rulers gain power by their wits and must retain it in the same way, and in which the penalties for failure are likely to be imprisonment, exile or death. The successful ruler is he who can attract loyalty, can control or destroy potential rivals, can induce in the population a sense of stability and permanence, if not actual well-being, and can reach some accommodation with powerful external political and economic forces.

As this reference to Machiavelli suggests, the techniques of personal leadership are essentially unchanging, induced by the nature of human beings and the logic of the recurring political situations in which leaders find themselves. Two basic styles of leadership have long been distinguished: the passive and the active, the fox and the lion, or (in Jackson and Rosberg's terms) the prince and the autocrat.[10] The fox or prince is a manipulator, one who does not seek to destroy politicians who represent potentially dangerous sources of support, but rather plays them off against one another while seeking to bring them into ever closer dependence on himself. He avoids committing himself, whenever possible, to any distinctive policy or course of action, but rather moves with the consensus and, when some bold stroke is called for, retains the ability to dissociate himself from it should it fail, leaving some subordinate to shoulder the responsibility.[11] It is a strategy which maximises choice, avoids risks, and is especially appropriate for a leader who starts in a weak position, surrounded by regional bosses or other powerful politicians whose support he cannot afford to alienate, and who then seeks steadily to build himself into a position of supremacy. It is the strategy followed, say, by Haile Selassie in Ethiopia, Kenyatta in Kenya or Senghor in Senegal. Its great advantage is its flexibility. Its weaknesses are partly that it requires great manipulative skill, and can come unstuck in the hands of a leader who lacks it, but more that in concentrating on day-to-day tactics it tends to lose sight of longer-term considerations. It is adapted, in Jackson and Rosberg's useful distinction,[12] to seamanship rather than navigation, staying afloat rather than getting anywhere, and the leader may find himself, like Haile Selassie, caught in a situation where manipulation can achieve nothing because what is at stake is the directionless inadequacy of this whole style of leadership itself.

The lion or autocrat seeks to dominate rather than manipulate. His instinct is to destroy or drive out rivals, rather than conciliate and undermine them. He surrounds himself with obedient followers, men without any substantial political weight of their own, often bureaucrats or technicians rather than politicians, whom he can dismiss at will should they show any sign of independence. It is the only style available to a leader with definite policy goals to which he is committed — and a style appropriate, therefore, to those nationalist leaders who waged a genuine struggle against colonial rule, rather than simply putting together a coalition to succeed it. It tends to restrict choice, in the same way that it restricts the political groups actively involved in government, and it leads easily to the creation of an embittered opposition whose leaders are in prison or in exile. It is, therefore, a risky strategy, and can only successfully be followed by a leader in a position of strength. It is the strategy followed, say, by Mrs Gandhi in India, Michael Manley in Jamaica, Banda in Malawi or Nkrumah in Ghana. Its great advantage is that it can, when directed to attainable goals, achieve results which are beyond the grasp of the manipulatory politician. Its weaknesses are that it can go dramatically wrong, especially in the hands of politicians such as Lumumba in the Congo (Zaire) or Ironsi in Nigeria who did not have a position strong enough to sustain this style of leadership, and paid for their mistake with their lives; and that the personal autocracy which it involves may be appallingly abused.

Jackson and Rosberg suggest two further styles of leadership, the prophet and the tyrant, but both of these are in my view better regarded as types of autocrat, distinguishable not by their style of rule but by the use to which they put it. The prophet is a leader whose efforts are directed towards achieving some public and national goal, and for whom, therefore, power is always secondary to the purpose to which it is put. The designation of Michael Manley of Jamaica, at least by his own party, the PNP, as the 'Moses' who would lead his people to the promised land, puts the point perfectly. Nyerere of Tanzania is perhaps the clearest example, and Sékou Touré of Guinea would certainly qualify; Jackson and Rosberg include Nkrumah of Ghana, altogether a more dubious case. Prophetic leadership is necessarily autocratic, since the leader must subordinate all other political forces and actors to his own single-minded pursuit of his goal, even though prophets like other leaders must be able to handle the day-to-day demands of government, though the autocracy of a Manley within the Jamaican two-party system never approached the near paranoia of a Sékou Touré. Revolutionary leadership — that of a Castro in Cuba or a Ho Chi Minh in Vietnam — may also be classed as prophetic, but this will be looked at in a later chapter. Tyranny, conversely, is autocracy abused, a system in which government becomes merely the instrument of the tyrant's personal whim, directed to his own gratification or survival. The African trio, Amin of Uganda, Bokassa of Central Africa and Macias of Equatorial Guinea, all of them overthrown in 1979, provide the best examples, though François Duvalier of Haiti also belongs on the list, and many third world leaders including Marcos of the

Philippines have an element of the tyrant in them. All in all, considering the scope provided for the abuse of power in third world political systems, it is surprising that the list is not longer. One reason is certainly that tyranny alienates external support, both because it is embarrassing to the regime's external patron — never more so than in the relations between France and the Emperor Bokassa of Central Africa — but also because the tyrant's behaviour becomes highly unpredictable and hence unmanageable.

This emphasis on leaders is justified because they matter. While the overall political character of third world states is to a large degree set by 'structural' considerations — their artificiality, their role in the world economy, their domestic social structure — these leave a lot of scope for personal government and indeed in some ways encourage it. One reason why Malawi is different from Tanzania is because one has had Banda while the other has had Nyerere. We shall also see later how leadership has affected economic change. Another way in which the personal nature of leadership becomes strikingly clear is in the 'court' or entourage with which leaders surround themselves. The term is appropriate in that this resembles the retinue of an early modern monarch — Henry VIII of England, for instance[13] — rather than anything so prosaic as an administrative staff. It is most obvious when the leader is on tour, in the motorcade of officials who follow him along the dusty roads, not because their presence is strictly needed but rather because it is expected, and because they themselves need to demonstrate their influence by their physical proximity to the leader. It is visible, too, in the line-up of ministers at the airport to pay their respects to the head of state on his return from foreign visits, or in the amount of time that regional governors or administrators spend in the capital in attendance on the president. In a patrimonial system and in large degree in a neo-patrimonial one too, *not* to be seen frequently in the company of the man at the top is interpreted on the one hand as showing disloyalty or disrespect, on the other as indicating a loss or lack of influence with him.

Within the court, there is thus a constant struggle for the leader's ear. A court is an inherently factional form of political organisation. If the leader is, in Jackson and Rosberg's terms, a prince, then factions will form about the different political groupings which the leader plays off against one another. Even if he is an autocrat, underlings will compete to demonstrate loyalty, or to impugn that of rivals, as well as to persuade him to endorse policies which they favour. This jockeying for position is reflected in purges or reshuffles, as posts are allocated to one faction or another. In Ghana in 1962, the 'old guard' of Nkrumah's CPP, nationalist bosses from the pre-independence days, were swept aside in favour of the 'young Nkrumaists', a new generation of more ideologically committed socialists; the next year, an assassination attempt against Nkrumah was used to cast doubt on the young Nkrumaists' loyalty, and the rump of the old guard returned to power. It is an atmosphere which breeds accusations of plots and counterplots, by no means all of them fanciful, and courtiers who fall foul of these may be imprisoned or even executed. More often, they are kept at arm's length until a turn of fortune's wheel brings them back into favour.

The critical problem faced by a personalist regime is that of succession. A change in leadership puts every position at risk until the new leader has established himself and reformed the court about him. This change can take place two ways, from within or from without. Change from outside, characteristically in the form of a military coup, may come suddenly and unexpectedly, and in any event, the court of the existing head of state is likely to be too committed to him to have much prospect of surviving his fall. Even then, though, the decay of a regime may be evident before the coup which gives it its *coup de grâce*, and in states such as Turkey or Argentina the coup has acquired a predictable and almost institutionalised role in the political process; politicians may then seek to dissociate themselves from the regime, in the expectation that the new government will need to look for political support among those least compromised by their role in the former administration.

Succession from within may be arranged by a group of kingmakers from the military or (more rarely) the governing party, or by the effective designation of a 'dauphin' by the ageing president. It is much easier for a prince to do this than for an autocrat. The prince is used to dealing with factions, and in naming a dauphin he is essentially giving his final accolade to the faction associated with the person who would constitutionally take over in the event of his own death or resignation. The succession of Tubman by Tolbert in Liberia, Kenyatta by Moi in Kenya, and Senghor by Abdou Diouf in Senegal are all examples, though in the first two cases (where the incumbent died in office) there was a moment of uncertainty before it became clear that the successor would take over peacefully. In such cases, a few individuals very closely associated with the old leader can be sacrificed in the interests of a new image or a publicised clampdown on corruption, together with anyone whose loyalty wavered at the moment of succession, but the old pattern can be reproduced without fundamental change. For an autocrat it is more difficult, since he cannot designate a successor without changing the nature of the regime or indeed announcing his own dispensability — hence the danger of any politician so much as speculating about the succession to someone such as Banda of Malawi. A prophet will, in addition, need to find someone committed to his own aspirations, while a tyrant finds himself riding a tiger from which he cannot dismount. It is not surprising that some autocrats, especially the tyrants, find themselves turning to the time-honoured solution of succession from within the family, as with Bokassa's make-believe empire or the Duvaliers in Haiti; the same tendency is not unknown within socialist states such as North Korea, or in Mrs Gandhi's India.

Maintaining a Ruling Coalition

Political leadership is a matter of strategy as well as of tactics. Strategically, the main challenge facing leaders is that of creating and maintaining a coalition of interests associated with their rule which is sufficient to keep them in power. The nature of this coalition will obviously vary according to the composition of the main centres of social and political power in any given country, but the process of coalition-building itself, and the success or failure of the resulting regimes, reveals characteristic and constantly recurring patterns. These patterns recur, moreover, regardless of the formal institutional or constitutional structure of the regime. The role of coalition-building is particularly obvious under liberal democratic systems of government, because these invest political competition with great publicity, and provide a formal mathematical mechanism through the electoral system, by which success can be established; at the same time, they affect the nature of the winning coalition by giving a high political weight to the simple counting of votes and hence to the political actors (such as rural patrons) who can deliver them. When the single-party state is imposed, or the army takes over, coalition-building becomes more furtive but is no less important. The size of coalitions can no longer be counted, nor the requirements of a 'winning' coalition specified; it becomes easier for small but well-placed minorities to seize power as well as to cling onto it, and coalitional 'weight' comes to be defined in terms of location and force rather than votes. But the logic of coalitional politics still remains in force: Sukarno, Nkrumah or the Shah, all proof against electoral overthrow, none the less fell because they could not maintain the support of a coalition of the weight required.

One common currency of coalitional politics is ethnicity. The vast majority of third world states are ethnically heterogeneous, and ethnicity provides a form of political identity — readily mobilised, as has been seen, through patron-client networks — which can be expressed both electorally and in other ways. Exactly how it works, however, depends primarily on the ethnic configuration of each particular state. In states with one dominant and central group, such as Sri Lanka or Burma, Ethiopia or Sudan, political power requires first and foremost that the ruler retain its allegiance; he can be overthrown at the centre, only indirectly threatened at the periphery. When the ruler is under severe pressure, therefore, he is likely to emphasise his connections with the central group, to which in any event he is likely to belong. On the other hand, the permanent exclusion of peripheral minorities from the political structure carries appreciable dangers too. In the case of Sudan and Ethiopia, it has led to long and bitter civil wars, in which the central government has lost control over substantial areas of its territory. The authority of the modern Burmese state fades out towards its mountainous frontier areas much as it did under the old pre-colonial monarchy. The politics of Sri Lanka is punctuated by outbreaks of Tamil violence. Provided that his central base is tolerably secure, the ruler then has a strong incentive to seek to incorporate or assuage peripheral groups in order to associate them with his government. In an unusually far-sighted and courageous application of this principle, President Nimairi was even prepared to accept regional autonomy for the Southern Sudan as the price for ending the long civil war with the north, and his authority in the south was then so great that he used southern soldiers as his personal guard against the possibility of his being overthrown by a northern coup in Khartoum. Over time, however, the need to maintain his northern support (coupled with increasing northern Islamic militancy and the difficulty of maintaining a stable regime in the south) produced a shift away from regional autonomy and renewed southern disaffection. A peculiar application of the same principle applies to the distinctive ethnic politics of South Africa, where the dominance of the Afrikaners among the white voting population gives them the position of a 'majority' group on whose support the government must rely. On the other hand, effective government requires the support of other elements within the white community, especially the English-speaking South Africans, and the possibility of accommodation at least with non-whites. Any movement towards accommodation in turn provokes the suspicion of 'verkrampte' elements within the Afrikaner population, and an anxious response by a government which cannot afford to lose its core support.

Other configurations produce different patterns of coalition-building. At one extreme, such as Malaysia, the dominance of the core (Malay) group is so assured that most of the critical political bargaining takes place within it, and it is left to the minority Chinese and Indian communities (which suffer the double disadvantage of alienness and of controlling no regional centre of their own) to associate themselves with it, only the occasional outbreak indicating the frustrations of permanent subordination. Another and potentially very dangerous pattern occurs where, as in Guyana, the population is almost evenly divided between two major groups, and the political structure reflects the dominance of one over the other. But the most complex form of ethnic coalition-building occurs when there are more than two major groups, and no single one has sufficient territorial numerical or coercive advantage to guarantee control. Coalitions then have to be constructed between potentially shifting groups, in which even fairly small groups may acquire a bargaining power which reflects their tactical import-ance. The convoluted patterns which result are most visible − at both national and regional levels − in large and complex societies such as India and Nigeria which combine a federal system with a multi-party liberal democracy.

Ethnic politics turns not only on numbers, but on the special advant-ages or disadvantages which groups may gain from differing patterns of incorporation into the economy or political system, often following from the socially discriminatory effects of colonial rule. A politically dominant minority, whether indigenous like the Tutsi in Burundi or immigrant like the whites in Rhodesia (Zimbabwe), is in a highly perilous position once political mobilisation occurs among the dis-advantaged majority, since this inherently threatens the minority's control and coalition-building outside the dominant group becomes all but impossible. Small groups which control much of the economy but lack political strength − the 'pariah entrepreneurs' − are also highly exposed since they can be extremely vulnerable to politicians, like General Amin with the Ugandan Asians, who wish to exploit both their wealth and their political unpopularity. Minorities whose strength lies in the bureaucracy and the professions are better able to assimilate politicians drawn from the majority groups, and can be hard to dislodge, since they control the very institutions through which poli-ticians need to exercise their power.

Ethnic groups, none the less, rarely form stable and internally coherent building blocks from which a coalition can be constructed. For one thing, even though the sense of solidarity imposed by a common ethnic identity can be considerable, it has to compete with other forms of political cleavage, notably those of class. But more importantly, ethnic identities themselves can be remarkably fluid. They are by no means necessarily laid down as some immutable grid which it is beyond the capacity of the individual to change. Individuals may sometimes pass readily from one group to another, or make use of a mixed ancestry or upbringing to associate themselves with different groups to maximise their personal advantage; politicians are often particularly well placed to manipulate their own ethnicity, treating it as a kind of badge or uniform designed to broaden or intensify their appeal according to the circumstances of the time. Ethnic groups themselves, far from constituting monolithic blocks, are frequently divisible into smaller groups whose own solidarity may be mobilised whenever it can be used as a resource in political competition. One reason why ethnic coalition-building can be extremely complex even in states with a dominant ethnic core is that the core group itself is likely to fragment, especially if it is well enough entrenched to fear little threat from minority or peripheral groups. A group which presents a united front at national level may break down into squabbling factions at regional and again at local level. This is no more than the logic of clientelist politics expressed through the medium of ethnicity.

Social and economic class, though readily regarded as an alternative to ethnicity in the mobilisation of political support, is in practice often better treated as an overlapping or indeed supplementary form of political cleavage. A great deal of ethnic competition is simply and directly concerned with access to economic benefits, and when — as very often happens — ethnic groups are in some measure economically specialised, it becomes pointless to draw a distinction between ethnicity and class. Even where ethnic differences are slight or blurred, and class might be expected to gain a compensating importance as a vehicle for political conflict, its impact is often mitigated by clientelist networks whch cut across class divisions, in the way which has been noted in the 'boss politics' of Latin American no less than North American cities.[14] None the less, there are states, especially in Latin America, where class is the essential vehicle for political competition, and the maintenance of a class-based coalition the condition for survival. This can work in different ways. One that has been often noted, especially among the more highly developed states of the southern cone of the continent, is the use of the military to bind together a middle-class coalition which would not be strong or united enough to govern without military leadership.[15] Since it is formed essentially as a defensive alliance, such a coalition may be extremely repressive against working-class or left-wing opposition, but is endangered by the ambitions of civilian politicians once the military leadership comes to be seen as either ineffective or unnecessary. In an analogous way, the fall of one of the few Latin American regimes to rely fairly unequivocally on a working-class base, that of Allende in Chile from 1970 to 1973, was promoted by the fragmentation of his always rather shaky coalition in the strikes of 1972-3, opening the way for military takeover. Another form of class coalition characteristic of smaller states especially in Central America consists essentially of an oligarchy, both urban and rural, with external (United States) support. While in a sense such a regime is maintained externally quite as much as from within, the leader's ability to retain the support of leading middle-class or oligarchical elements may be of vital importance in enabling him to draw on external assistance, as illustrated especially in the fall of the Somoza dynasty in Nicaragua in 1979, and perhaps also of Batista in Cuba in 1959.

But class as an element of coalition-building extends beyond the categories of 'working' or 'middle' class familiar from industrial states. In many third world societies the most important class division, if 'class' is defined in classic Marxist fashion, by reference to the means of production, is that between urban and rural dwellers. During the nationalist period, when the electoral systems established by departing colonial powers offered victory to the group of politicians who could most successfully mobilise the numerically overwhelming rural vote, leaders such as Gandhi in India and Senghor in Senegal profited from their ability to extend their movements beyond the cities. Subsequently, urban dwellers (the 'bourgeoisie' in the broadest and most literal sense of the word) have gained from their strategic location, and the ability to retain at least the acquiescence of the towns is often essential to leaders' survival. The fall of the Shah of Iran in 1979, of Haile Selassie in Ethiopia in 1974, or of Ayub Khan in Pakistan in 1969, in each case after their authority had been shattered by urban unrest, demonstrate a degree of urban power which also helps to explain the common bias of economic development programmes towards the cities at the expense of the countryside. Occasionally, a leader such as Perón in Argentina is able to create a base for support in a populist movement which provides a political outlet for the urban masses — the 'descamisados' or people without shirts — which counterbalances the strength of the army and much of the urban upper class within a still essentially right-wing ideology.

Another aspect of urban coalition-building is the role of professional and institutional groups which are heavily based in the towns. The most important of these by a long way is usually the army, whose support is essential to the survival of any regime whether military or civilian. Its role, especially when it takes direct control of government through a coup d'état, will be examined in a later chapter. The civilian bureaucracy rarely figures in any very obvious way in the maintenance or overthrow of governments because its position is rarely threatened: it is a part of the governing coalition permanently in power, and the phrase 'bureaucratic authoritarianism' has been coined to describe a regime maintained essentially by the power of its own servants. Other occupational groups may matter too. The power of the professions, led in this case as usual by the lawyers, was best demonstrated by their ability to thwart the ambitions of the Ghanaian military leader, General Acheampong, to institutionalise his regime in the mid-1970s. The Shah of Iran's fall was promoted by the disaffection of the commercial classes represented in the Bazaar, while the withdrawal of support for President Marcos by businessmen in the Philippines in 1983 likewise indicated a significant weakening in his position.

Trade unions are another mechanism for orchestrating urban interests, especially at times of potential unrest produced by falling real living standards. The importance of unions will obviously vary markedly in relation not only to underlying social conditions such as the level of urbanisation and industrialisation, but also to the extent to which deliberate efforts have been made to organise workers in pursuit of political goals. The highly politicised trade union organisations of the southern cone of Latin America represent one end of a continuum, at the other end of which are states where unions are almost non-existent. Nor are trade unions only an urban phenomenon, rural unions being especially important where large-scale plantation agriculture is controlled by multinational companies. Within the towns, an almost continuous tension between government and workers often expresses itself in a cyclical process: following any threatening expression of urban disaffection, the government seeks to control the unions by a mixture of centralised organisation imposed from above, and measures to assuage immediate grievances and co-opt union leaders into the governing coalition; as the effect of these concessions wears off, and as leaders acquire an increasingly governmental position divorced from the concerns of their members, so further grievances build up and a new generation of leaders arises to articulate them; the whole process is then repeated, possibly after a change of central government has produced a new set of national leaders who in turn want both the support and the control which co-optation offers. Rank-and-file control over the leadership is a problem in any trade union organisation, but specifically in a third world context it provides one indicator of the 'autonomy' of working-class organisations, and hence of the extent to which political activity is organised on a class rather than a clientelist basis. Where the class basis of politics is weak, the union may be seen by its leaders as a launching mechanism to project them into the elite. Sometimes, the leaders themselves are graduates who look to the union in their search for a political base; less educated leaders may seek to remedy this weakness by taking themselves off on courses abroad; at worst, they may just abscond with the funds.

A final urban occupational group with a high level of political visibility are the students. Articulate, ambitious, often idealistic, and concentrated in a small number of institutions permitting easy mobilisation, they are often at odds with the government as well as with the administrators of their own colleges who are usually subject to close political control. Issues, sometimes of astonishingly apparent triviality, may escalate following reactions on each side into a full-blown riot or demonstration with anti-governmental overtones. Since students do not in themselves have any very substantial resources at their disposal, such demonstrations can usually be suppressed without much difficulty by the government's riot police, generally ill-educated peasants who may take a positive delight in wielding their batons against such an identifiable elite; colleges and universities can be closed, and the students dispersed to their homes or the countryside — where isolation and the need to gain their qualifications will force them into submission. Where a regime is already weak, however, a student demonstration may display its lack of nerve, or prompt more powerful groups to show their solidarity, thus leading to the collapse of the regime. Even apparently powerful military governments, such as those in Sudan in 1964 or in Thailand in 1973, have fallen in this way. At the very least, then, student demonstrations provide a challenge to which the regime must respond.

One way in which the governing coalition can be orchestrated, though by no means an essential one, is through a political party. Parties, indeed, are better regarded as coalitional umbrellas than as organisations expressing coherent sets of interests which can gain institutional identities of their own. This helps to explain the ease with which they can divide, reform, accumulate converts, change their names, and encompass a wide range of factional and ideological differences. Though the coalitional form of parties may be most obvious when they are fighting electoral battles against one another — as for instance in the break-up of the old Congress, the formation of Janata, and the subsequent triumph of Congress (I) in India — it is no less the case when there is only a single party in the field. Both KANU in Kenya and TANU (subsequently CCM) in Tanzania have provided a formalised system of popular elections between party members which aimed to ensure that members of parliament would bring with them a degree of local support which in turn would help sustain the government. The party equally serves as a mechanism for distributing at least a modicum of jobs and development allocations to its supporters. In a very large and diverse political society, such as India or Brazil, a party may be almost indispensable for keeping some kind of control over this process — one reason, perhaps, why parties have survived in Brazil even under military government. Even where parties have negligible functions in rallying support, they help to signify a formal acceptance of the regime and to identify its principal patrons. The reason why parties are so readily abolished when a new regime (especially a military one) takes over is because this identification then becomes an embarrassment, as the patrons seek to establish new ties with whoever now holds power at the centre.

How Regimes Fail

Third world regimes are a good deal less unstable than popular mythology would have it. It is true that the majority of third world states have experienced military coups since 1960 — an aspect of politics discussed in Chapter 7; but this is more a matter of the way in which governments change than of the frequency with which they do so. Africa especially provides, along with several cases of chronic instability, examples of leaders who have held power uninterruptedly for twenty years or more: Haile Selassie of Ethiopia, Sékou Touré of Guinea, Houphouet-Boigny of Ivory Coast, Nyerere of Tanzania, Kaunda of Zambia, Banda of Malawi. Peaceful succession from one ruler to another is by no means rare — Senghor to Diouf in Senegal, Kenyatta to Moi in Kenya, Ahidjo to Biya in Cameroon — and Africa can even boast the longest continuously governing political party in the history of the world: the True Whig Party of Liberia from 1878 to 1980. In maintaining themselves in power, third world leaders and regimes have several advantages. The power of the state, generally much greater than that of any other organised political force within society, enables regimes to insulate themselves against (or, put more crudely, forcibly suppress) potential rivals; the condition for survival is then that the regime retain the support of the state's own officials, overwhelmingly the greatest danger being that of overthrow from within. Given that stability often depends on the skill of individual rulers, the effective leader of a well-established regime may manipulate clientele networks so as to create an expectation of permanence, while expectations of change are blunted by the fact that most of the population quite rightly suppose that the nature or composition of the government is not something which they are ever likely to be able to control.

There are obviously countervailing reasons which help to account for instability. At the most basic level, dependence on an international economy over which they have very little influence makes regimes vulnerable especially to recession in the western industrial economies; the weakness of national identities with their corresponding concepts of political authority impedes the formation of effective institutions through which political demands can be processed and mediated; while the substitution for such institutions of particularist clienteles helps to breed a sense of alienation which may surface, for example, in riots. Other reasons for instability are tactical rather than deep-seated, and help to explain the differences between stable states and apparently similar neighbours with a high level of regime turnover. Failure, like success, can be self-reinforcing. In states such as Ghana or Bangladesh, which have had a high incidence of instability, it becomes extremely difficult for regimes to establish the sense of their own permanence which is itself an important element in their survival. Conversely, a leader who emerges unscathed from a period of chaos, such as Nimairi in Sudan or Mengistu Haile-Mariam in Ethiopia, may be ascribed that 'fortuna' which Machiavelli sees as the most precious attribute of a prince. Individual leadership skills are equally vital, as an earlier section has shown, and either a nationalist movement or a coup may throw up a leader who has very little conception of what his job requires.

The most difficult problem in political management is that of responding to a shrinkage in the ruling coalition. The shrinkage is almost inevitable. All governments, whether military or civilian, single- or multi-party, raise expectations when they come to power that they will be most unlikely to fulfil. Sometimes the coalition cracks almost immediately, as in the break-up of the Patriotic Front alliance between Mugabe and Nkomo in post-independence Zimbabwe; at other times, it may be spread over several years. The defection of previous supporters immediately affects the regime's sense of security, and is likely to provoke a strong reaction. Both single-party and military regimes share an ideological tendency — even though couched in rather different terms — to regard themselves as the embodiment of an ideal of national unity, dissent from which is treasonable; all opposition must then be incorporated or suppressed. In a multi-party state, defection to the opposition or some other challenge to the government such as an adverse court decision is readily seen as threatening the government's control; if allowed to go unpunished, it may be taken as reflecting the government's weakness, and lead to a progressive erosion of support as the opposition's star rises, and prudent folk align themselves on the side of the likely winners. The initial defection in any event is likely to have taken place at a time of government unpopularity.

The normal and obvious government response is to increase the level of repression. Force is what it possesses and its opponents lack. Sometimes, and especially under multi-party political systems, this can be done through legal manipulation without physical coercion. Laws can be passed to deprive dissident members of parliament of their seats, or to require a by-election when a member crosses from one party to another (the same law being rescinded when an opposition representative wishes to join the government). More often, direct repression is called for, including some measure such as Mrs Gandhi's state of emergency in 1975, or martial law in the Philippines in 1972, which enables the government to imprison its opponents. At a further level of escalation, government forces may be unleashed against regions or ethnic groups sympathetic to the opposition, as in the stationing of the notoriously brutal Fifth Brigade in Nkomo's Matabeleland base area in Zimbabwe in 1982. All of this raises the stakes. It may succeed in imposing some kind of order, or may trigger a further level of dissident reaction. It is easy enough, from the security of western liberal societies, to condemn government overreaction as being foolish as well as wrong. Certainly government repression is often counterproductive, springing from a leader's individual pique and alienating groups whom a wiser strategy might have reincorporated into the ruling coalition. At the same time, the bases for insecurity are real. Like a hypochondriac whose protestations of illness are ascribed to a fevered imagination until suddenly he dies, the plots which a leader sees everywhere look ludicrous until one succeeds. Events like the overthrow of Maurice Bishop in Grenada in October 1983, and his subsequent murder and the invasion of the island, look like farce until they suddenly degenerate to tragedy. What distinguishes successful leaders is perhaps as much as anything a sense of how far it is safe to go.

A leader's fall may simply be a matter of rank bad luck. Though Bangladesh is an exceedingly difficult country to govern, General Zia ur-Rahman had made as good a job of it as any, and his assassination by the commander of a garrison which he was visiting in 1981 seems to have reflected merely personal enmity and ambition rather than any more basic defect in the regime. More often, there is an evident source of failure, which the leader's fall reflects and exposes, and which may arise at one of a number of levels. It may emerge either in the city or in the countryside, and in each of these cases may take one of two principal forms. In the city, the two forms are archetypally expressed in the riot and the coup. While the coup may reflect little more than the ambition or disaffection of the person who leads it, it often more basically expresses the discontents of the bureaucracy or, in the larger and more institutionalised third world states such as Chile or Argentina, those of the armed forces as a corporation. Coups and their resulting military regimes are examined in Chapter 7. Riots, on the other hand, generally start at the bottom and work up; initiated by some group such as the students, trade unionists or the unemployed urban mob, they may spread to reveal unsuspected depths of discontent even with apparently deeply-entrenched regimes, and make the urban centres (and especially the capital) practically ungovernable. At this point, conservative commercial interests whose sympathies would normally lie with the regime may move over to the opposition as the best means of maintaining their position. The regime may then fall to a military takeover prompted by the bureaucracy's need to restore order, or even as in the case of Iran to a government essentially placed in power by the mob itself; even if the regime succeeds in weathering the riots – which of their nature are likely to be of fairly short duration since the rioters depend on the urban environment which they are disrupting – this will often be at the expense of concessions (either to the rioters or to the armed forces) which seriously weaken its standing and lead to its overthrow a few months later. Only a regime with the wholehearted support of the armed forces is likely to survive serious urban rioting with its power intact.

Failure in the countryside is much less immediately apparent, since regimes are not overthrown there. The government continues to survive in the capital, and – much more easily than when faced by urban discontent – can often get external military assistance to suppress rural opposition. Rural opposition can, however, go on for a long time, and in the process pose a more basic threat to the state's effectiveness and survival than the short-term riots of the cities. One form this can take is that the government may simply lose effective control over large tracts of the countryside, degenerating into a 'broken-backed state' whose authority in much of its official territory is at best no more than titular. The classic Weberian definition of a state as having a monopoly of the legitimate use of force within its frontiers would deny many third world states over substantial periods of time the status of being 'real' states at all. The broken-backed phenomenon has been most evident in the Southeast Asian states such as Burma to which the term was originally applied,[16] but can equally be found at various times in African states (such as Zaire, Ethiopia or Sudan), and Latin American ones (such as Colombia during the 'violencia' of 1948-64). It is most characteristic of states in which peripheral peoples assert their independence of a dominant core controlled by a central regime which they cannot expect to overthrow, but may also be prompted by a combination of general bureaucratic inadequacy and rural discontent, and by local warlords sustained especially by the drugs trade. The second form occurs, still more dangerously for the central regime, when the countryside is used as a base area for the armed overthrow of urban government. This, the classic rural revolutionary strategy, is considered in Chapter 8.

Notes

1. *L'Essor Hebdomadaire* (31 March 1964), quoted and translated in F. Snyder, *One-Party Government in Mali* (Yale University Press, 1965), p. 90.

2. These categories are adapted from C. Young, *Ideology and Development in Africa* (Yale University Press, 1982).

3. World Bank, *World Development Report 1981* (Oxford University Press, 1981), Table 5.

4. B. Amonoo, *Ghana 1957-1966: The Politics of Institutional Dualism* (Allen & Unwin, 1981).

5. See, for example, Ayi Kwei Armah, *The Beautyful Ones Are Not Yet Born* (Heinemann, 1969), pp. 155-7.

6. See H. Bienen, *Tanzania: Party Transformation and Economic Development* (Princeton University Press, 1967).

7. I. Wallerstein, 'The Decline of the Party in Single-Party African States' in J. La Palombara and M. Weiner (eds.), *Political Parties and Political Development* (Princeton University Press, 1966).

8. N. Kasfir, *The Shrinking Political Arena* (University of California Press, 1976).

9. J.A. Schumpeter, *Capitalism, Socialism and Democracy* (Allen & Unwin, 1943), Chapter 22.

10. R.H. Jackson and C.G. Rosberg, *Personal Rule in Black Africa* (University of California Press, 1982).

11. See for example, C. Clapham, 'Imperial Leadership in Ethiopia', *African*

Affairs, vol. 68, no. 271 (1969), pp. 110-20.

12. Jackson and Rosberg, *Personal Rule in Black Africa*, p. 18.

13. The court politics of Henry VIII is brilliantly described in Lacey Baldwin Smith, *Henry VIII: The Mask of Royalty* (Cape, 1971).

14. See S.W. Schmidt *et al., Friends, Followers and Factions: A Reader in Political Clientelism* (University of California Press, 1977).

15. The classic exposition of this view is J. Nun, 'The Middle-Class Military Coup' in C. Veliz (ed.), *The Politics of Conformity in Latin America* (Oxford University Press, 1967).

16. The phrase is from H. Tinker, *Ballot Box and Bayonet: People and Government in Emergent Asian Countries* (Oxford University Press, 1964).

5 MANAGING THE ECONOMY

The Politics of Economic Management

This chapter is not directly concerned with the economic plight of the third world — a subject, however important, about which a great deal has already been written. It is concerned with the management of the economy as a political problem facing third world governments. This problem is often presented in terms of the strategies for economic development between which governments can choose, especially in so far as these can be related to 'socialist' or 'capitalist' development paths. These are certainly part of it: many third world states have had a real (though variable) degree of choice, and the options which they have selected have had a significant effect on the well-being or otherwise of their peoples. But these choices have had to be made, not only within the context of an international economic system which imposes constraints of a broadly familiar kind, but equally within the context of the third world state structure itself.

By far the most important priority of economic management is the maintenance and consolidation of the state, and alternative capitalist or socialist (or even Marxist) development strategies may be much better regarded as different means for attaining this common goal, than as serving in their own right as the principal objective of government action, or as defining the key types of different social and political systems in the way that they are usually taken to do in comparing developed industrial states. Economic development policies are state development policies. At their simplest and most basic, they are concerned with getting and spending: with raising the money which is needed to run the state, and especially to meet the demands of groups within the society who depend on state allocations, notably those government employees who present the principal threat to most third world regimes. In the process, they provide a mechanism for reallocating resources towards those who have political power, and away from those who lack it. More generally, economic management is concerned with political control. The two main control mechanisms open to any government are the imposition of force and the manipulation of economic reward, and in states where authority is fragile and force consequently often dangerous and difficult to impose, economic manipulation provides a vastly preferable option. This in turn places a premium on the degree of control which the state is able to exercise over the economy: over patterns of production and distribution, and over the benefits to be gained from the allocation of employment opportunities and the extraction of a surplus or profit for the state's own use. The rhetoric of socialism which comes so readily to third world governments is often most plausibly regarded as an ideological mechanism for justifying increases in their own power. Since the most profitable and easily controlled areas of economic activity are those concerned with external trade and especially export production, economic management provides the clearest and most literal example of the role of the third world state as broker between domestic and external interests. Control of the economy is thus intimately linked to external relations, and provides a ready indicator of the government's autonomy *vis-à-vis* the outside world. A 'banana republic' is a state whose domestic economic management has been co-opted by external companies to a degree that deprives the state of autonomy even in the conduct of its own internal affairs. This is, however, an exceptional and limiting case; most third world states have been able to acquire a degree of control over their economies which, though highly variable, disproves any simplistic notion of the state as merely the product and plaything of external economic forces.

One useful indicator of the relationship between economic management and political control lies in the priority which economic development has as a political goal of government. It is readily assumed, especially by development economists, that since economic underdevelopment is the principal problem (and indeed defining characteristic) of third world states, so development must be the overriding goal of their governments. Often, perhaps usually, this is not the case.[1] Politicians everywhere have multiple and competing goals and calls on their attention, and in third world states these will characteristically include a fairly high priority for symbolic goals (geared either to personal or national self-esteem), for national political goals including notably the maintenance of state integrity and, most important of all, for staying in power. All these goals will of course eventually be served by a successful programme of economic development. In the short term, they compete with it. The most general source of competition is that economic development calls for investment, whether in economic or political terms, which clashes with the immediate demands of consumption. This does not just mean using precious funds to keep the army happy or defeat a secessionist war. It means not endangering the consumption patterns of urban groups, and thus shifting funds from the countryside to the cities – a problem which will be examined later. It also means that the political system will often be structured in an economically ineffective way. To stay in power, as we have seen, it is often necessary to build a political coalition geared to maintaining a balance among a number of competing interests, which is inherently at variance with any attempt to impose any single strategy. Put slightly differently, the type of political system which is cheapest to run is one which does not seek to enforce its own policies, or offend established interests or attitudes, but which merely reacts in an *ad hoc* way to the most pressing demands made on it. Several studies of economic development planning have made the point that, quite independently of the value of plans in themselves as instruments of economic development, any plan is difficult to implement because it requires a centrally-directed structure of government which is at odds with the determination of departmental ministers or local officials to run their own show.[2] The president is too busy (and very likely too wise) to direct the implementation of the plan himself; a minister of planning is no more than one among equals, with no authority over the ministers of agriculture, transport or public works; a minister of state in the president's office has the central position, but is most unlikely to have the political clout to whip other politicians into line. But all these are simply reflections of the fact that any economic development programme requires both great determination and, still more importantly, effective political institutions.

Exactly the same problem is reflected on the ground in the way that development projects are 'skewed' by political considerations. The 'wrong' roads are built, the showpiece development project placed in a clearly uneconomic location. Whether this is the result of a process of consensual policy making which requires that every region feels that it is being treated fairly, or more crudely of a minister putting funds into his own constituency, it reflects the impact of a neo-patrimonial social order. Its salience is increased by the fact that development funds, especially in the form of foreign aid, provide one of the very few sources of discretionary finance which hard-pressed governments have available in allocating rewards and maintaining political allegiance. What, from the foreign aid giver's viewpoint, is an attempt to relieve hunger or promote health (or possibly, even then, provide orders for recession-hit domestic industries), is from the recipient's viewpoint a potential source of control whose political implications cannot be avoided. This simple fact lies behind much of the righteous indignation of recipient governments about the 'strings' with which aid is 'tied'.

The actual priority given to economic development goals varies widely. For some leaders, such as Houphouet-Boigny of the Ivory Coast, they take a pre-eminence which relegates issues of national autonomy to a subsidiary position. For others, such as Nyerere in Tanzania or Banda in Malawi, they form part of a set of policies geared to some broader concept of national development. Bureaucratic authoritarian military regimes may likewise see 'monetarist' development policies as tying in not simply with economic efficiency but equally with the need to weaken political opponents such as trade unions. Often, as has already been suggested, economic policy is more a matter of *ad hoc* reaction than of conscious strategy, while for rulers such as Haile Selassie of Ethiopia (regardless of the obligatory rhetorical gestures in that direction), it is hard to see it as having much meaning at all, except for the vital need to generate revenues to maintain a centralised state machinery. Even where economic development goals are downplayed or deliberately rejected, however, this is not necessarily a matter for condemnation. When Sékou Touré said in rejecting de Gaulle's referendum in 1958 that Guineans preferred poverty in liberty to riches in slavery, or Samora Machel at considerable cost closed the Mozambique border with white-ruled Rhodesia, each was expressing a legitimate moral choice of a kind that external commentators can only respect.

Getting and Spending

Government Revenues and External Dependence

The most important political fact about the revenues of third world governments is their dependence on international trade. Unlike industrial states, which raise the greater part of their revenue from domestic economic transactions (especially from income and sales taxes), most third world governments rely on external transactions. This is not, on the whole, because third world states are more heavily involved than industrial states in production for the international market. In 1979, exports amounted to 20 per cent of the gross domestic product of middle- and low-income countries, as against 19 per cent for industrial market economies.[3] While a few countries, such as the major oil exporters like Saudi Arabia and Kuwait, or entrepôt states like Singapore, are very heavily involved in the international market, most third world governments tax foreign trade simply because they can control it much more easily (and at much lower political cost) than internal production. In this, they continue the precedent of the colonial state, which encouraged export production partly at least to provide a tax base for the administration itself. Straightforward import and export duties are only one form, and often not the major one, taken by this reliance on trade. Especially in mineral-producing states, a second form consists of levies on multinational corporations, through royalties, profits taxes or profit-sharing agreements. Thirdly, the state can raise its own profits by creating international trading monopolies, which give it an economically favoured position as the sole provider of imported consumer goods, or more often as the sole buyer of cash crops from farmers which it resells overseas; the same outcome results from the state's nationalisation of foreign multinationals, which it may run itself, or else farm out to a foreign management (often the original owner) which receives a fee for its services. A fourth highly important source of state revenue consists of direct external transfers in the form of aid or loans from international, governmental and private sources; these gain political significance both from the disproportionate share which they comprise in the discretionary development budget and, in the case of loans especially, from the government's urgent need to stabilise either its own income and expenditure account or its balance of external trade. Further external revenue-raising devices include the manipulation of foreign exchange rates and special income taxes or fees on expatriate employees. The external element in government income is often diffi-cult to calculate because it is lumped in with other revenue sources in published accounts, but by way of example, the governments of two small West African states, Liberia and Sierra Leone, derived between 60 per cent and 80 per cent of their income in the late 1960s and early 1970s directly from external transactions,[4] even though exports accounted (in Sierra Leone) for no more than 24 per cent of gross domestic product. For many states, and especially the major oil pro-ducers, an even higher proportion of revenues is likely to be derived from international trade.

This dependence on externally-generated revenues has direct political consequences.[5] The most basic is that it becomes almost impossible for most third world states to contemplate any strategy for economic development which would involve any substantial reduction in their participation in international trade. There are a few exceptions. China and India have huge domestic markets, rely on exports for only 4-6 per cent of gross domestic product, and raise by far the greater part of their revenue internally. Other states with a low dependence on exports, such as Turkey and Brazil, have a high dependence on external capital inflows. In general, a reduction in foreign trade involves a shift in the tax base of the state onto the domestic market and this in turn implies an increase in the government's administrative and coercive capacity: domestic revenue is difficult to extract, and any government obliged to increase its reliance on it will have to reckon with the possibility of riots in the cities, withdrawal of the peasantry from market production, and a surge in black marketeering. The Burmese government did its best, with a drop from 20 per cent to 8 per cent in exports as a percentage of gross domestic product between 1960 and 1979, but has been obliged to reverse the policy in its search for government revenue.[6] Elsewhere, only a government with the iron determination and control over its population of the Khmer Rouge has been able to produce any substantial reduction. Two other states where exports have sharply dropped as a percentage of gross domestic product, Ghana and Uganda, provide evidence not of self-reliance but, on the contrary, of a collapse in government capacity. On the whole, third world governments have a positive interest in encouraging production for the world market in order to increase their revenue base, and this explains why even self-confessedly 'socialist' regimes have often proclaimed extremely liberal investment policies, and maintained close relations with transnational corporations, especially in fields such as mineral production where technological and marketing factors call for vertically integrated structures for extraction, transport and processing. In Guinea and Angola, for example, bauxite and oil production under transnational control provide the income without which socialist policies would be all but impossible in other areas of the economy, or indeed the political system. Regardless of their ideological bickering, governments and transnationals share an interest in maintaining uninterrupted production, which is sometimes sharply demonstrated by the transnational's ability to call on government help in preventing any disruptive action by the workforce.

A second consequence of revenue dependence is that governments have an equally strong interest in policing their own economic frontiers. This is true in the most literal sense. The more income the government extracts from international trade, the more worthwhile it is for both producers and consumers to circumvent it by smuggling. Smuggling is a very substantial problem for any continental third world government except the very largest. It is simply a matter of economic rationality. If export produce can be sold for more, or imported goods bought for less, across the border, then (allowing for the cost of transport) they will move. The dramatic decline in production figures for Guinean agriculture in the years after independence in 1958 is probably due less to any real fall in production than to the crops being sold in ways which evaded the Guinean state. Cocoa accounted for some 25 per cent of Togo's total exports by value in 1978, very little of which was locally produced: it came across the border from Ghana.[7] It is then in the government's interest to intensify border patrols, which in turn are less likely to stop smuggling than to increase its 'transport' costs, whether by evading the patrols or by bribing them.

One of the main differences between 'socialist' and 'capitalist' governments lies in their determination to police their economic frontiers not just in this literal sense but in a broader one, a touchstone of this being the maintenance of a non-convertible national currency. A non-convertible currency increases the state's control capacity, especially by impeding the export of capital, but at the cost of increasing the benefits to be gained by smuggling — whether directly by selling goods for a currency which is worth something externally, or indirectly by exchange control circumventions of one sort or another. Sierra Leone, whose principal export is diamonds, has been obliged to maintain a convertible currency because these are so easily smuggled that the government has to pay even illegal diamond diggers a fair economic price for their stones on a 'no questions asked' basis. Nonconvertibility also has the effect of shifting real income from the countryside to the towns, in ways which are discussed in a later section.

Another aspect of policing arises from the relationship between governments and transnational corporations. While these have a common interest in maintaining mineral production (save in managing the rate of depletion, where the government may take a more longterm view than the corporation), they have directly opposed interests in sharing out the profit. The result is a running battle in which the government seeks to extract an increased surplus through its use of state powers, which the corporation seeks to evade through its use of technical expertise. The government's weapon of last resort is nationalisation without compensation, while the corporation's is the threat of pulling out altogether, but both of these ultimate deterrents carry enormous costs to the user: the government will be forfeiting the chance of attracting other foreign investment, while the transnational will be abandoning what is usually a large fixed investment and assured source of supply. Other forms of nationalisation may not be unwelcome to the corporation, provided it retains control of day-to-day management. '51% nationalisation' involves the government taking a formal controlling interest which gives it a half share in profits and the power to impose specific policies (on indigenisation of senior staff, for instance), but at the same time lowers the political vulnerability of the transnational by putting it in partnership with the government, which will then see the corporation's affairs from a management point of view. The transnational has innumerable avenues open to it for trying to circumvent government control, many of which involve artificially running down profits on the local side of its operations by internally transferring funds to its home base or wherever profits taxes are least; such mechanisms include depreciation rates, transfer pricing (where the corporation transfers goods at an artificial price between its own subsidiaries) and management or consultancy contracts. Faced by a baffling array of technical arguments, the third world government may simply have to demand more money and hope that its extortions do not actually lead the protesting transnational to pull out. The degree of direct interference by transnationals in the domestic politics of the host state is generally much less than popular demonology would have it, the role of United States transnationals in smaller Latin American states providing most of the exceptions. Corporations can rub along with governments of any political persuasion and have no political goals beyond the admittedly important one of freedom to run their own operations.[8] Intervention in domestic politics is an extremely risky game which they are generally wise to avoid, though 'sweeteners' to government officials in one form or another may be a normal part of running the business: the highly placed politician who is invited to join the board, the law firm with government contacts which is offered a retainer, donations to worthy causes which are close to the interests (and very likely the pockets) of local officials in the area where they operate, are all part of the transnational's daily life. While these all provide evidence of the symbiotic relationship of government and transnational, however, they indicate the government's (or ruling elite's) capacity to extort benefits from the corporation, quite as much as the other way round.

The final, and in many ways most important, political implication of external revenue dependence arises from the simple uncertainty of revenues which are directly or indirectly derived from trade in international primary products, which fluctuate unpredictably in price and quantity. In principle, third world states stand to make gains as well as losses, as in the great oil boom of the mid-1970s which gave enormous windfall revenues to third world oil producers (and corresponding losses to oil consumers). In practice any benefit is easily outweighed by the effects of unpredictability, including governments' ineradicable tendency to make optimistic projections in times of boom which leave them badly exposed in times of slump. Equally, export revenue drops take place at times of recession in the industrial states which are then all the more reluctant to bail out third world governments. The problem is familiar enough to need no further emphasis, and has been discussed at length in widely circulated sources such as the Brandt reports.[9] Its effects on government revenues and freedom of action should simply be noted.

Government Spending and Internal Transfers

In one sense, government expenditure is simply the converse of government income, and raises similar problems with regard to external dependence. Overexpenditure increases reliance on outside aid, and in a few ex-colonial states the cost of maintaining the bureaucracy has been such that they have needed straightforward assistance in balancing the current budget (rather than development aid) from the former colonial power. Some forms of spending, such as armaments, create dependence on the supplier. The more interesting issues raised by government spending, however, concern the classic political question, 'who gets what?', and the effects of the state structure in transferring benefits between groups within domestic society. One point here is the tendency for government consumption to increase at the expense of private consumption in the overall distribution of the national product. Between 1960 and 1979, public consumption as a percentage of gross domestic product increased from 9 per cent to 11 per cent in low-income and from 11 per cent to 13 per cent in middle-income states, though the same rate of increase, from 15 per cent to 17 per cent, occurred in the industrial market economies. There was some tendency, though not a very great one, for the rate of increase to rise in the 1970s by comparison with the 1960s.[10] These crude figures include a number of states, mostly African, where the government share of consumption more than doubled over the two decades (Argentina, Burundi, Ethiopia, Jamaica, Liberia, Somalia, Zambia), offset by others, mostly Asian and Latin American, where it increased more slowly or declined. Contrary to a great deal of well-meaning propaganda, there has been no evident tendency for expenditure on defence to take any increasing share of government spending, or to rise at the expense of 'social' goals such as health and education.[11] The World Bank's figures are incomplete, but show a proportional decline in defence spending between 1972 and

1978 for both low-income and middle-income countries. There are no comparable figures for the main oil-exporters, several of which spent heavily on armaments from their 1970s bonanza.[12]

Where government spending matters most, however, is in its physical and social distribution, rather than its distribution between different sectors of government. By far the greater part of such spending goes to pay the salaries of state employees. In physical terms, this means that it goes overwhelmingly to the cities, and especially to the capital city. In social terms, it means that it goes disproportionately to the modern educated elite. Both of these points are more easily grasped than measured. In smaller third world states with 'primate' cities, government is essentially an affair of the capital, in which all the ministries are concentrated. The various districts or provinces each have their local bureaucracies, often gathered into one single building at the regional headquarters, but these are puny by comparison: even a key rural sector of government, such as agriculture, may be represented at local level just by the district agricultural officer and his assistant, while the qualified staff are concentrated into the central ministry, and make only occasional field trips into the provinces. Social services such as schools and hospitals are likewise concentrated, providing the capital both with the major sources of state employment and with the benefits they provide. In large third world states such as Brazil, India and Nigeria, exactly the same process is pushed down the scale. Each of these has a federal system of government, and each 'state' (in the sense of the main regional units of which the federation is composed) has its own substantial bureaucracy. One of the main reasons for the constant demands in Nigeria, say, for the creation of new states by dividing the existing ones, is that this automatically leads to the establishment of a new state capital with its bureaucracy and its obligatory social services. Equally, while government employs large numbers of poorly paid people in menial positions, it is also *par excellence* the preserve of the elite, whether as administrators, educators, army officers or, indeed, businessmen for whom government contacts and contracts are essential to survival.[13] Government spending thus reinforces the distribution of political power discussed in the last chapter.

The same goes for economic development policies which are as readily equated with urban/rural and state/subject divisions as with any ideological approach to development conceived in left/right terms.[14] One of these is the underpricing of rural produce, as against the overpricing of urban produce. Infant industries which require a high level of protection oblige the consumer to pay an inflated price for an

often low quality product, compared with goods which could otherwise have been imported. This may be justifiable as a spur to industrialisation, but contrasts sharply with food pricing policies, where the
authorities are obliged to maintain low urban prices even where this leads
to a high level of imports and the decay of the domestic agricultural
sector. This is because governments cannot afford to raise prices for
urban consumers because of the risk of political repercussions, a point
sharply made by the Monrovia rice riots of April 1979 which led to the
fall of the Liberian True Whig Party regime which had been in power
for over a century, or the Tunisian food riots of 1983.[15] The other
principal rural product, cash crops, is taxed through government monopoly purchasing at prices below the world market resale price.[16] Likewise, a non-convertible national currency is not simply a concomitant
of a 'socialist' development policy which requires control over capital
movements. It also has redistributive effects arising from the fact that
the currency will inevitably be overvalued (and sometimes grossly
overvalued, by ten times or more) by comparison with its free market
rate of exchange. Farmers will (unless they can smuggle their crops
abroad) be paid by government in comparatively valueless local currency for goods which it then resells for convertible currencies on the
world market. Imported consumer goods which form part of the elite
urban life style will be comparatively cheap in local currency terms;
and while governments will have to ensure through some form of
exchange control that this does not lead to an unrestricted flood of
imports (such as happened in Ghana with 'open import licencing'
under the Busia government after 1969), the controls themselves provide copious opportunities for enrichment. An import licence easily
becomes a licence to print money.[17]

This broad picture, obviously enough, overlooks many of the differences between third world states in economic size and endowment.
It equally ignores variations that arise as a result of deliberate policy
choices. The economic fate which follows from pursuing the tendencies
discussed in this section – and especially the cumulative effect of
taxing the rural and productive sectors of the economy in favour of
government and urban consumption – is potentially so disastrous that
at some point they will have to be controlled or reversed. Governments
are caught between the short-term dangers of urban and external
dependence, and the long-term dangers of following the line of least
resistance. They may confront the policy choices raised by this
dilemma either sooner or later, depending on their foresight, and their
economic and political strength or freedom of action. They may do so

in different ways, depending in some measure at least on their own ideological choice. The main possible forms of response are discussed in the next section.

Strategies and Structures of Economic Control

Within the constraints imposed by the structure of the state on the one hand, and of the international economic system on the other, third world leaders and governments do have some element of choice in the management of their economies. That this choice, surprising though it may seem, is none the less genuine, is demonstrated first by real differences in the ways in which comparable third world economies are in fact organised and run, and secondly by perhaps even more dramatic differences in the degree of success or failure which they have achieved. In economic as in political management, what has made choice possible has been the low level of existing institutionalisation, and since institutionalisation is a fair measure of effectiveness, their choice follows from weakness rather than from strength. One indicator of this is that it is on the whole the African states, which according to most indicators are the least economically developed of the third world,[18] that have had the most evident degree of choice, while even for them the options have tended to close as the years go by: Nkrumah had a freedom of manoeuvre in Ghana at independence in 1957 which has progressively been denied his successors as the economy has slid further and further into stagnation and decay. At the other extreme, Latin American regimes, though scarcely more locked than African ones into the international economy, have had to operate within a constricting mesh of established interests, perhaps breakable only by revolution on the Cuban scale. The contrast between socialist or even Marxist regimes in Africa, and the failure of the Allende government to manage vested economic interests (domestic no less than external) in Chile, provides an example.

In so far as regimes have choices, then, what choices do they have? Basically, and this harps back to the point about institutions, it is a choice of the form of organisational structure through which the economy is chiefly to be managed. And even though economies (like anything else) do not fall neatly into slots, there are two main groups of contenders, each of which may be divided into two further principal forms. The first (and highly conventional) breakdown is between private (or 'capitalist') structures on the one hand, and governmental (or 'socialist') ones on the other, though an immediate warning is needed that neither term means quite the same thing as its equivalent in industrial states. The capitalist category then splits into indigenous or domestic as against external or transnational capitalism, while for the socialist one I would adapt Crawford Young's terms, populist as against Marxist.[19] Few if any national economies fall exclusively into a single category. The ability of transnationals to coexist with governments of almost any ideological persuasion has already been noted, and alliances between the state and either indigenous or transnational capital are frequent. The Marxist variant is the most distinct, since it implies a more thoroughgoing system of social and political, as well as economic, management than the others; where it is combined with transnational capital, this tends to be confined to distinct enclaves, and virtually no accommodation is possible with indigenous capital, except at the lowest level of peasant farming or petty trade. There are none the less distinctive kinds of organisation involved in each case, and policies and strategies of economic management appropriate to each. All that is possible in a thumbnail survey of this kind is to sketch out the main alternatives.

Foreign and Indigenous Capitalism

The age of *laissez-faire* capitalism is so long gone from the industrial west that it may scarcely be necessary to point out that it is virtually non-existent in the third world too. Only in Hong Kong, where a small and almost entirely alien colonial administration provides for little more than basic law and order functions, does such a system operate; and while this might be taken as evidence that the state is more of a hindrance than a help to third world development, the special circumstances of Hong Kong prevent any plausible generalisation. Elsewhere, the state is very closely involved in economic policy and, as in many industrial capitalist states, this involvement is necessary for the economy to operate in its present form. In a state such as Brazil, where a very large part of economic management is directly undertaken by state corporations, it is scarcely plausible to speak of private capitalism at all. What capitalism means, then, is that the principal organisations which conduct the day-to-day business of the economy are privately owned and managed.

In the majority of third world states, this ownership and management come initially from foreign sources, possibly because the society lacks an indigenous entrepreneurial tradition, but equally because economic development is closely associated with overseas trade, and requires technology, capital and forms of organisation which have to be imported; metropolitan companies also have the initial political advantages provided by colonial control. In keeping with these origins, a high level of direct external management is generally associated with the simplest economies, geared to export production especially of minerals, though external capitalism is also often associated with export-directed processing, import-oriented manufacturing and assembly of foreign products under licence, and professional services such as banking, accounting, publishing or architecture. What it offers to the government is the possibility of large-scale foreign investment, especially during the initial stage of establishing the business, coupled with fairly efficient operation and hence, during boom periods at least, the possibility of very rapid growth in the economy and thus the government's revenue base. Its corresponding disadvantage is a low level of control, at the day-to-day operational level through the various devices already noted by which the company may evade payments to government, through the management of the company in response to its global interests which may take very little notice of its importance to the national economy and, at the most general level, through the government's need to maintain business 'confidence', which in practice may be equated with not doing anything which adversely affects external economic interests. It is through this implicit pressure much more than direct interference that the external economy's control over domestic political options is normally exercised. Where the external share in the economy is sufficiently large and long-established, it forms common interests with a section of domestic society which may then be termed a 'comprador bourgeoisie'. The value of this term — which refers in Latin American usage to the local agent of a foreign business — lies precisely in its application to local interests dependent on external capital, which can usefully be distinguished from a 'bureaucratic bourgeoisie' dependent on control of government, and a 'national bourgeoisie' dependent on indigenous capital. The relationship between government and external capital, comfortable enough during periods of economic growth, comes under severe strain during periods of recession when the government is caught in a revenue trap which leads it to squeeze transnationals whose own profits are declining, and the local unemployed look to the jobs which have been filled by foreigners. Since external capital is almost bound to be politically unpopular, what then matters is the government's willingness or capacity to maintain an alliance with a group which is easily treated as a scapegoat for economic problems, during a period of recession which threatens its own survival. Unless the government is either strong enough domestically to persist with an open externally-oriented economy, or so weak internationally that it has no freedom to change it, it will be strongly tempted to close off the economy by restricting the employment of foreigners and outflow of funds, and insisting on a larger share in management either on its own behalf, through nationalisation, or on that of domestic capitalists.

Indigenous capitalism depends overwhelmingly on the existence or creation of a domestic capitalist class, without which it becomes merely a means for the government to use its powers to channel funds into the pockets of its own members and their associates, acting in a private capacity. In some areas, mostly in Asia, but to some extent in North and West Africa, a tradition of capitalism may be implicit in indigenous trading patterns, and especially the structure of long distance trade. Another way in which a capitalist class can grow, especially in Asia and Latin America, is through the extraction of a surplus from land ownership which can be invested in urban industrial and commercial ventures. But overwhelmingly the most important impetus for the creation of a capitalist class comes, paradoxically in a way, from government, which is needed to sustain an environment in which private entrepreneurs are protected both from foreign capitalists and from government itself. The most obvious way in which indigenous capitalism depends on government help is through straightforward tariff protection and direct import controls, without which few domestic industries would be able to get under way. These are readily compatible with the government's interests both in raising revenue from tariffs and in increasing local production, although without further measures they may simply lead to external companies assembling goods locally. A second range of measures call for indigenisation of employment and control, in its crudest form just by expelling foreigners, but more often by deliberate action to restrict foreign ownership and management of key areas of the economy. Where there is any substantial foreign ownership of agricultural land, this is usually the first area to be attacked, most obviously in states such as Kenya or Zimbabwe where colonial farmers have threatened indigenous political control. Other measures include prohibitions on employing foreigners in posts for which qualified local nationals are available, total exclusion of foreigners from specified areas of the economy such as retail trade, and legislation requiring subsidiaries of foreign companies to be reconstituted as local companies with indigenous equity participation.

Government action is equally needed to provide indigenous capital with a favourable domestic environment, especially since the product of the indigenous private sector is normally strongly oriented towards domestic consumption. In the first place, the government may have to provide private capitalists with capital, usually through loans from a state-funded investment bank. Exclusion of foreigners from the home market, whatever form it takes, helps to increase the profitability of local producers at the expense of local consumers. Encouragement of private sector agriculture requires high maintained prices from government buying agencies, with the effect (in the short term, at least) of reducing the government's resale profit or even calling for subsidies. Government contracting can be used to provide an assured market for local businessmen. In all but a very few third world states private capital is thus so dependent on the state that a symbiotic relationship develops in which the state controls indigenous businessmen, who in turn seek to manipulate the state to serve their interests. Often, the same groups and individuals are involved in each, with politicians and civil servants running businesses on the side through relatives and nominees, or sometimes indeed quite openly: in Liberia before the 1980 coup there was no secret about one Minister of Defence's share in a firm which supplied uniforms to the army, or a police chief's ownership of a taxi business. While small businesses proliferate, even in a huge country such as India the major industrial and commercial enterprises are concentrated in very few hands. Is private enterprise anything more, then, than a device by which governments create wealth for their supporters at the expense of local consumers, while reassuring the United States of their ideological respectability? The answer varies, certainly, from case to case. But in so far as it is negative, this must rest in large part on the equally negative point that indigenous capitalism provides the only way of managing the economy which does not consign it either to foreigners whose interests may be very far removed from local ones, or to governments whose record of direct economic administration has often been appalling. It may in fact be the least of three evils.

State Socialism

'Socialism' as an ideology of economic management is so closely attuned to the interests and attitudes of third world governing elites that its popularity needs no further explanation. At its crudest, it offers to place control over the economy in the very hands which, at independence, have just gained control over government; but quite apart from its appeal both to personal interest and to nationalist rhetoric, it has more respectable arguments in its favour. In states where the indigenous capitalist class is weak, or where it is closely associated with external interests, state control offers the only means by which the economy can be brought under indigenous supervision. It is equally necessary for the government to control the economy if it is to make any effort to realise many of the aspirations which lay behind the nationalist movements — a theme often expressed in former British colonies in terms of a need to 'seize the commanding heights of the economy' which explicitly looked back to the British Labour government of 1945-51. The state, too, had a capacity to raise large capital sums, either locally through taxation or externally through aid, which easily outstripped local private companies, and had a bargaining strength in dealing with foreign capital which local companies likewise lacked. And if, after all, private capitalism required constant state intervention to ensure its profitability, why should the state not reap the benefits of its own measures, and in so doing further its own national goals rather than the individual self-interest of private businessmen? These are all broadly nationalist reasons for state intervention, characteristic of political systems with single or dominant nationalist parties, or of the more left-wing-oriented of the two parties in liberal states such as Jamaica or Sri Lanka. They owe very little to any 'hard' class or Marxist analysis, of the kind found only in a small number of revolutionary states, and are fairly summed up in Young's phrase as 'populist socialism'. African states such as Ghana, Guinea and Tanzania, Arab ones including Egypt, Algeria and Iraq, and in South Asia Sri Lanka before 1977, Burma, and, in some respects, India, all provide cases. South America, with its strong infusion of both multinational and domestic capitalism, provides fewer examples, Peru under the Velasco government between 1968 and 1975 being the clearest; but as already suggested in the case of Brazil, the role of the state in economic management may produce similar practical effects, even though the rhetorical element of populist socialism is lacking. Indeed the use of the state as an agency of economic management by right-wing military regimes echoes the way in which colonial administrations often took direct control of sectors of the economy which back in the metropolitan state would have been left to private enterprise.

The two most characteristic economic features of populist socialism are a non-convertible currency and the prominent role given to state corporations or 'parastatals' in managing the economy. While there is no possibility of closing the economy by cutting it off from the outside world (and usually no desire to do so), the limited degree of closure provided by a non-convertible currency is essential to provide the government with sufficient control over the national economy and especially to inhibit the flight of private savings which any socialist development strategy normally induces. Two states which opted for populist socialist policies while members of international currency communities, Guinea in West Africa and Tanzania in East Africa, found it necessary to withdraw from these and set up currency barriers against their neighbours. One common result is a loss of domestic confidence in the currency which may well be both cause and effect of government deficit financing − or printing money to pay its bills. Another result is smuggling. Along with a non-convertible currency goes a necessarily complicated set of foreign exchange controls, designed to pay for essential imports without siphoning out savings, and to discriminate between imports which, in the government's view, really are essential, as against those for which there is merely a high domestic demand. Populist socialist governments are usually actively hostile to indigenous capitalism, and where any substantial domestic capitalist economy exists, as in India, this will be subject to state controls. Import licencing in itself is an effective form of control, especially for domestic manufacturers who rely on imported machinery, parts or raw materials; dependence on credit from state-owned financial institutions is another. In India production licences are needed for manufacturers, in order to ensure that production fits in with national plans, while large enterprises are subject to special controls under monopoly legislation. Since each set of controls requires a bureaucracy to administer it, and provides economically rational entrepreneurs with an incentive to circumvent it, the opportunities for corruption are multiplied. Administrators acquire an interest in maintaining controls which they have to be paid to operate, and which they may be paid again to turn a blind eye to. Populist socialist regimes often display a paradoxical preference for foreign transnationals over domestic capitalists, partly because they simply cannot do without the technology, investment and revenues which the transnationals provide, but also because they present no domestic political threat. Among all African regimes, for example, few can have fallen victim to such a collection of dubious foreign adventurers as the Nkrumah government in Ghana, in the form of management contracts for government corporations, or suppliers' credits on disadvantageous terms for prestigious but unnecessary investments. The grandiose dreams of ambitious national leaders can provide easy opportunities for jet-setting businessmen in search of a quick profit.

Parastatals, often to be found operating under acronyms like NNPC or composite names like Petrobras or Pertamina (to take the national petroleum corporations of Nigeria, Brazil and Indonesia respectively) provide the instrument through which the state runs the economy itself. In some cases, the parastatal name is a façade behind which a transnational management continues to run the business on straightforward commercial lines as the government's agent or partner, but more often parastatals are set up and run by indigenous nationals. How well they are run depends to a large extent on the availability of qualified and competent managers, and on the nature of the political and economic control imposed from the centre. While a country such as Brazil has a large pool of highly qualified experts and administrators, the small civil services of newly independent African states have often been hard put to it to cope with the ordinary political and administrative tasks which independence gives them, let alone run the economy as well. Political control is equally important. A telling comparison of state farms in neighbouring Ghana and Ivory Coast shows how the Ghanaian ones, used as much as anything as instruments for political patronage, were run with disastrous incompetence, while the successful Ivoirian farms were run on a commercial basis by qualified managers, many of whom were French.[20] Both at the top and lower down, parastatals provide a high proportion of secure and well-paid jobs, and the temptation to use them to pay off political debts is great. With little of a private company's immediate incentive for profitability, and access to the borrowing resources of the state, it is easy enough for a parastatal to build up − often quite unknown to the government − an astonishing level of debt. Certainly not all of them operate at a loss: some work under such favourable guaranteed monopoly conditions that they would find it very hard to, while most countries with a large parastatal sector show a wide variation in the efficiency of individual corporations and a few real success stories. But it is hard to find a country where the parastatal sector as a whole runs at a profit, and a combination of managerial inefficiency and the fatal fascination of prestigious large-scale projects can lead to staggering losses. By the time that Pertamina's mismanagement forced itself on the Indonesian government's attention in 1975-6, the corporation had run up liabilities of over $10 billion. Brazil, building the largest dam on earth at a cost of $16 billion, found itself short of funds when the predicted surge in demand for electricity failed to materialise; half-a-dozen smaller dams, some of which could have been cancelled if necessary, would have served the purpose at far less risk.[21] In many respects, the economic inefficiencies and political constraints which characterise third world parastatals are not so different from those of the socialist bloc or nationalised industries in the west, though the weakness of the managerial ethos and the poverty of the countries concerned may make their effects much worse. In some countries, notably Brazil, parastatal-led investment has helped trigger a rapid rate of precarious growth. Overall, however, Young's figures suggest that populist socialist regimes in the third world have achieved a lower level of economic growth than capitalist ones,[22] and while there may be compensating advantages in social equality, these are much more evident in cutting the living standards of the few at the top, than in raising those of the many at the bottom.

Though a few third world regimes combine Marxist-Leninist rhetoric with populist socialist economic management — and even, in Benin and Congo, with membership of the franc zone — populist socialism should be sharply distinguished from any thoroughgoing attempt to institute a revolutionary Marxist economic order. While this too is statist in approach, it calls for a much more intensive level of compulsion and command, a very different kind of domestic political structure and, in the case of the two clearest examples, Cuba and Vietnam, for member-ship of Comecon and a reorientation of economic links towards the Soviet bloc. Since these in turn essentially require a domestic revolu-tion, such economies are more appropriately examined as part of the later chapter on revolutionary regimes.

Political Repression and Economic Control

Control of the economy means control of the people in it. The theme of this chapter has been that economic policy is a central political issue concerned with the creation of benefits on the one hand, and their dis-tribution on the other. While the allocation of economic rewards may in some degree compensate for the imposition of force, some forms of economic management — and especially, of course, those that entail the withholding of rewards from important political groups — will call for force. This is not simply a matter of privileged groups repressing exploited groups so that they can enjoy their disproportionate share of benefits, though that certainly enters into it. Repression may equally be needed to transfer resources from consumption (or immediate benefit) to investment (or hoped-for future benefit) or to impose some more efficient structure of production.

While general links between economy and political structure are easy enough to sketch out, their specific application is a much trickier matter. The link is clearest in the case of revolutionary Marxist regimes whose structures of economic and political management are scarcely distinguishable from one another, and which call for a very high level of political repression, at any rate in their initial stages: first of all to dispossess the existing dominant economic groups, secondly to force the people into new forms of economic organisation subject to central command, and thirdly to withhold current consumption in favour of investment. Additional repression may be needed to pay for the costs not just of domestic control, but equally of such states' very high propensity to become involved in international conflict. Elsewhere, the relationship is much less clear. Populist socialist regimes lend themselves easily to a rhetoric of identification of leader with nation, in which opposition of any kind is identified as the work of traitors and saboteurs; but then in both Sri Lanka under the Bandaranaike governments and Jamaica under Michael Manley, such regimes operated within the framework of a liberal democratic state. That both Manley and Mrs Bandaranaike lost elections to opposition parties explicitly committed to the reconstruction of the economy on capitalist lines demonstrates both the genuinely liberal nature of the political system, and the failure of populist socialism to generate lasting popular support. At the other end of the spectrum, while a liberal political system is often regarded in western industrial states as the natural accompaniment to a capitalist economy, the same is not true of the third world. Sri Lanka and Jamaica (under the Jayewardene and Seaga governments) are both capitalist and liberal, but President Banda's Malawi combines an aggressive commitment to capitalism with a political structure every bit as authoritarian as that of any of his socialist neighbours.

States at a fairly early stage of capitalist development can certainly operate successfully at a low level of political repression, as Ivory Coast and Kenya help to demonstrate — though the aftermath of the failed Kenya coup of 1982 also helps to indicate that repression may increase as growth declines. It is at later stages that the problems arise, most explicitly expressed in O'Donnell's view — with the southern cone of South America particularly in mind — that the survival of both national and international capitalism requires the creation of a bureaucratic-authoritarian state capable of repressing the popular sections of the society.[23] Most obviously appropriate to Chile and Argentina, the model might equally be applied in some degree to Brazil and possibly Mexico, and outside Latin America to Turkey and to South Korea under the Park regime of 1961-79. Where the model is least plausible, however, is in its assumption that bureaucratic-authoritarianism is needed to maintain a specifically *capitalist* economy. Though the links between capitalism, domestic class structure and political repression in post-1973 Chile are easy enough to draw, capitalist repression in one context may perhaps better be seen as not essentially different from socialist repression in another. Economic change gives rise to competing groups between which governments may find it extremely difficult to mediate, especially in the uncertain international economic and political conditions in which modern third world states seek to survive. Any attempt by the state to promote radical economic change is likely to exacerbate domestic conflict, and in the process require it to choose sides, both between domestic rivals and between alternative sources of international support. Both the promotion of economic change, and the desire to maintain its domestic and international autonomy, are likely to lead the state to strengthen, if it can, its own authoritarian structure. Chilean and Cuban authoritarianism may thus be different (albeit very different) sides of the same coin. Whether such an authoritarian state, of a capitalist or a socialist kind, actually will lead to economic development is a much more uncertain question.

Notes

1. See C. Leys, 'Political Perspectives' in D. Seers and L. Joy (eds.), *Development in a Divided World* (Penguin, 1971).

2. See, for example, R.C. Pratt, 'The Administration of Economic Planning in a Newly Independent State: the Tanzanian Experience, 1963-66', *Journal of Commonwealth Political Studies*, vol. 5, no. 1 (1967).

3. World Bank, *World Development Report 1981* (Oxford University Press, 1981), Table 5; these figures exclude India and China, which have exceptionally low export dependence, and also the major oil exporters, which have exceptionally high dependence.

4. C. Clapham, *Liberia and Sierra Leone* (Cambridge University Press, 1976), pp. 101-2.

5. See I. Wallerstein, 'The Range of Choice: Constraints on the Policies of Governments of Contemporary African Independent States' in M.F. Lofchie (ed.), *The State of the Nations* (University of California Press, 1971).

6. *World Development Report 1981*, Table 5; for Burma, see J. Silverstein, *Burma: Military Rule and the Politics of Stagnation* (Cornell, 1977), p. 165.

7. See *Africa South of the Sahara 1982-3* (Europa, 1982), p. 1086.

8. R.L. Sklar has elaborated this point in terms of 'the doctrine of domicile', in *Corporate Power in an African State* (University of California Press, 1976), pp. 182-8.

9. Brandt Commission, *North-South: A Programme for Surival* (Pan, 1980); *Common Crisis: Co-operation for World Recovery* (Pan, 1983).

10. *World Development Report 1981*, Tables 4, 5.

11. Ibid., Table 24.

12. See Stockholm International Peace Research Institute, *Yearbook on Armament and Disarmament* (Alquist & Wiksell, annual).

13. See, for example, S. Amin, *Le Monde des Affaires Senegalais* (Presses Universitaires de France, 1969).

14. See, for example, M. Lipton, *Why Poor People Stay Poor: Urban Bias in*

World Development (Temple Smith, 1977).

15. See also Lipton, ibid., pp. 67-8 and Chapter 13.

16. See P.T. Bauer, *Dissent on Development* (Weidenfeld, 1971), Chapter 12.

17. See D. Goldsworthy, 'Ghana's Second Republic: A Post Mortem', *African Affairs*, vol. 72, no. 286 (1973), pp. 8-25; R. Jefferies, 'Rawlings and the Political Economy of Underdevelopment in Ghana', *African Affairs*, vol. 81, no. 324 (1982), pp. 307-17

18. See, for example, *World Development Report 1981*, Tables 1, 6, 7, 9, 20, 21.

19. See C. Young, *Ideology and Development in Africa* (Yale University Press, 1982); Young has only one capitalist category, and uses the terms Populist Socialist and Afro-Marxist for the two socialist ones.

20. Jean M. Due, 'Agricultural Development in the Ivory Coast and Ghana', *Journal of Modern African Studies*, vol. 7, no. 4, (1969), pp. 637-66.

21. *The Economist*, London (12 March 1983), 'Brazil: A Survey', p. 6.

22. Young, *Ideology and Development in Africa*, Chapter 6.

23. G. O'Donnell, *Modernisation and Bureaucratic Authoritarianism: Studies in South American Politics* (University of California Press, 1973).

6 MANAGING THE EXTERNAL POLITICAL ARENA

External Relations and the Third World State

Any attempt to place third world states in the context of global relationships must start by emphasising their dependence on and their
penetration by external interests. It is not simply that on any index of
international power and status, third world states come consistently at
the bottom of the table; it is more that they were for the most part
created by the external world in the first place, in the form of colonialism, and continue to be bound into it by economic, strategic and
cultural links which they can break only with great danger and difficulty. Any chart of the flow of economic transactions, or still more
sensitively of armaments, demonstrates the umbilical cord through which
the third world is bound to the industrial states. Less easily measured,
but equally significant, is the way in which these transactions create
and sustain domestic political groups whose interests tie them to the
outside. In this sense, the traditional dichotomy which separates
domestic from external politics and policy simply does not exist.

Yet across the linkages forged by external penetration and dependence falls the barrier created by the state itself. Even though this state
is itself usually an external creation, it falls at independence into the
hands of indigenous elites who thus acquire an interest in its preservation. The external relations of underdeveloped states thus raise in acute
form the tensions between the vertical flow of transactions to and from
the industrial metropoles, and the horizontal barrier, more or less
effective, which the state places across their path. Very few states
indeed seek to use that barrier to prevent the flow of transactions, and
seal off their society from the outside world; to do so would be both
against their interests and beyond their capacities. What governing
elites seek to do, rather, is to manage the flow so far as they can in
order to maintain their own security and achieve their other goals.
Their position is the precise equivalent of that of local politicians who,
especially during periods of electoral competition, act as brokers
between their own communities and national centres of power. It rests,
on the one hand on their degree of local authority and control, on the
other on the privileged access which this gives them to the higher levels
of the national or international hierarchy. The way in which they carry

113

out this task defines the kind of government which they are, and has a major part in determining their failure or success.

It is exactly this relationship between the state as an external creation, and the state as the power base of domestic political elites, that accounts for the survival of even the most feeble of third world states, in defiance of that Hobbesian view that sees the international system as a conflictual arena in which the weakest go to the wall. Jackson and Rosberg have argued that *juridical* statehood (international recognition) is more important than *empirical* statehood (capacity to control and defend territory) in explaining why Africa's weak states survive;[1] but this in turn reflects the fact that juridical recognition provides the key mechanism through which the alliance between domestic rulers and outside supporters is maintained.

State, Class and Dependence

The Foreign Policy of State Preservation

It follows that the first priority of external relations in all third world states is the maintenance of the state itself, since this provides the *raison d'être* of governing elites and the base from which their power derives. The more successfully they can establish their position as gate-keepers, controlling flows across their frontiers in either direction, the stronger is their brokerage position, the better are the bargains they can strike on one side or the other, and the greater the 'commission' they can extract in terms of personal benefits or freedom of political action. Control over external relations thus depends on sealing off the state politically, just as control over revenues from external trade depends on sealing it off economically — the two being indeed, no more than different aspects of the same relationship with the outside world. A ruler who controls his state, and who can thus offer diplomatic support, strategic location or access to economic opportunities within the state to one of the industrial metropoles, will in turn be able to exchange these benefits for economic aid and investment or military assistance, which will help him to maintain his domestic hold. The leader of a weak and divided state will be able to strike few bargains, because of external lack of confidence in his ability to keep them, unless he is prepared to subordinate himself almost entirely to his external protector. The broker may be a genuinely independent operator, capable of making deals on all sides with whichever partners he chooses, balancing these against one another so as to reduce his dependence on any one of them; or he may subside into the client of a dominant patron, with his very survival dependent on following his mentor's wishes.

The central importance of state preservation becomes clearest when it is threatened. When Biafra declared its independence from Nigeria in 1967, or Ethiopia seemed to be falling apart under the combined blows of Somali invasion and Eritrean secession ten years later, the vital and overriding objective for the government of each state was external military support. In Nigeria's case, state unity was re-established with the aid of arms purchases from different sources, chiefly the Soviet Union and the United Kingdom. This left Nigeria at the end of the war in a very much stronger international bargaining position than Ethiopia, which could obtain its arms from only one source (the Soviet Union), which could not afford to purchase them outright and which, in addition, needed direct intervention by some 20,000 Cuban troops and accompanying Soviet military advisers before victory could be achieved. The Ethiopian and Nigerian civil wars also illustrate an important paradox in the external dependence of third world states: that size does not always mean strength. When a state is artificially created (though in Ethiopia's case by internal expansion rather than external colonialism) large size will almost automatically carry with it a high degree of internal ethnic and regional diversity, leading to domestic conflicts which provide opportunities for outside intervention. Zaire, Sudan and Angola in Africa, and Indonesia and Pakistan (especially before the Bangladesh secession) in Asia provide further examples. India and the large Latin American states, with their greater degree of internal unity, have proved less vulnerable.

External assistance to opposition movements thus raises the most strident protest from governing elites, such as the South African support for the Unita guerrilla movement directed against the MPLA government in Angola after 1976, or the tangle of claims and counterclaims about external aid for opponents of Central American regimes in the early 1980s, whether in the form of Soviet/Cuban subversion of the right-wing government of El Salvador, or United States subversion of the left-wing government of Nicaragua. In the context of the state-centred politics of the third world, external intervention on behalf of regimes established in power at the centre acquires a legitimacy which similar intervention on behalf of their opponents lacks. This is logical enough: in an area of potentially very high instability, one is stabilising, the other destabilising; governments which themselves are heavily dependent on external assistance, are quick to denounce any such assistance to their opponents, and to claim that essentially domestic opposisition — in the form of student riots, for instance — is externally directed.

For the most part all states, whether third world or industrial, are content to abide by the conventions of statehood. States provide a framework of order which is scarcely less essential to industrial states seeking influence in the third world than it is to the local governing elites themselves. The western capitalist states, responsible for establishing the pattern of third world statehood in the first place, equally have an interest in maintaining it; they have no interest whatever in a collapse of state effectiveness which could only jeopardise their economic linkages with the third world and the other legacies of colonialism and dependence. The Soviet Union and its allies, less committed to the *status quo* as such, none the less find it vastly more convenient and effective to act whenever possible through official central governments than to foster opposition to them. Support for the governments of Ethiopia and Angola, for example, has permitted them a level of intervention and influence which would never have been possible outside the conventions of support for existing regimes; even in the much more doubtful case of Soviet intervention in Afghanistan, it is the Soviet claim to be assisting an indigenous central government that gives its presence whatever colouring of legitimacy it possesses. The Vietnamese intervention in Kampuchea is in many ways comparable.

There has thus developed a convention of respect for existing states which, save in a few exceptional cases such as South Vietnam and possibly Belize, is almost universally adhered to. One expression of this is the recognition of existing international boundaries. It is paradoxical but perfectly logical that this recognition should be most closely adhered to in that part of the third world, Africa, in which the boundaries themselves are most blatantly artificial. The regional grouping of all independent African states, the Organisation of African Unity, agreed very early in its existence that the boundaries inherited from the colonial partition of Africa should be respected. The reason is that where a state is defined by its boundaries, rather than by any historic sense of internal nationality, these acquire a status which they do not have when they are simply lines of demarcation between national entities recognised as existing in their own right. The frontiers between Iraq and Iran, for instance, or between Vietnam and Kampuchea, may be regarded as legitimate matters for dispute in so far as there are Arabs living in territory defined as Iranian, or Khmers in territory defined as Vietnamese. But whether one is Ghanaian, Ivoirien or Voltaique is definable only in terms of which side of the border one happens to live. Nationality is definable only in terms of statehood.

Nationalism and Foreign Relations

Whereas the state provides a clear and unambiguous basis for external relations, the nation forms a very much less certain one. A state interest can be defined easily enough; a national interest is hard to pin down even in those cases where a nation could be said to exist. The contrast between the two is most cruelly acute in the case of the one African people who have a clearly defined sense of national identity independent of territoral boundaries, the Somalis. A nomadic people — which in itself diminishes their respect for fixed frontiers — they share a common culture, religion and language, and despite internal divisions would by any criterion be said to constitute a 'nation'. They were divided by a process of imperial partition, in which they were in no way consulted, among five different territories, two of which were entirely Somali in population and united at independence in 1960 to form the Somali Republic. A third, Djibouti, later gained separate independence under a Somali-dominated government. Somali attempts to incorporate into the Somali state the large number of ethnic Somalis living in Ethiopia and Kenya have not only been resisted by these two states — both larger and more powerful than the Somali Republic — but have also run sharply up against the convention of respect for existing boundaries adhered to by all other African states and by all the major external powers. The ultimate disillusionment came for the Somalis when the Soviet Union, which had previously armed and trained a large Somali army as a means of establishing a presence in the Horn of Africa, switched sides and supported the Ethiopians as soon as this army was used to liberate the Somalis living within Ethiopia. This was not simply a matter of exchanging a weak client, Somalia, for a strong one, Ethiopia; it also put the Soviet Union on the right side in its dealings with the rest of Africa. The United States, instantly sought by the Somalis as a counterweight, was prepared to provide aid to defend the existing Somali state, but emphatically not to unify the Somali nation. Elsewhere, too, the nation has got nowhere when confronted by the state, the clearest example being that of the Kurds of north-west Asia, divided among five independent states and with a majority in none of them, whose perennial revolts against their various occupying powers have so far achieved nothing and do not look likely to.

A second and rather different way in which the idea of a nation may underlie the external relations of third world states is through attempts by governing elites, accepting their inherited international boundaries, to forge a greater degree of autonomy and coherence among the people within them. This too may create tensions across the frontiers when national feeling is fostered internally by directing it against 'aliens', or by assaults on the ethnic identity or autonomy of peoples who straddle the border. Just as Khmer nationalism in Cambodia (Kampuchea) under the Lon Nol regime before 1975 was directed against the Vietnamese, so Vietnamese nationalism has equally been turned against the Chinese within Vietnam; Chinese communities throughout Southeast Asia have indeed frequently been a convenient target for nationalist solidarity, most violently in Indonesia after 1965, with obvious consequences for relations with Peking. In most cases, however, much the most important implication of indigenous nationalism is its inherent tendency, in a penetrated state, to push the regime into confrontation with the external powers on which it is most heavily dependent. While the maintenance of an effective state is an objective which both external powers and indigenous elites have in common, a strong sense of nationalism is likely to reduce the influence of external powers both directly by threatening specific interests within the third world state, and indirectly by giving indigenous governments a stronger and more articulate local base. This in turn constrains the kind of relationship with the outside world which the regime is permitted to maintain. This leaves governments with a choice between fostering and building on this nationalism in order to strengthen their domestic support, at the risk of creating conflict and instability in their external relations; or on the other hand accepting the implications of dependence at the potential cost of losing domestic support. This dichotomy is of course too stark and simple. Sometimes the two sides may be reconcilable without much difficulty. Neither internal nationalism nor external dependence is as monolithic as this formulation implies, and it is often possible to arrange an accommodation in which essential elements of each can be preserved. But there is enough in it to make it useful at least as a starting point for examining the foreign policy dilemmas of third world governments.

This clash between indigenous nationalism and external dependence was clear first of all in the nationalist movements themselves. The more 'nationalist' such movements were, both in their anticolonialism and in the intensity of their insistence on the unity of the colonised peoples, the more concerned they were after independence to remove any continued elements of colonial domination, and the more strained their relations with the former colonial power. This was most obvious in the single state, North Vietnam, which gained independence through a war of national liberation led by an indigenous Communist Party, and it was clear to a lesser degree in states including Algeria and the Portuguese territories in Africa which were led by former guerrilla movements of a more straightforwardly nationalist rather than explicitly Communist kind. The French imposed a particularly stark choice between nationalism and dependence (unlike the Portuguese who offered no choice at all) by the strength of the postcolonial linkages which they sought to maintain; and when these were rejected, as happened in Guinea, this left a legacy of bitterness in relations between the two states which further intensified Guinean nationalism. Colonies in which the nationalist movement was divided, or in which it could scarcely be said to be 'nationalist' at all, graduated easily into the client states of their former metropoles. In some such states, especially in Southeast Asia, successor elites needed the tacit or active support of the colonial power in order to be able to take over at independence at all, as was the case in varying degrees in Malaysia, the Philippines and (most extreme) South Vietnam, and outside the region in Guyana and Cameroun. In these cases, too, the relationship of dependence continued, while in states such as Kenya or Nigeria it would be fair to speak not so much of 'dependence', as of a natural alliance of interest and outlook between the colonial regime and its successors. A similar alliance has grown up between France and the former French colonies in Africa. The colonial policies of assimilation and association helped to produce similarities of outlook which were strengthened after independence by the maintenance of a common currency zone, French willingness to provide military assistance to threatened African regimes, and the high priority which African affairs received from successive governments in France. A close presidential concern for Africa was established by de Gaulle and maintained especially by Giscard d'Estaing and Mitterand. It takes institutional form in the Franco-African summits, held alternately in France and Africa, which have provided a much more effective forum for French diplomacy than Commonwealth meetings have done for Britain, and which have been expanded to include a high attendance even from non-Francophone African states.

The converse relationship between nationalism and the rejection of dependence is not just a matter of turning the former colonial regime into an appropriate bogeyman, in opposition to which the nation can be defined. It is rather that the establishment of state control and the creation of national identity call for changes in social, cultural, political and economic institutions associated with the colonial regime, and this frequently involves a real clash of interests. Whereas in western capitalist countries a government policy of increasing state control over central areas of the economy is for the most part a matter of nationalising domestically-owned businesses, for third world states it almost invariably involves the expropriation of the local assets of a foreign multinational corporation, in the nature of things one most likely to be based in the former metropole. Even when decolonisation itself goes smoothly, resentments against the ex-colonial power smoulder on, and may come to a head very rapidly as a result of a change in leadership or some symbolically charged political incident, such as the anti-British feeling which followed the assassination of the Nigerian head of state, General Murtala Mohammed, in 1976, or a number of issues raised by the new Malaysian Prime Minister, Mahathir Mohamad Iskandar in 1981. An analogous relationship exists between Latin America and the United States, based on the level of United States' economic dominance but intensified by the cultural clash between Hispanic south and Anglo-Saxon north. Latin American nationalism carries with it an almost automatic rejection of, or at least ambivalence towards, the United States, most stridently exemplified by Cuba but present also for example in reactions to the Falklands crisis of 1982, easily presented as a colonial intrusion into Hispanic South America of an Anglo-Saxon nation supported by the United States. Anti-Americanism becomes, indeed, almost the equivalent of anticolonial nationalism in non-colonial states with established regimes closely allied with the USA, as happened in most spectacular fashion after the fall of the Shah, and also less dramatically in Ethiopia with the deposition of Haile Selassie. In those comparatively few third world states where it has gained a similar position of dominance, the Soviet Union has been subject to exactly the same reaction, as has happened in Egypt, Somalia and, most violently, Afghanistan. The relationship between patron and client is a tense one, in that the two sides have rather different interests, and each is liable to demand more from the exchange between them than the other is prepared to give; the client in terms of support, the patron in terms of control. In Somalia, President Siyad called for an unlimited Soviet commitment to Somali foreign policy goals at a time when the Russians in any event had an interest in transferring their patronage to Ethiopia. In Iran and Afghanistan, the Americans and Russians respectively found themselves committed to an unpopular local regime.

In all these cases the idea of nationalism, though useful up to a point, is none the less misleading. Nationalism is not, save in the rhetoric of leaders, the united feeling of a single people. It is a set of demands, put forward by some groups within the state, and either opposed or less enthusiastially pursued by others. Such groups may be defined in either ethnic/regional or class terms. Ethnically speaking, nationalism is characteristically the cry of majority or central peoples who use it as a means for controlling their peripheries — of central Burmese against Chins or Karens, central Amharas against Eritreans and Somalis. It asserts both the values of the dominant people as national values, and the legitimacy of central state domination over potential secessionists. In an expansionist state like the Somali Republic the same logic works the other way round: nationalism is particularly associated with those Somali clans whose members stretch across the frontiers into Ethiopia and Kenya, and whose full incorporation would increase the weight of those clans in domestic Somali politics.

Class and External Support

This ethnic/regional definition of nationalism clearly matters in a state's relations with its neighbours, but is no more than a matter of chance in its relations with external powers: at one moment it is the United States which (to put it crudely) supports Amhara domination in Ethiopia, at another the Soviet Union. At this point, class — despite all the caveats already made about the dangers of using it as an explanatory variable in third world politics — is likely to be more helpful. At any rate some correlations can be made. Established traditionalist regimes, based on a surviving monarchy or on a dominant landowning or chiefly class, are almost invariably closely allied with the western industrial states, and especially the United States. The list is too long to be seriously challenged: Thailand, Saudi Arabia, pre-revolutionary Ethiopia and Iran, pre-coup Liberia, the more conservative regimes in Latin America, and those ex-colonial regimes like Malaysia or Nigeria in which the government at independence draws its main support from traditionalist leaders controlling an unmobilised peasantry. It is not simply that such regimes are automatically pro-western by virtue of a natural ideological affinity, though certainly they have every reason to be naturally anti-Communist, in that any kind of Marxist ideology would challenge their position as a ruling class. It is also, I think, that a traditionalist regime can be sufficiently confident about its own control over its people not to fear that this will be undercut by its patron. It is likely to be confident — perhaps overconfident — of its brokerage role, able to accept the benefits of American support while keeping the Americans at arm's length in its dealings with its own society. At the other extreme a regime based on a mobilised peasantry is equally likely to be allied with the Soviet Union – again, perhaps, because it feels the need for protection against capitalist takeover just as traditionalist regimes fear Communism. Vietnam and Cuba may serve as examples here; one obvious exception, Khmer Rouge Kampuchea, is readily explained by regional rivalry with Vietnam.

The trouble with this formulation is that it does not cover that large majority of third world states which are governed by what are loosely describable as urban bourgeoisies. These span almost the full range of foreign policy options from close dependence on western capitalism through a substantial number of non-aligned states to alliance with the Soviet Union, though they do not include any states which are fully Marxist-Leninist in the sense both of being ruled by a Leninist party and of being incorporated into Comecon (CMEA). One can, I think, infer that an urban bourgeoisie needs economic linkages with western capitalism as a source both of markets for local production (principally of primary products but also so far as possible of manufactured goods) and of supply of sophisticated manufactures and other goods for their own consumption. Equally, they do not possess the degree of local control required to displace taxes on international trade by a direct levy of a surplus from the population as a means of sustaining themselves, and this commits them to trading patterns which inevitably are mainly with the west. A western trading orientation, however, does not necessarily carry with it either a pro-western foreign policy or military dependence on the west. It may work quite the opposite way round: Ethiopia has been forced to expand its production of cash crops for sale to the west in order to repay, in US dollars, the Soviet Union for military assistance in its 1977-8 wars in the Ogaden and Eritrea.

Immediate military need will clearly have a determining effect on foreign policy, while financial crisis can be almost as important. Military needs may be supplied by any of the major powers, the Soviet Union having established its position as an international patron through its rapid and effective supply of both arms and troops to the MPLA in Angola in 1975-6 and to the military government in Ethiopia in 1977-8. Among western states, France and the United States have been the most ready to intervene militarily to protect their clients. Economic crisis, unlike military need, almost invariably increases dependence on the west, since most third world states' debts are due to western sources, and in any event the Soviet Union has no foreign exchange to spare; economic support for Cuba is an experiment unlikely to be repeated.[2] In addition, the foreign policy stance of a regime may be affected by aspects of ideological outlook which are by no means all readily reducible to the social base of the regime.

Discounting these intervening variables, however, foreign policies may in some degree be explained by examining the relative strengths of the different elements within the urban bourgeoisie, and the relationships between them: the bureaucratic bourgeoisie, drawing its strength from its control of the state; the national bourgeoisie, derived from indigenous capitalism; and the comprador bourgeoisie, dependent on its linkages with multinational corporations and international trade. The first of these, it may be postulated, can be expected to favour a non-aligned diplomatic stance, as the means, along with state control of the domestic economy, by which the autonomy of the state and those who control it can best be achieved; this stance may be modified by military regimes which place a high value on access to imported weaponry. A comprador bourgeoisie is in essence the local representative of the western capitalist economies, and where it exists in any strength will favour close alliance with them; primarily a Latin American phenomenon, as the Spanish origin of the name suggests, it exists as a significant force in any state with a high level of multinational engagement in the economy, and may be ascribed some role, for instance, in the westward shift of Zambian foreign policy in the 1970s away from the non-aligned stance initially established by President Kaunda. A national bourgeoisie occupies something of an intermediate position, on the one hand closely linked to the international capitalist system through its need for capital, raw materials and markets, on the other forced into protectionism by its need to defend its local base against much more powerful multinationals; its influence is signalled by high protective tariffs and measures prohibiting foreign participation in specified areas of the economy, Nigeria since the end of the civil war in 1970 being one of the best examples.

But these three groups, of course, are not separate and distinct. Their political and economic activities are often closely linked, with politicians acting both as private national capitalists and as link men with international businesses, and the foreign policy outcome in any given case will reflect the numerous elements in their international bargaining position – the structure of the local economy, their degree of political control, the country's diplomatic and strategic importance – as they seek to strike the best bargain they can get with the outside world. In addition, the bourgeoisie as a whole may have interests in common, especially when threatened by other domestic classes. The dependence of Latin American middle-class regimes on the United States may be the result, not so much of the pre-eminence of comprador over bureaucratic and national elements, as of the challenge to the bourgeoisie as a whole from populist or proletarian forces. The overthrow of the Allende government in Chile, and its replacement by the Pinochet regime, is often ascribed at the level of demonology to the machinations of the United States' Central Intelligence Agency. Whatever the CIA's immediate role, the episode as a whole is much more satisfactorily explained in terms of the threat presented by Allende's measures to the Chilean middle class (by their incompetence, perhaps, as much as their Marxism), and their need to call on the United States for support against domestic upheaval. José Nun's classic study of the Latin American middle-class military coup makes much the same point in a more general context.[3] In much of the rest of the third world, and especially in Africa, there is very little effective threat to the control of politics by the urban bourgeoise, and the need for this to unite in search of external support does not, therefore, arise.

Personality and Leadership in Foreign Relations

I have left until last the role of individual decision makers in the formulation of third world foreign policies because its importance is easily exaggerated. The antics of an Amin or a Ghaddafi attract a degree of attention which might lead one to suppose that the foreign relations of Uganda or Libya were the simple playthings of their leaders. So in a way they are, but they are playthings which can only be used and understood within the structure which determines how the game may be played. Certainly it is true that the state-centredness of the domestic political structure, and the pre-eminence within the state machinery of the head of state himself, turn the making of foreign policy into a personal much more than an institutional process. Immediate constraints on the regime's external policies are likely to arise only when that regime is itself so weak that a false move would offend vested interests powerful enough to displace it – the case perhaps of the Argentine military junta during its conduct of the Falklands crisis in 1982. When the regime has a fairly firm domestic base, and the state itself is not subject to any immediate threat of external intervention, then the head of state does indeed have a great deal of latitude in managing external relations. The minister of foreign affairs, and the ministry itself, are usually little more than agents and advisers of the head of state. When the advice is not welcome, he can turn elsewhere. Nkrumah in Ghana conducted much of his foreign policy, especially within Africa, through the African Affairs Secretariat attached to the presidency itself, as a means of bypassing the ministry which he regarded as steeped in colonial attitudes. General Murtala Mohammed in Nigeria, looking for a more radical foreign policy after ousting General Gowon in 1975, turned for advice to a group of young academics. African leaders in particular have gained a great deal of latitude from the fact that their continent has for the most part not been subject to the same intense conflicts, backed by external intervention, as the Middle East and Southeast Asia, and has escaped the degree of great power hegemony that characterises Latin America. When, for example, Zambia under President Kaunda opted after independence for a foreign policy actively directed at weakening linkages with the still white-ruled territories of southern Africa, whereas President Banda in neighbouring Malawi took precisely the opposite course, these differences could ultimately only be explained – despite a number of important other factors in each case – as the personal choice of the leader concerned.

The leader's role in foreign policy also arises from the fact that the patron-client links which constitute the core of many third world states' relations with the industrial world are often in large measure *personal* links with the leader, rather than institutional ones with the state. The leader is not simply the symbol of national identity, though to the outside world Tanzania comes to seem synonymous with Nyerere, Cuba with Castro, Iran with the Shah; he is also the person who makes the deals, deals which are concerned with his own position and security as well as with 'national' foreign policy. President Nasser in Egypt, for example, acquired a standing throughout the Arab world and the third world as a whole which greatly strengthened his ability to retain his independence from his external backers, especially his sources of military equipment and financial aid. His successor, Sadat, who was in any event scarcely in a position to conduct the same kind of foreign policy as Nasser, chose to reverse Nasser's approach, adopting a stance of dependence on the west which had at least the advantage of inducing the west, and especially the United States, to provide levels of assistance which would not have been forthcoming to a leader less totally committed to them. Following Sadat's assassination, itself in many ways a reflection of the domestic dangers attendant on external dependence, his successor President Mubarak had in turn some freedom of action in deciding whether to restore the links with other Arab states which Sadat could never have mended, whether to retain the American alliance (automatically placed in question by the death of its architect), whether even to resume Nasser's connection with the Soviet Union. Throughout this period Egypt's fundamental problems did not change, but individual leaders had a substantial freedom of action in deciding how to manage them, and in turn stood or fell according to whether their approaches worked.

A final reason for the prominence of leaders in the conduct of external relations is quite simply that it is fun. The annual heads of state meetings of the Organisation of African Unity and the triennial summits of the Non-Aligned Movement, the visits to Moscow or Washington or the United Nations, the chance to hobnob with great world leaders like Castro or Mrs Gandhi, all provide welcome relief to men whose everyday life is a constant struggle with the intractable problems of small, poor and feeble states. Some leaders spend much of the year on the move, in a constant round of diplomatic visits limited only by the danger that the leader's absence abroad provides the best opportunity for ousting him at home: the cruellest revelation of the gap between diplomatic pretensions and domestic capacities was the overthrow of Nkrumah in 1966 by a military coup in Ghana, carried out while he was in Peking trying to arrange a settlement to the war in Vietnam. The OAU's annual summit imposes a substantial burden on the host state, but this has not prevented the leaders of several of Africa's smaller states from undertaking the task, since in turn this provides them by convention with the chairmanship of the organisation for the following year, and the gratification of acting as the titular leader of Africa. President Tolbert of Liberia died in the job, victim of a coup to which the strain on state revenues imposed by the OAU summit was at any rate one contributory factor.

But much of this personal diplomacy is the icing on the cake. The rhetoric of non-alignment, or of Arab, African or Latin American solidarity, is a long way away from the linkages which anchor third world states in their station in the international system, and even apparently considerable shifts in global alliances, from pro-western to non-aligned to pro-Soviet, may take place without bringing any corresponding change in trading patterns or the structure of domestic production. The two small West African states of Congo and Benin combine Marxism-Leninism with membership of the franc zone, and Ethiopia's military dependence on the Soviet Union does not jeopardise her adherence to the Lomé Convention with the European Community. The most personalist and independent policy must come to terms, over time, with the realities of economic and strategic dependence, and there are many regimes which start with a flourish of independence but come to adapt themselves to the requirements of survival. Guinea's foreign policy has been a constant search to compensate for the glorious gesture of independence with which she rejected France in 1958; Bolivian nationalism after the coup of 1964 slowly found its way to an accommodation with the United States. Where a maverick foreign policy maker survives over some considerable period there is generally some solid backing behind him: in the case of Colonel Ghaddafi of Libya, for example, an apparently firm domestic base (though such appearances often turn out to be misleading), the economic independence provided by oil revenues, and the military protection provided by a working alliance with the Soviet Union. Mavericks without such protection often come to grief. The Emperor Bokassa of Central Africa tried his luck to the extent of publicly insulting an emissary of his patron, President Giscard d'Estaing. Both the Khmer Rouge regime in Kampuchea and General Amin in Uganda so cut themselves off from external support (in very different ways) that when invaded by their neighbours they had no effective patron to turn to. The Khomeini regime in Iran similarly invited invasion from Iraq, having dramatically broken its links with the United States while putting nothing in their place, but proved able to see off the invader without need for external help. The freedom of third world leaders from immediate institutional constraints, in external as in domestic politics, does not release them from structural constraints which are none the less dangerous for being less precisely identifiable.

South-South Relations

The previous section has concentrated on relations between third world states and the superpowers and former colonial metropoles, because these are the ones which matter most. Many of the relationships between third world states themselves, for which the term 'south-south relations' has been coined, derive their importance from the role of the industrial north. The effect may be either to divide third world states or to unite them. On the one hand, divisions between the superpowers feed through into conflicts between their third world clients, and consequently into alliances between third world states which find themselves in the same camp. Cuban assistance to the MPLA in the Angolan civil war of 1975-6, and to Ethiopia in the Ethio-Somali war of 1977-8, was made possible only by the logistical support which Cuba received from the Soviet Union; in just the same way, Morocco intervened in Zaire in 1977 with help from France and the United States. The United States has been especially anxious to gain support from its regional clients for any intervention in the western hemisphere, as for example in the role of other Caribbean states in the Grenada invasion of 1983. Local conflicts almost inevitably take on an east-west dimension, most dramatically in the Middle East and Southeast Asia. On the other hand, a display of unity by third world states enables them to improve their position in bargaining with the industrial world, and this has helped to promote a rhetoric of south-south unity exactly analogous to the unity promoted by the nationalist movements in seeking to bring pressure on colonial regimes. Even before most of them became independent, third world leaders were quick to recognise the advantages which they could gain from a united front in dealing with the industrial world, a recognition commonly dated to the first Afro-Asian summit at Bandung in Indonesia in 1955. In demanding the liberation of territories still under colonial rule, they could combine their own anticolonialism with the common interest which they all had in increasing the number and weight of fellow third world states in the global political system. But the unity which they demanded was unity of a strictly limited kind, and after independence its limitations became increasingly clear. It did not involve any surrender of state sovereignty to form regional or continental unions, any serious threat to northern (or rather western) interests, or any serious attempt to replace existing ties by a south-south alliance conceived in ideological, economic or security terms. There was too much at stake. State leaders depended on state sovereignty, and their economies depended on existing patterns of north-south trade. Third world states as a whole, and regional or functional coalitions among them, have had some success in improving their bargaining capacity when this could be done at little risk to their vital interests, but have shown no sign of threatening their lifelines to the north.

The Third World Coalition

This has been clear enough from the experience of the broadest of the third world political groupings, the Non-Aligned Movement. Meeting triennially (with one gap in 1967) since 1961, the Movement includes all African states (with the obvious exception of South Africa) and the great majority of Asian ones, but only a small though growing number of Latin American countries. Since the African states belong automatically by virtue of their membership of the OAU, their presence provides no index of 'non-alignment' in any but a purely institutional sense of the word, including as it does states heavily committed to the west such as Ivory Coast and Malawi, and states such as Djibouti in which French troops are permanently stationed. At the other extreme, Cuba has been an active member, and host to the 1979 summit, despite membership of Comecon and close military ties with the Soviet Union. As one might expect, therefore, there is a substantial degree of variation between non-aligned states in their diplomatic stance on issues which affect relations between the western and Soviet blocs, reflected for example in their votes in the General Assembly of the United Nations.[4] There is, however, a much higher level of cohesion between them on 'colonial' issues, such as policy towards white rule in Southern Africa, with which the Palestine/Israel issue has also come to be associated. Though such issues involve a degree of rhetorical anti-westernism, they do not jeopardise either economic or strategic links with the west. On the one recent issue on which anticolonialism could be readily associated with an anti-Soviet stance, the Russian invasion of Afghanistan in late 1979, only a small group of easily identified Soviet clients voted with the Russians (Cuba, Ethiopia, Grenada, Vietnam) and the majority of non-aligned states voted against, though a significant number of the more radical third world states were absent or abstained. Logically enough, however, the Karmal government placed in power by the Soviet Union was in favour of the invasion, and this points up the central paradox of the non-aligned position. The movement can in general terms deplore intervention by industrial states in the third world, and give diplomatic support to liberation movements against colonial rule or to third world governments threatened by industrial states; but when intervention meets with the approval of the regimes which gain from it, the non-aligned can only persist in their disapproval at the cost of denying the right of the governments of independent states to take whatever action they deem necessary to preserve their sovereignty and security.

Increasingly, and especially since the oil price rises enforced by the Organisation of Petroleum Exporting Countries (OPEC) from 1973 onwards, the goals of the third world coalition have turned to economic issues. The year of the price rises, which seemed (meretriciously as it proved) to offer third world states the chance to exercise substantial economic influence in their bargaining with the north, saw also the Algiers Non-Aligned summit which set in train the demands for a new international economic order. Both OPEC and the NIEO were precise counterparts in the international sphere to the domestic bargaining between third world governments and locally operating transnational corporations discussed in the last chapter. Neither was intended to disrupt a pattern of north-south trade which all parties took for granted. All that was sought by third world states was an increase in their control over that trade, and in the share of the profits from it that came their way. The same goes in a much more direct way for the Afro-Caribbean-Pacific (ACP) group of states set up to negotiate the form of association between themselves and the European Community under the Lomé Conventions of 1975 and 1980. The shift in global economic conditions since 1973, which has enabled the industrial states to reassert their strength, has been sharply reflected in a loss of third world bargaining power and the collapse of most of the expectations from third world collective bargaining which were built up in the mid-1970s.

Regional Associations

Similar problems of internal sovereignty and ideological diversity arise in third world regional groupings. There are four principal regional organisations of third world states, each defining its membership in a rather different way. The Organisation of American States, including as it does the United States and the twenty Latin American states (a relationship described by a former Guatemalan president as 'the shark and the twenty sardines'[5]) serves very largely as a forum within which to raise and regulate relations between the two, and in this sense can scarcely be regarded as a third world organisation at all. Its expulsion of Cuba from membership in 1962, after which only Mexico among OAS states continued to maintain diplomatic relations with Castro's government, helps to emphasise the United States' role within it, even though it is an arena in which the USA often has to adopt a defensive stance against a sense of Latin solidarity over issues such as the Panama Canal Zone or US support for Britain in the 1982 Falklands crisis. A further feature of the OAS is that it has refused (on the insistence of its Latin members) to admit any new state which has a territorial dispute with existing members, the effect being to exclude former British colonies such as Guyana and Belize, and this in turn prevents the use of the Organisation to settle such issues. Even disputes between existing members, such as that between Chile and Argentina over islands in the Beagle Channel, have been sent for external arbitraton.

There is no continent-wide Asian organisation, a fact which is scarcely surprising since Asia possesses neither the geographical compactness nor the continental sense of political identity which in different ways characterise both Africa and Latin America. The Association of South East Asian Nations (ASEAN), includes only five states (Thailand, Malaysia, Singapore, Indonesia and the Philippines), and its formation at the height of the Vietnam war in 1967 helps to indicate its origin as a grouping of broadly pro-western states which felt threatened by developments in the region. Despite its usefulness as a vehicle for the co-ordination of foreign policies, especially over relations with Vietnam and the associated regimes in Laos and Kampuchea, it has no military functions and – like all such organisations – has its capabilities reduced by disputes among its own members.

At the other end of the continent, the Arab League has the advantages of linguistic, cultural and religious solidarity, and of a common external enemy in the form of Israel. Unlike either the OAS or ASEAN, moreover, it is genuinely non-aligned as between the western and Soviet blocs, with members drawn from consistently pro-western states such as Jordan and Saudi Arabia, and from Soviet-leaning ones such as, at varying times, Iraq, Syria, Egypt and Libya. In a way, the amount that its members have in common may have helped to intensify disputes between them, by promoting at least among the more radical states a sense of a 'correct' Arab posture, and a consequent sense of the legitimacy of intervention in the internal affairs of states whose governments did not share it. Maintenance of a common line among some twenty states with different external alliances in an area of very high international conflict would in any case have been difficult. The one critical element was hostility to Israel, and in this respect the Arab states of North Africa proved able to extend Arab diplomatic support by linking the Israel and South Africa issues within the Organisation of African Unity. Egypt's recognition of Israel – at a time, paradoxically, when almost all of the black African states had broken diplomatic relations – was thus the one act incompatible with membership, and since Egypt has more than twice the population of any other Arab state, and also substantially the largest Arab armed forces, this subsequently paralysed the organisation.

By far the largest third world regional organisation in terms of membership, and in many ways the most effective, has been the Organisation of African Unity. Formed in 1963, it superseded the rival groupings with which the newly independent African states had previously been associated and included all independent African states apart from South Africa, bridging in particular the divides between Arab north and black south, francophone and anglophone, and radical and conservative. Its charter has no mechanism by which a member state can be expelled. The price for such an all-inclusive body was acceptance of the twin principles of non-intervention in the internal affairs of other member states, and the sanctity of the international frontiers inherited from colonialism. From the second of these, as we have seen, only the

Somali Republic dissented. The first was a rebuff to those nationalists, led by Nkrumah, who saw the hallowed principle of African unity in terms of a continental political union, leading ultimately to a United States of Africa. It made clear that this was to be a union of states, in which the government of each state was to be permitted to pursue whatever policy it wished, at any rate internally. This also rapidly came to imply the acceptance by OAU of whatever regime exercised effective power within a member state, regardless of how it had come to power. Master Sergeant Doe of Liberia, who seized power in 1980 by assassinating the OAU's current chairman, President Tolbert, was for a while denied a place in OAU meetings, not so much because of his coup but because of the revulsion aroused by the public execution of Tolbert's ministers which followed it. After a visit by a mediating group of senior heads of state, he tacitly agreed to change his ways. In external policy, while imposing no restrictions on relations with superpowers or former colonial metropoles, the OAU did successfully maintain a stance of unremitting hostility to the white governments of South Africa and Rhodesia (Zimbabwe), and to the remaining colonial regimes in Africa, especially the Portuguese; several African states retained effective economic and diplomatic contacts with the white regimes, and some were in no position to avoid them, but only President Banda of Malawi openly flouted the organisation on the issue. The OAU's limited capacity to bind its members to follow common policies when these diverged from their vital interests soon became clear, however, when only a derisory number of states implemented an OAU recommendation to break off diplomatic relations with Britain following the unilateral declaration of independence by the Smith government in Rhodesia in 1965; such a move threatened links with the former colonial metropole to an extent that few states were prepared to accept.

The OAU has had some success in resolving disputes between its members, generally through the mediation of senior African statesmen led by the Organisation's current chairman. By its insistence on maintaining the existing boundaries, and by its opposition to secessionist movements, it has also helped to restrict external intervention in the continent by defining one side in conflicts as illegitimate, while favouring the other. In the Nigerian civil war this worked to the advantage of the federal government, while after the Somali invasion of Ethiopia in 1977 it helped to justify the Derg's call for Soviet and Cuban help. African states were much more evenly divided over the Angolan civil war of 1975-6, but the MPLA was favoured both because of its superior claim to be considered the 'central' government, and because of its opponents' increasing reliance on South African support. In all these respects the OAU has favoured the position of states and central governments – it has been referred to indeed as a governments' trade union. The issues which it has manifestly failed to resolve have been, first, those which turn essentially on north-south economic and security links with which it is powerless to interfere and, secondly, those in which support for existing governments provides no adequate guide.

One form which this second problem has taken has been the dilemma presented by governments which blatantly offend against the most basic conceptions of human rights – a problem all the more embarrassing in that the African case against the white minority governments of southern Africa has been based on a moral claim for human equality, and lays itself open to charges of hypocrisy if black African governments do not condemn fellow African regimes which on the face of it are equally bad. One response, fostered by President Jawara of The Gambia, has been an attempt to draw up an African charter of human rights approved by the OAU, but the enforcement of such a charter against member governments would run directly against the principle of non-interference in domestic affairs on which the OAU is founded. President Nyerere of Tanzania was prepared to take direct action to overthrow President Amin in the 1978-9 invasion of Uganda, an action which clearly flouted OAU principles (despite some legal colouring provided by previous Ugandan incursions into Tanzania), but which was accepted as a *fait accompli* by other member states. Another dilemma arises when a state has no effective central government at all, and the OAU is left to choose or arbitrate between rival claimants. In Angola the dilemma was eventually settled by the victory of the Soviet-supported MPLA, but in the Chad civil wars of 1978-82 the OAU found itself much more directly committed. Anxious on the one hand to preserve order and prevent bloodshed, on the other to avoid committing itself to supporting any of the eleven factions principally involved, it despatched a peacekeeping force which was intended to keep the contestants apart, but not to fight on behalf of the nominal central government of President Goukhouni. In effect, it helped to provide a safe area within which the forces of Goukhouni's main rival, Hissen Habre, could regroup before attacking the capital, after which the OAU force was withdrawn. A third dilemma derived from the same general problem arose in former Spanish Sahara, which after Spain's withdrawal was claimed (and in part occupied) by Morocco, despite armed opposition from the indigenous Polisario movement, backed by several other African states, which proclaimed its separate independence as the Saharawi Arab Democratic Republic (SADR) in 1980. The OAU admitted the SADR to membership in 1981, since it was by then recognised by a majority of member states, but Morocco's supporters were numerous enough to prevent the assembly of the necessary two-thirds quorum at the next annual OAU summit at Tripoli, Libya in July 1982.

These cases all show the inadequacy of the simple acceptance of existing states and governments as a principle by which to regulate relations between third world states. It is a principle which assumes that difficult issues about what *are* states and governments will not arise, or if they do will be settled either internally or through extra-continental intervention. Analogous cases arise elsewhere in the third world, for example with the independence of Belize (whose territory, like Sahara's, is claimed by a neighbour) or the Vietnamese invasion of Kampuchea (similar in some respects to Tanzania's invasion of Uganda). What is ultimately at issue is the capacity of third world states to maintain a stable pattern of international relations among themselves, without direct intervention by the industrial powers, and this is far from having been achieved.

The Emergence of Regional Powers

The 1970s and early 1980s have in fact seen a substantially increased level of intervention by their neighbours in the internal politics of African and Asian states, as the immediate post-independence linkages between the new states and their former metropoles have on the whole declined. One form which this has taken has been the emergence of regional powers which tacitly or explicitly claim the right to concern themselves with the form of government in other states in the region, and which consequently build up their own external clientelist connections. One of the first clear manifestations of this change was the Indian invasion of what was then East Pakistan in 1971, to destroy West Pakistani control and set up the new state of Bangladesh; by this act, uncontested by any of the major industrial states, India established herself conclusively as the dominant regional power. In Southeast Asia, Vietnam has since the end of the war in 1975 secured a position of regional dominance still more clearly based on military superiority, first through the unification of former North and South Vietnam, then through the conquest of Kampuchea and the establishment of a client government in Laos, and finally through the vastly greater size and effectiveness of her armed forces than those of the ASEAN states. In the Middle East, Israel has long occupied the paradoxical position of a militarily-dominant regional power unable to establish relations with her neighbours, except through direct invasion or the support of local forces like the Maronite militia in Lebanon.

Regional powers in Africa have been slower to emerge, both because of the principles established by the OAU, and because the larger and potentially more powerful African states have almost all, as already noted, been crippled by internal divisions. The main regional power has indeed in a sense been South Africa, whose economy gives her a dominant position in southern Africa, and who has been no less willing than Israel to intervene militarily in neighbouring states. Among the black African states, by far the leading candidate for regional power status has been Nigeria, by virtue of her size, her oil revenues and the access of national confidence which followed the end of the civil war in 1970. But though active diplomatically in many ways — in Southern African issues, in establishing the Economic Community of West African States, in negotiating the Lome Conventions with the European Community — Nigeria has avoided direct involvement in her neighbours' affairs, save in the unavoidable case of Chad. Guinea by contrast has despatched troops to protect the governments of Sierra Leone in 1971 and Liberia in 1979, while Senegal used the attempted coup in The Gambia in 1981 to secure a Senegambian confederation in which she holds a position of unchallengeable dominance. Tanzania is rather poorer and not substantially larger than her East African neighbours, but has been willing to despatch troops both to Uganda and to the Seychelles.

In some degree, therefore, third world states are progressively building up relationships among themselves, which for the most part supplement rather than displace their relations with industrial states. These relationships are useful to governing elites, in that they can be used for mutual protection both in improving their bargaining position with the industrial states, and in helping to secure their domestic hold on power; but they show no sign whatever of displacing state sovereignty and elite control by any form of supranational confederation at regional, continental or global level, except in so far as this is achieved by military domination and dependence. States whose governments depend on the military protection of their neighbours, like The Gambia, Kampuchea and Afghanistan, are in rather greater danger of absorption than those which depend on the protection of more distant powers.

Notes

1. R.H. Jackson and C.G. Rosberg, 'Why Africa's Weak States Persist', *World Politics*, vol. 35 no. 1 (1982), for a more general discussion, on a regional basis, of the role of foreign policy in third world states, see C. Clapham (ed.), *Foreign Policy Making in Developing States* (Saxon House, 1977).

2. See C. Coker, 'Adventurism and Pragmatism: The Soviet Union, Comecon and Relations with African States', *International Affairs*, vol. 57, no. 4 (1981), pp. 618-33; and P. Wiles (ed.), *The New Communist Third World* (Croom Helm, 1981), Chapter 1.

3. J. Nun, 'The Middle-Class Military Coup' in C. Veliz (ed.), *The Politics of Conformity in Latin America* (Oxford University Press, 1967).

4. See P. Willetts, *The Non-Aligned Movement* (Pinter, 1978).

5. See E. Kaufman, 'Latin America' in Clapham (ed.), *Foreign Policy Making in Developing States.*

7 SOLDIER AND STATE

The Coup

Military coups and the military regimes which follow from them are so much a feature of third world politics that their presence or absence in any given region might almost be taken as a rough and ready touchstone of third worldliness. Like all political generalisàtions, this one is subject to exceptions. Within Europe, coups have taken place since 1960 in Greece and Portugal — both of which may count among the more 'third worldly' of European states — and the installation of a military government in Poland in December 1981 demonstrated that the army cannot aways be insulated from a direct political role even in Marxist-Leninist states. The difference between industrial states, either capitalist or Communist, and the third world is none the less striking. Fully three-quarters of the twenty Latin American regimes have had military coups since 1960, the only exceptions being the socialist state of Cuba, the peculiar family dictatorship of Haiti, and three countries (Mexico, Costa Rica and Venezuela) which appear to have achieved a stable balance of civilian political forces. Just on half the states in third world Asia, and rather more in Africa, have had military coups and governments over the same period, even though (since many states did not become independent until after 1960) these have been less at risk. Within each continent, there have been regions in which military intervention has so far been very limited or non-existent, leaving an increased incidence of coups in other regions. None of the eight African states south of a line from Angola through Zambia and Malawi to Mozambique has yet experienced a successful coup, in part perhaps because of the delayed independence of the former Portuguese colonies and Zimbabwe, in part because the South African presence may inhibit coups in the three former High Commission territories. In Asia, the traditionalist states of the Arabian peninsula provide the largest coup-free zone, though the constitutionalist regimes of India, Sri Lanka, Malaysia and Singapore have also maintained civilian control over the army. In general, and especially in Africa, the absence of military government reflects the skills and good fortune of a civilian political leader, rather than anything inherently inconducive to military intervention in the state which he governs. The successful coups in

Liberia in 1980 and Guinea in 1984, and the unsuccessful ones in The Gambia in 1981 and Kenya in 1982, all indicate the vulnerability of regimes which had often been regarded as among the most stable in Africa. In some cases, such as the francophone African states of Senegal, Ivory Coast and Gabon, coups may be inhibited as much as anything by the support which the regime receives from an external power. The only substantial area of the the third world which has as yet had no military governments is the English-speaking Caribbean, many of the states in which have only recently become independent. Even here, there has been one non-military coup (in Grenada), and the army has had to be disbanded in Dominica.

The incidence of coups has called forth numerous attempts at explanation, which between them have run the full range of social science theorising. Some have sought statistical correlations between those states in which coups have and have not taken place,[1] while others have taken a general conceptual approach backed by citing particular examples.[2] Some have looked for explanations at a global level, some with reference to given continents and regions, and some by examining the circumstances of individual states. These have gone a long way towards explaining the conditions in which coups are likely to occur, and suggesting the underlying features of third world politics which help to give rise to them. Economic dependence, for example, is clearly related to political instability through the existence of a significant (but not universal) correlation between coups and rapid drops in the value of exported primary products.[3] Of greater direct concern for this book — which in any event is not concerned with the appraisal of the enormous literature in this field — are the studies which seek to link military intervention to general underlying features of the politics of third world states, notably Finer's concept of political culture, and Huntington's concepts of institutionalisation and its converse, praetorianism. The idea of political culture is an elusive and in many ways an unsatisfactory one, but fundamentally it is linked — as Finer uses it — to the notion of legitimacy.[4] A society with a developed political culture is one in which there is a broadly-held belief in a certain kind of political structure, in which leaders are selected according to a given procedure, or exercise power in accordance with given standards as to what is legitimate or right. This structure may be a liberal democratic or Marxist-Leninist or traditional religious one, but it must give an element of moral backing to a regime which cannot be supplied by simple force. One way in which this is significant is that a high proportion of third world states which have not seriously been threatened by coups have been those in which some such sense of legitimacy can be discerned: liberal democratic in Sri Lanka or Jamaica, Marxist-Leninist in Cuba or Vietnam, traditional in Nepal or Saudi Arabia. Not that this legitimacy can be relied on to preserve these regimes for all time: legitimacy itself lays down standards which must be respected if it is to survive, and traditional and liberal democratic values are especially vulnerable. A second way in which it is significant is that a high proportion of third world states are artificial and subject to rapid and disruptive change, both of which make it extremely difficult to generate widely accepted political values. Military intervention then takes place because there is no moral constraint which prevents it.

Huntington's emphasis is on political organisation rather than political values.[5] An institutionalised society is one in which there are effective political mechanisms for reconciling and implementing demands, the most appropriate of which are political parties. Political parties or equivalent institutions will certainly prevent many kinds of demand from being presented at all — indeed one of the ways in which they most effectively maintain order is by keeping things off the political agenda. It is essential, however, that they should be what Huntington terms 'autonomous', that they should not simply act as the mouthpieces of particular sections of the society, such as ethnic, religious or class groups. Implicit in this is some conception of a national or public interest, overriding sectional interests, and this in turn takes one back to some notion of shared values. By the same token, shared values are unlikely to survive for very long unless there is some institutional mechanism in which they are embodied. A praetorian society is one in which there are no effective institutions, and in which social groups take direct political action to achieve their goals — a free-for-all in which the army is likely to be most successful because it largely controls the instruments of force. The incidence of military takeovers can thus be seen as following either from the polarisation of third world states on ethnic lines, resulting in army intervention on behalf of one ethnic group or to impose order on all of them, or else from the decay of political parties and the imposition of personal rule which often characterise the post-independence period.

Both Finer's and Huntington's approaches may be modified by, but are not essentially at odds with, the neo-patrimonial structure of third world politics already suggested. The absence of effective political institutions in Huntington's sense need not directly lead to a praetorian clash of social forces, because political demands may instead be mediated through personal leadership and patron-client networks. Such networks are, however, unable to serve the functions which Huntington requires of institutions, precisely because, being essentially private in nature, they cannot generate a sense of legitimacy. Within a neo-patrimonial system, there is nothing much to distinguish a leader who owes his position to a military coup from one who owes it to an election. The essential basis for his power is in either case that he *has* power, and can use that power to make deals with those people and groups whose support he needs. This is the main reason why, for many purposes, it may not matter all that much whether a regime is civilian or military, or why it often becomes rather difficult to distinguish the two.

There is, however, a more basic reason for the salience of the military in third world politics than either Finer or Huntington suggests, and this arises from the centrality of the state. In countries where the state is itself by far the dominant source of organised power, control of the state by any agency external to it becomes extremely difficult, and a military coup represents the ultimate refinement of the process by which the state is taken over by its own servants. Sometimes indeed a coup can be seen as the result of actions by the incumbent government which threaten the interests or self-image of the bureaucracy. The Ghanaian coup of January 1972, for example, followed hard on government austerity measures which cut housing and motor car allowances for senior civil servants (including army officers) and, through a drastic devaluation of the currency, threatened their access to the imported consumer goods on which an elite life style depended More often intervention is occasioned, or at any rate justified, by reference to more general political goals or ideals, such as the incapacity, dishonesty or ethnic favouritism of the regime. The most effective general explanation of the nature of military regimes is, therefore, likely to be one which calls on the interests and attitudes of the bureaucratic bourgeoisie, and relates these to the particular circumstances of the state concerned.[6] Variations will of course occur when the military leadership is differentiated from the rest of the bureaucratic bourgeoisie in ethnic, class or generational terms.

The Military Regime

In many respects, as I have suggested, it may make little difference whether a regime is a military or a civilian one. In states where participation in politics is in any event low, and there are few if any generally accepted moral principles which would distinguish 'legitimate' from 'illegitimate' government, what matters is simply that it *is* the government. Even when the government in power was initially elected by some reasonably free and fair procedure, it frequently entrenches itself in such a way that there is no effective chance of displacing it, so that participation may well be low, regardless of the formal status of the regime. Military regimes are often regarded as depending on force for their tenure of power, but exactly the same may be true of civilian ones, which equally have the army and police at their disposal to suppress opposition. There is little evidence to suggest that military regimes as a group depend more than civilian ones on the actual exercise of force — rather than the ultimate threat of it — in order to stay in power. President Marcos in the Philippines and Mrs Gandhi in India have controlled opposition through martial law and state of emergency, despite themselves heading civilian governments. Some military regimes have indeed needed to impose their rule through a systematic use of force, especially some of the Latin American military governments, such as those of Chile and Argentina, and it may be suggested that once a society has reached a given level of sophistication, military rule will be less willingly accepted and will need to be more brutally imposed; I will return to this argument later, but in any event it is one which depends on the structure of the society rather than on military government in itself. Military regimes may well have a better than average chance of throwing up a homicidal maniac such as Bokassa or Amin, but the civilian government of Macias Nguema in Equatorial Guinea shows that they have no monopoly in that respect; while in terms of the systematic use of coercion to transform a society, few regimes can compare with the Khmer Rouge in Kampuchea, which is better regarded as a civilian movement brought to power through guerrilla warfare than as a proper military government.

Nor, popular stereotype to the contrary, can military governments validly be classified as inherently conservative or right wing. Many of them certainly are, and the reasons for it will be examined, but military coups may also give rise to radical nationalist regimes like those of Nasser in Egypt or Ghaddafi in Libya, and on occasion to governments which at least claim to be Marxist-Leninist, as in Benin, Congo and Ethiopia. The early belief that military regimes in black Africa were inherently neo-colonial in origin and policy, given some colouring by the 1966 coup against Nkrumah in Ghana, has proved unable to survive the belligerent nationalism of the Nigerian military government after

1975, or the messianic populism of the regimes led by Flight Lieutenant Jerry Rawlings in Ghana. Looked at across the board through cross-national aggregate surveys, there is little to distinguish military from civilian regimes in terms of most kinds of government policy output, though they do – in keeping with the view of their bureaucratic interests outlined in the previous section – have quite a marked tendency to increase government spending on the military itself.[7]

In so far as any general characteristics of military regimes can be distinguished, it would seem most plausible to look for them either in some distinctive set of military *attitudes* towards politics and political issues, or in the distinctive form of *organisational structure*, the army itself, which the regime used in order to gain power, and on which it relies, initially at least, in order to keep it. Since the structural and ideological features of the military are closely linked, for example through the emphasis placed on obedience and *esprit de corps*, the effects of each are likely to be mutually reinforcing. Many of the characteristic attitudes of the military emerge in stereotyped form in the justificatory announcements which follow the coup, including notably a belief in discipline, efficiency, honesty and national unity. At its simplest, the conception of government which follows from this might be summed up as the theory of *right orders*, the belief that if there is anything wrong, what is necessary is to give the right orders to deal with it. Underlying this is a set of idealised assumptions: that the objective to be achieved is clear and generally agreed; that the structure responsible for carrying out the orders is disciplined and efficient; and that the objective is within the structure's capacity to achieve. What follows from it is 'operation' government, the definition of clearly defined political tasks – to restore the economy, to achieve self-sufficiency in food production, to stamp out corruption, to create national unity – to which government should be directed. The people with whom military leaders explicitly contrast themselves are, then, the politicians, seen as devious, dishonest, factionalist, self-seeking players of sterile games which can only harm the country; and beyond this, it is not dificult to see a distaste for the whole 'political' way of doing things: for bargaining, negotiation, manipulation and, more generally, for political organisation.

Such a simple set of attitudes is likely to work only in a fairly unsophisticated political system, and any military ruler who seeks to put it into practice in a system where there actually are important political bargaining groups is likely to find himself in trouble. One

classic and tragic example is that of the first Nigerian military government of Major-General Ironsi between January and July 1966. Brought
to power as the incidental by-product of an aborted coup in which he
was not directly involved, he identified the country's principal problem
(with some justice) as regional and tribal division, and set out to deal
with it through central government actions (such as the Unification
Decree which abolished regional civil services), the effect of which was
to intensify the insecurity of regional and ethnic groups which readily
suspected him of acting for the advantage of his own people. Barely six
months after coming to power, he was assassinated in a regionally-
inspired counter-coup which led to ethnic killings in the army and the
country as a whole, and set Nigeria well on the way to the civil war
which broke out a year later. Few military leaders are quite so naive.
Those who remain in power for any length of time have perforce to
adapt themselves to the realities of political life, and many do so with
considerable skill. The senior officers of forces with well-established
traditions of political intervention, such as those of Thailand or Argentina, readily develop into a sophisticated group of soldier-politicians
whose factional manoeuvres are in many ways not qualitatively
different from those of the leaders of a civilian political party: they
need to look after their supporters, form coalitions, decide when and
whether to enter or leave the government and decide what policies to
support when they are in it.

The approach to politics implicit in these attitudes is none the less
reinforced by the organisational structure of the military, and its role as
the armed wing of the bureaucratic bourgeoisie. Its hierarchical structure
on the one hand lends itself to carrying out clearly defined tasks, and
on the other is placed under great strain by any form of politicisation
which encourages the questioning of orders from above, or the
formation of rival ideological groups. The maintenance of organisational cohesion is the single most important dilemma facing military
governments, and one which will be examined in the next section. Its
role as an agency of the state leads the military almost invariably to
adopt a managerial approach to political problems. It is an attitude, for
example, which lends itself easily to a monetarist approach to economic
policy, and even in markedly left-wing regimes it leads to a socialism
of state intervention rather than one of popular participation. What is
interesting is the way in which essentially the same attitudes and
interests lead the military, at different stages of social and political
mobilisation, into stances which can be classed at opposite ends of the
left-right ideological spectrum. In this respect, Huntington's encapsula-

tion of the ideological position of the military is unsurpassed:

> As society changes, so does the role of the military. In the world of
> oligarchy, the soldier is a radical; in the middle-class world he is a
> participant and arbiter; as the mass society looms on the horizon,
> he becomes the conservative guardian of the existing order. Thus,
> the more backward a society is, the more progressive the role of its
> military; the more advanced a society becomes, the more conserva-
> tive and reactionary becomes the role of its military.[8]

What happens in effect is that the military remains the same, wedded to
an elitist conception of nationalism and efficiency, while the society
changes round it, so that views which are radical in one context move
across to become conservative in another. Huntington's three categories of breakthrough, guardian and veto coups, with the appropriate
military regimes which follow them, provide a corresponding typology
of military governments which, while not universally applicable, encom-
passes a very wide range of cases in a neat and conceptually economical
way.

The breakthrough coup occurs when the military — and especially
the middle and lower ranks of the officer corps — is frustrated by the
continued tenure of power by what it feels to be an outmoded and
ineffective traditionalist elite. It is a once and for all affair. The
monarch or ruling oligarchy needs to build up a westernised state apparatus in order to consolidate power, both internally and often against an
encroaching external colonialism. Over a period, not only effective
power but also the dominant concepts of legitimacy come to favour the
new bureaucratic elite, whose takeover is directed to demands for efficiency and rapid modernisation. The formula which constitutes
'modernity' will vary with the period and the circumstances. For
Mustafa Kemal and his colleagues in Turkey after 1923, it was conceived in essentially western liberal terms — with the effect of keeping
the Turkish military broadly loyal to a somewhat idealised conception
of western liberal democracy, down to the present day. For Nasser and
the free officers in Egypt after 1952, it was seen very much in the light
of the more radical nationalist parties of the period, with an emphasis
on 'socialism' of a statist kind, opposition to imperialism, national
control of resources, and the additional element supplied by Arab
unity. Mengistu Haile-Mariam and the Derg in Ethiopia after 1974 put
it in terms of Marxist-Leninist scientific socialism, aided though this
was by the need for Soviet military support, and impeded though it was

by the regime's reluctance to compromise its independence by building up the institutional infrastructure of a Marxist-Leninist state. Other variants include the Thai coup of 1932, which retained the monarchy while severely restricting its political powers, and the Libyan coup of 1969, which called on Islamic fundamentalism in place of Nasser's earlier emphasis on a largely secular Arab nationalism. Such break-through coups thus form a distinctive group, the usefulness of Huntington's categorisation being indicated by the fact that the easily identifiable Libyan and Ethiopian examples have occurred since his book appeared. They lead to radical regimes confident of the legitimacy of their own tenure of power, which may civilianise themselves, as in Turkey, but which feel under no obligation to hand over to any other civilian political elite. Taking place for the most part in traditional polities with an existing sense of national identity, they often succeed in extending and modernising this to a remarkably effective degree.

The guardian coup occurs in states in which the new urban middle class already enjoys effectively unchallenged control. It does not, therefore, involve the definitive replacement of one ruling class or elite by another, or lead to any irreversible change in the political structure. It may simply be the army's turn to find a seat in a game of musical chairs. The reasons which lead the military to take over from a civilian regime, or which equally frequently lead one group within the army to oust another group already in possession, are many and various, and may not be particularly important. Any government is vulnerable at times of economic crisis or when its popularity is low for any other reason, especially if it has offended the interests of the bureaucratic elite. A government which, like that in Nigeria in January 1966, has clearly proved incapable of maintaining political order is ripe for over-throw by one that feels it can do better. Corruption and dictatorship, almost invariably given as justifications for intervention, may some-times actually serve as reasons for it. A government of one ethnic com-plexion may be overthrown by soldiers of another, or still more simply, an officer such as Amin in Uganda in 1971 or Acheampong in Ghana the following year may seize power because he wants it for essentially personal reasons.

A military regime of this kind will have no inherent tendency to be either more radical or more reactionary than the government it displaces — except in so far as it may feel the need to react against its predecessor's policies, whatever these may have been. It will show the normal range of policy variation which might follow from the electoral victory of the opposition in a liberal democratic system. In Ghana after the 1966 coup, the National Liberation Council reversed Nkrumah's policies of state socialism and non-alignment in favour of a much closer political and economic relationship with the west, just as did the Seaga government after defeating Manley in the Jamaica 1980 election. In Nigeria after 1975, the new Murtala Mohammed regime was both more radical at home and more anti-western abroad than the previous (and also military) Gowon one. Military regimes no less than civilian ones will feel the need to make populist gestures designed to bolster public support, while looking after the interests of those sections of the elite on which their power chiefly depends. On the whole, guardian regimes are concerned to do much the same kind of thing as their civilian predecessors, but to do it better. The political rhetoric of this kind of government is filled with the language of the doctor and the school-master. It tends to see itself (as in Nigeria) as a 'corrective government', to call itself a National Reformation Council (in Sierra Leone) or a National Redemption Council (in Ghana). It launches clean-ups against corruption, and applies doses of stiff medicine to cure the economy, usually with the stated intention that once the cure or course of education has been successfully completed, the patient or pupil will be released to look after himself.

The veto coup takes place when social mobilisation has reached a stage which presents a real threat to the interests of the bureaucracy, and more generally to the interests of the middle classes which by this stage are likely to have become well developed and firmly entrenched. What it vetoes is mass participation, especially through left-wing parties with policies of drastic social change. It is thus inherently conserva-tive, and is likely to seek the support of the United States against opposition which is correspondingly likely to be backed by the Soviet Union or by its regional allies such as Cuba or Vietnam. One distinctive feature of a veto regime is that since it faces large-scale and broadly-based opposition, it will need to take appropriately repressive action if it is to impose itself successfully. A breakthrough coup, by contrast, only needs to dispose of a fairly small governing clique (though it may do so in a brutal manner), while a guardian coup can frequently (though by no means always) take place without any bloodshed at all. One indicator which Huntington uses for the growth of veto coups in Latin America is, therefore, the steady increase during the three decades after 1935 in the percentage of coups involving a substantial degree of violence, from 19 per cent in 1935-44, to 32 per cent in 1945-54, to 67 per cent in 1955-64.[9] The degree of repression required by the military regimes in Chile after 1973 and Argentina after 1976 helps to confirm the validity of the veto coup as a device intended to restrain popular participation. As these cases suggest, the veto coup has been primarily a Latin American phenomenon, very largely because it is in Latin America (and especially in the larger and richer states) that the social developments which give rise to it have been most marked, but analogous interventions have taken place in Turkey and Greece, while the Thai coup of 1976 and the Indonesian military takeover in 1965 might also be included. A veto coup is not necessarily a once and for all operation, because the conditions that give rise to it do not go away: the Turkish military has intervened three times at approximately ten-year intervals since 1960. What matters is whether, on the one hand, the military can succeed in instituting a political system that safeguards its essential interests, or on the other, the forces of mass participation succeed in making the military's political position untenable, and in reducing it to a position of subordination to the government. If neither happens, the state may be caught, as in Chile and Argentina, between the irresistible force of the military and the irremovable object of the mass, with correspondingly violent consequences.

These types of coup are useful as general indicators of the social bases and political orientations of military regimes, not as hard and fast categories. Guardian regimes especially are subject to a wide range of variation which may affect their political stance. Whereas breakthrough coups are almost always the work of junior officers and veto coups of senior ones, guardian coups can come from any level in the military hierarchy, from generals down through the officer corps to non-commissioned officers and even private soldiers. This may influence the radicalism of the regime, in as much as senior officers are likely to be politically to the right of junior ones (though privates and NCOs, as in Sierra Leone in 1968 and Liberia after 1980, may be so lacking in the necessary self-confidence and educational skills that they rely heavily on civilian advisers, and the same may not apply). The lower the level in the military hierarchy from which the coup group is drawn, moreover, the greater the difficulty of securing the institutional unity of the army – a problem considered in the next section.

Rank also influences military regimes through the pronounced tendency of military hierarchies to fall into generational sets, in which age grades (which correspond with rank as each set moves up the ladder of promotion) are differentiated by their origins, training or institutional experience. Those recruited under one regime may have been selected by different criteria from those recruited under another; prewar, wartime and postwar officers may have had markedly different formative experiences. Generational differences are then reinforced by the tendency of soldiers to consort socially and politically with their own peer group, in contrast to the formalised hierarchy of operational command. These differences are particularly marked in ex-colonial armies, though certainly not confined to them. The first generation of indigenous officers in what were to become the armies of the newly independent African states were selected by the colonial rulers from among the senior NCOs, this being the highest rank that any African had then been able to reach. Men of long army service, little education and limited political outlook, they often proved inadequate to the task of running a modern state, as in their different ways did Ankrah of Ghana, Ironsi of Nigeria and Amin of Uganda. A later generation, still under colonial rule, were recruited from the better-qualified school leavers or sometimes even university graduates, and sent to metropolitan training establishments followed by direct entry into the officer corps. A self-conscious elite, rapidly promoted as the officer corps was Africanised in the last years of colonialism and early years of independence, this group most often showed the attitudes which led some observers to view the military as an inherently neo-colonial institution.[10] Afrifa in Ghana, who rose from brigade major to head of state over the three years from 1966 to 1969, put his admiration for colonial institutions with embarrassing candour:[11] 'I was thrilled by Sandhurst . . . the best part of my life — learning to be a soldier in a wonderful and mysterious institution with traditions going back to 1802.' Officers recruited after independence were less likely to be sent to colonial training institutions, and often found promotion blocked by a senior generation only a few years older than themselves. Since the armed forces provided the main channel through which the post-independence generation reached positions of political leadership, they sometimes found themselves, like Murtala Mohammed in Nigeria or Flight Lieutenant Jerry Rawlings in Ghana, the spokesmen for resentments at continuing dependence which were widely spread through the whole society.

A further source of generational cleavage may arise from changes in the ethnic balance of the army. British colonial armies were famed for their recruitment of soldiers from 'martial races', generally peoples living away from, and hostile to, the main centres of education and social change in which opposition to the colonial regime was greatest; officers recruited just before independence were likely, in contrast, to come from areas in which education was most widespread; in either case, people from the most prosperous areas were least likely to join the army. Post-independence governments sometimes deliberately introduced ethnic criteria for officer recruitment, either to ensure that the army reflected the balance of peoples in the country as a whole, or more crudely to bias it in favour of the group which provided its own political base. This was likely to favour central rather than peripheral regions, and majority groups rather than minorities: the lowland Burmese, for example, rather than the hill peoples on whom the British had relied. Once these differences are turned to direct political relevance by the advent of a military regime, the result can be extremely explosive, as most obviously in the Nigerian coup of July 1966 and the civil war of 1967-70.[12]

Finally, military regimes − like any other − are subject to a wide range of variation due to national circumstances or the personalities of their leaders. The peculiar experiment in autonomous socialism adapted by the Burmese military government under Ne Win after 1962 was in some measure the result of a characteristically Burmese isolationism, in some measure the reflection of the origins of the Burmese army (and of Ne Win himself) as an anti-colonialist movement during the Second World War. The Indonesian military regime owes its pro-western stance to its rise to power following the abortive Communist coup and its need for western economic aid, just as the Marxism-Leninism of General Siyad's government in Somalia could be ascribed to Soviet support during the coup which brought it to power, and to the continued need for Soviet military aid (until 1977) for use against Ethiopia. As a military regime settles down, moreover, it finds itself confronting the same intractable problems as its predecessors, dealing with the same political groups and forces, shuffling the same limited policy options. It is the way in which it interacts with these political forces that chiefly determines whether it remains a specifically 'military' government or metamorphoses itself into something rather different and more broadly-based, and that determines, indeed whether it remains in power or goes the way of the regime it overthrew.

The Political Dilemmas of the Military

Regardless of the type of coup, and the structure and political outlook of the resulting government, there are two characteristic problems which confront all military regimes. The first of these is the problem of the regime's relationship with the military itself, the second that of its relationship with that constellation of forces, institutions and individuals which makes up 'ordinary' or civilian politics. The first is gener-

ally the most immediately pressing, though it is the second which ultimately determines the political future of the regime, and the possibility
of any peaceful transformation into, or transfer of power to, a civilian
system of government.[13]

The Politics of the Army

When the army goes into politics, so too does politics come into the
army. The degree of insulation from political affairs which can be
maintained under a civilian regime is no longer possible once army
officers control the state and are directly responsible for political decisions. For one thing, it is the armed forces which have enabled the
government to take power, and which therefore constitute the political
base of the regime, in a far more direct way than is true even of a
civilian government which depends on a high level of military force.
The armed forces become the nearest equivalent – and in many ways a
very inadequate one – to a civilian political party. Political decisions
are easily seen as being taken on the military's behalf, and become the
subject of debate within it. The ideological attitudes of the leadership, which are of only indirect importance when it is not immediately
involved in government, now come to matter. The political interests of
the armed forces – perhaps simply over questions such as pay and conditions, perhaps over broader issues – can be directly represented. Conversely, matters which might previously have been regarded as internal
to the military come to take on a political dimension: questions of pro-
motions, of who commands units and where they are stationed, of the
standing of officers from different regions or ethnic groups, or of those
with different political outlooks, are liable to scrutiny within the forces.
The effect can be extremely damaging to the coherence and effectiveness of the military as a fighting force.

In this respect, the level in the armed forces from which the coup is
launched is critical. Senior officers, especially if they act together, have
the best chance of using the armed forces as a springboard into government, while insulating them from the most corrosive effects of political
involvement. In a large army, like the Turkish, in which military takeovers are characteristically directed by the chiefs of staff, it makes very
little difference to the ordinary soldier, or even the junior officer,
whether the army is 'in power' or not. All that happens is that the most
senior generals are promoted out of the army into governmental posts,
and someone else takes their place. Only if the regime directly involves
them in action of a politically controversial kind is there likely to be
much trouble. Otherwise the main danger which the military ruler

faces is from his immediately subordinate officers, especially if these feel that he has proved incapable of handling a political crisis, or has taken some action likely to bring the armed forces into disrepute. Brigadier Lansana in Sierra Leone was deposed within two days of taking power, once his subordinates realised that his entry into politics was guided by party considerations. Ayub Khan in Pakistan was ousted by his army commander, Acheampong in Ghana by the fellow members of his ruling military council, in each case essentially because of a failure to deal with civilian political unrest. Galtieri in Argentina was forced to resign by the armed forces in the aftermath of military defeat.

If the coup is led by junior officers, or still more so by NCOs, it becomes not only a coup but also a mutiny against the military command, and the danger to the unity of the armed forces is much greater, especially if senior officers have been killed in the process. This accounted for much of the bitterness which followed the Nigerian coup of January 1966, and led to the much more widespread killing of officers in the counter-coup in July. The privates' coup in Sierra Leone in 1968 led to almost the entire officer corps being marched off to jail wearing nothing but their underpants, an episode which contributed to a degree of fragmentation which left the army incapable of any coherent political action, with the result that the next attempted coup collapsed in fiasco. Such events have led some observers to question whether African armies especially should be properly regarded as organisational entities at all, rather than being simply described as groups of armed men in uniform. This is to exaggerate, though equally the stereotype of the military as a disciplined hierarchy may be no less wide of the mark. In states in which institutions are in any event weak, militaries have generally proved substantially more effective than many other forms of organisation, notably political parties, while none the less proving unable to survive immersion in the corrosive fluid of politics.

Military regimes have devised a distinctive attempt to counter the effects of politics on the armed forces, in the form of collective leadership. This on the face of it runs counter to the principle of command hierarchy, generally seen as essential for successful military operations, and contrasts sharply with the almost complete absence of genuine collective leadership in civilian governments. It indicates, in its own peculiar fashion, the military's recognition of the importance of representation. The form which this collective leadership takes does vary, however, according to the nature of the regime, the structure of the military, and the level within the armed forces from which military intervention has come. In its classic form, the junta is composed of the senior officers of the principal formations; characteristically, the chiefs of staff of the army, navy and air force, with the army, as the largest and politically most important force, enjoying the dominant role. This is appropriate to a veto regime, as exemplified by Argentina, Chile and Turkey, in which intervention takes place from the top and each member of the junta serves as the representative of his own force, some-times subject to removal should he lose the confidence of his subordinate officers. The problems of decision making in a junta under extreme stress, and the political constraints on its members, were sharply revealed by the behaviour of the Argentine military during the Falklands/Malvinas crisis of 1982.

The military council is rather a different kind of body, though directed to essentially the same goal of maintaining the cohesion of the armed forces. Characteristically African rather than Latin American, and occurring under guardian rather than veto regimes, it follows from the need to consolidate control and political support after the seizure of power by junior officers or other ranks who cannot automatically command the obedience of the military. Sometimes the council consists of the group of like-minded soldiers who launched the coup in the first place, while at other times this group is consciously enlarged to include other officers whose support is considered essential. The National Liberation Council which held power in Ghana from 1966 to 1969, and its successor the National Redemption Council of 1972 to 1979, are examples of the type. In each case, the Council removed its own Chairman — Ankrah of the NLC, Acheampong of the NRC — when (though in different ways and in different degrees) they showed signs of personal political ambitions which threatened the Council's cohesion. Whereas juntas almost invariably represent military units, military councils are frequently composed in such a way as to represent regional or ethnic groups in the country as a whole. The National Reformation Council of 1967-8 in Sierra Leone explicitly comprised two officers from each of the country's four main administrative sub-divisions, while the Federal Military Council in Nigeria after 1966 included the regional or state governors who were almost invariably natives of the area they governed. They were thus intended not only to preserve balance as between units, but to inhibit the fragmentation of the army (or indeed the country) on ethnic lines.

The most distinctive and peculiar of all collective military govern-ments was the original Derg in Ethiopia. Formed before the final overthrow of Haile Selassie as a parliament of the armed forces, it comprised an officer, a non-commissioned officer and an ordinary soldier from each of the forty-two principal units, successfully counteracting the Emperor's attempts to retain control through his well-practised technique of divide and rule. Highly efficacious for its original purpose, it was much too unwieldly to serve as an instrument of government, and suffered successive purges including the execution of its first two chairmen. Mengistu Haile-Mariam, who had long been the dominant figure within the Derg, then became its almost undisputed head.

In a similar (though usually less violent) way, a single leader often emerges from the collective leadership as the regime becomes established. A collective leadership is almost always temporary. Sometimes, as with Nasser among the Free Officers in Egypt after 1952, or Ne Win in the Burmese military government after 1962, a dominant figure is present from the start. Sometimes, like Gowon in Nigeria after 1966, he is thrown up by events. Many military regimes never make any pretence at collective leadership. But when there is no dominant leader, it is all the more likely that the military, regarding itself as no more than a caretaker administration, will hand over to a new civilian government.

Civil-Military Politics

This raises the second dilemma of the military: its relations with civilian political groups. In a sense, what is at issue here is the adequacy of the bureaucratic state. The civil bureaucracy, linked to the military as it usually is by similarities of origin, attitude and interest as fellow members of the state apparatus, rarely provides any threat to military government. Much more often, it benefits from military rule, sheltering beneath the protective umbrella provided by the army while it gets on with the business of administration unimpeded by intrusive politicians. The army for its part relies on the civilian bureaucracy for guidance in fields — such as economic management — where it lacks expertise, and for respectability in 'fronting' for the regime, both in its contacts with the rest of the population in regional administration and in its diplomatic connections with the outside world. To the extent, then, that the military and civil bureaucracy can manage the government without serious challenge, the state is sufficient unto itself as a source of political power. The resulting political structure is aptly described as one of bureaucratic authoritarianism, a phrase which has in particular been applied to the military governments of southern Europe and the southern cone of Latin America: a government of generals at the top, PhDs in the technical policy-making positions immediately beneath them and security police at the bottom, a combination best exemplified by the Pinochet regime in Chile.[14]

This government of the state, by the state, for the state is, however, rarely if ever realised in its pure form. Much more often – and certainly in Chile – the army itself tacitly represents broader political sections of the society, even if these in turn rely on military protection. The first step in sorting out the structure of civil-military relations under any military regime is thus to determine what these sections are; they provide the core constituency from which alliances with other civilian groups must subsequently be constructed. If there is no such core constituency, or if it is progressively alienated or restricted by the actions of the military leadership, then the regime itself is likely to be short-lived. As often as not, it will be replaced from within the armed forces, like the governments of General Gowon in Nigeria in 1975 or General Acheampong in Ghana in 1978, by a new military regime which promises to act more in tune with civilian political demands.

The nature of the social groups to which the military owes its core support varies widely in keeping with the social structures of third world states themselves. At their simplest they may be tribal or ethnic, especially in countries where military recruitment patterns under colonial or independent governments have favoured one such group over others. In Uganda, for example, Amin's core support rested on his own Kakwa people, and he found himself forced back into ever-closer dependence on them as his regime was progressively weakened by political repression and economic collapse. Though Mohamed Siyad Barre's government in Somalia was never so ethnically based – nor so repressive – as Amin's, none the less he depended in particular on the three clans (Marehan, Ogaden and Dulbahante) to which he was related by blood or marriage, and drew on them increasingly for support when his regime was under pressure, for example after defeat by Ethiopia in the 1977-8 war. Outside Africa, ethnicity is very much less important, simply because it rarely forms the basis for conflict over state control; even where ethnic conflicts exist, as in much of south-east and north-west Asia, or in Latin American states with a high Amerindian population, control of the state is rarely at issue, resting unchallenged with a dominant or central group.

The immediate aftermath of military takeover is generally a reaction of shock; often, if the experience of the preceding civilian government has been sufficiently chaotic, one of relief. Unless it has had to fight

its way into power against organised opposition, the army can generally rely on a period of grace in which to sort out its priorities and – if
it has sufficient foresight – to lay the foundations for a more durable
regime. This is equally a period of shock for the military itself, in which
it has to grapple with what are often an entirely new range of problems,
and to define its position in terms both of its own ideology and of the
civilian groups with which it will work. Often it seems enough to seek
an alliance of convenience with whatever politicians were opposed to
the ousted regime, thus establishing (provided it was sufficiently unpopular) a broad base of support for the new one. Exceptionally, even the
old regime is brought in on the act, as in Liberia in April 1980 when
the new People's Revolutionary Council co-opted three ministers from
the government whose president it had just assassinated. The disparate
range of political opinions which this technique produces can rarely be
kept together in a single government for long. As political choices are
forced on the government – over economic management, foreign relations, the nature and duration of military rule itself – so some groups of
politicians will be expelled from the government or deprived of influence within it, and others may tacitly withdraw their support or make
it conditional on some programme for demilitarisation. In the process,
the military defines it options and its ideological stance, while civilian
politicians regroup and re-orient themselves in response to the new
state of affairs.

The most basic choice facing the military is whether to go or to
stay: whether to establish some form of civilian government to which
power can be transferred (by a process often very similar to that by
which it had previously been transferred from the colonial administration to the new nationalist government), or to remain in office while
trying to build up a permanent political base. Almost every military
regime claims when it takes over that its rule will only be temporary,
but achieving temporariness is a much more difficult matter. Sometimes the claim is clearly fraudulent, or the leader discovers attractions
in office which he is reluctant to give up, but there are more deep-
seated problems in finding a successor regime which can form a fairly
effective government without at the same time threatening the interests
which the military regards as vital. A veto regime, called into existence by the military's desire to protect dominant class or state interests
against a threatening expansion in popular participation, will almost
inevitably be long-lived, since the conservative sectors on whose behalf
the army intervenes will be unable to retain control without its continued support; at most, there may be a facade of civilian govern-

ment. Breakthrough regimes, seeing the army at the centre of the process of modernisation which it is their mission to promote, are equally unlikely to withdraw except after a long period, the deliberate distancing of the Turkish army from power under Kemal Atatürk being in this respect an exception. Any fairly prompt and voluntary handover to civilians is, therefore, only likely to take place under guardian regimes, and these equally face problems in finding an acceptable successor. Where, as in Pakistan in 1977 or Bangladesh in 1975, the army ousts the electorally dominant party, it finds itself riding the tiger: any reasonably democratic transfer of power will restore a government resentful at its previous dismissal, and all the more embittered in both these cases by the killing of its previous leaders, Bhutto in Pakistan and Mujibur Rahman in Bangladesh. Any alternative civilian government would probably need to rely on a level of army support which would make it military in all but name.

Where a potential civilian alternative is available, there are certainly attractions to the military in handing over to it, the main one being the hope of avoiding further political strain on the armed forces. Civilian leaders, scenting the possibility of a return to barracks, are likely to make this a condition for their continued co-operation, though at the same time they must not alienate the military so much as to make it veto their claim on the succession. In several cases, such as Ghana in 1969 and 1979, Nigeria in 1979, or Turkey in 1961 and 1973, demilitarisation has led to a peaceful transfer of power to an elected government with fairly broad popular support. As all of these cases show, however — each of them ending within a few years in further military intervention — the problem doesn't end there. The post-military regime struggles under potentially crippling disadvantages.[15] One is that the structure of civilian politics — especially the party system — will almost inevitably duplicate that which has already been found wanting. Old politicians will return, with their old followers and their old rivals, very often paying off old scores and resuscitating local conflicts. The mechanistic assumptions of military leaders that the defects of the former civilian regime can be dealt with by constitutional engineering, and the banning of undesirable practices such as tribalism or corruption, are unlikely to be realised. In addition, the new civilian leaders will have to cope with the army itself: owing their power to it, yet wanting to assert their independence of it, their relations with it are likely to be strained. The military forms a permanent opposition, ready at any moment to take over, and the pattern of political expectations is accordingly transformed; where opponents of the government once looked to opposition parties, they now look to the military, and ambitious officers see themselves as potential rulers. Sometimes it works the other way round, and the government itself knocks on the door of the barracks in search of support against civilian rivals. In any event, the military has become a lasting factor in political calculation.

Staying in power, on the other hand, requires the military to look for fairly long-term sources of political support, and this almost invariably involves it in some kind of clientelist strategy, in which it uses its control of the state to buy support from compatible interest groups and leaders. Not only is this in any event a common pattern of third world politics; it is also well adapted to the military's commitment to the state structure, its hierarchical organisation, and its inability to cope with more genuinely participatory forms of political mobilisation. Since such a clientelist system will have to operate on the military's (or its leader's) terms, much depends on whether civilian politicians of sufficient weight are prepared to accept it, and this in turn depends on the 'autonomy' of civilian political organisations: the extent to which they must ultimately look back to their own supporters, rather than depending on access to state benefits. The inability of the Argentine military to develop a clientelist political base, for example, may partly be ascribed to the degree of autonomous mobilisation achieved especially by the Peronist movement, in contrast with Brazil, where the military government after 1964 was able to co-opt civilian politicians in a much more successful way. Similarly in Ghana in the mid-1970s, General Acheampong's attempt to set up a permanent structure of civil-military rule under the title of 'union government' foundered on the refusal to participate of autonomous professional associations, whereas in Zaire General Mobutu's apparently ramshackle regime has managed to survive remarkably well. The Zairean case also indicates the importance for many military clientelist regimes of external support. Any clientelist regime will need some access to external sources of economic benefits and sometimes of military assistance, but this need is often all the greater for military governments whose domestic political support is slight – and even sometimes non-existent.

Occasionally, and especially in the case of breakthrough regimes, military rulers aim at a system of joint civil-military rule which goes beyond simple clientelist co-operation, and attempt to form what might be called a military party state. The distinctive feature of breakthrough regimes is that they seek to expand popular participation in order to mobilise support against the oligarchical structure which they have overthrown. They see 'the people' as potential allies rather than enemies, and they are usually led by radical junior officers. This leads to the formation of groups such as the people's defence committees in Rawlings' Ghana, or to the urban and peasant associations in revolutionary Ethiopia, and in some cases to the creation of a national political party, such as the Burma Socialist Programme Party. In a way, this kind of regime seeks to carry out in reverse order the same process as revolutionary or nationalist parties which form guerrilla armies in their struggle for power, with the result that if they win the army and party are closely integrated within the state that they control. Some of the features of this kind of regime will be examined in the next chapter. However, the problems are greater when the army and the state apparatus of which it forms part predate the formation of the party, and it is easy for even breakthrough regimes to fall back on political organisation of a conventionally clientelist kind.

Even though military regimes and leaders face, from their own perspective, a choice between demilitarisation and seeking to institutionalise their rule, it does not follow that either option will necessarily be successful in producing any stable or effective system of government. Military regimes, because they do not necessarily even start their period in power with any assurance of political organisation or support, are more likely than civilian ones to reach a state of impasse, in which no acceptable solution appears to be available either by staying in power or leaving it. At one level, as already noted in the case of the Gowon regime in Nigeria or the Acheampong one in Ghana, the impasse may arise from the fact that the particular leader or leadership group has been boxed into a corner from which there is no escape, in which case the removal of a few individuals may reopen the political options for the new military government which then takes over. More seriously, the impasse may arise at the level of the military as a whole, in its dealings with civilian institutions. This has especially been the case with Latin American veto regimes which, as in Chile and Argentina in the early 1980s, have felt obliged to cling to power in the face of declining civilian support because of their fear of the consequences of handing over. Finally, and most dangerously of all, impasse may result in the fragmentation of the very state machinery of which the military forms part. Having intervened to protect the interests of the state apparatus against civilian political threat or mismanagement, the army may itself all but destroy those interests by introducing into the bureaucracy a level of politicisation (especially of an ethnic kind) which it cannot withstand. The most dramatic instances of state collapse have almost all taken place under military rule. Nigeria came close to this point in 1966-7, only to be saved, paradoxically enough, by the integrative effects of a three-year civil war. Uganda and Chad have gone over the brink, and have only been patched together again, partially and uncertainly, with a high level of external intervention. In Afghanistan, external intervention in support of an unpopular military/Marxist regime has intensified the level of fragmentation, while the military takeover in Bangladesh has placed enormous strain on a governmental structure which was in any event (after the split from Pakistan in 1971) fragile and newly formed. Military intervention emphasises the importance of the state in third world politics, but also its fragility.

Notes

1. See, for example, R.H.T. O'Kane, 'A Probabilistic Approach to the Causes of Coups d'Etat', *British Journal of Political Science*, vol. 11, no. 3 (1980), pp. 287-308.

2. See, for example, S.E. Finer, *The Man on Horseback* (Pall Mall, 1962).

3. O'Kane, 'A Probabilistic Approach'.

4. Finer, *The Man on Horseback*.

5. S.P. Huntington, *Political Order in Changing Societies* (Yale University Press, 1968), Chapter 4.

6. See, for example, R.E. Dowse, 'The Military and Political Development' in C. Leys (ed.), *Politics and Change in Developing Countries* (Cambridge University Press, 1969).

7. R.D. McKinlay and A.S. Cohan, 'A Comparative Analysis of the Political and Economic Performance of Military and Civilian Regimes', *Comparative Politics*, vol. 8, no. 1 1975), pp. 1-30.

8. Huntington, *Political Order in Changing Societies*, p. 221.

9. Ibid., p. 230.

10. See R. First, *The Barrel of a Gun* (Penguin, 1970), pp. 73-89.

11. A.A. Afrifa, *The Ghana Coup* (Cass, 1966), pp. 49-50.

12. C.H. Enloe, *Ethnic Soldiers: State Security in Divided Societies* (Penguin, 1980).

13. This section draws heavily on C. Clapham and G. Philip (eds.), *The Political Dilemmas of Military Regimes* (Croom Helm, 1984).

14. See J.J. Linz, 'An Authoritarian Regime: Spain' in E. Allardt and S. Rokkan, (eds.), *Mass Politics* (Free Press, 1970); and G. O'Donnell, *Modernization and Bureaucratic Authoritarianism* (University of California Press, 1973).

15. See J.B. Adekanye, 'The Post-Military Regime in Africa' in Clapham *et al.*, *The Political Dilemmas of Military Regimes*.

8 THE REVOLUTIONARY STATE

Revolution and the Third World

A revolution is a rapid, violent and irreversible change in the political organisation of a society. It involves the destruction of the existing political order, together with the myths which sustain it and the men which it sustains, and the creation of a new order, sustaining new men and sustained by new myths. This change may well result from, and will certainly lead to, other and dramatic developments in the economy and social structure, but what is central to revolution is its *political* element. What revolutions are basically about is the exercise of power, and the ideas and institutions through which this is achieved. They do not follow inevitably from any preceding set of conditions; and the social transformation to which they lead, though certainly a critical element without which no revolution can be said to have taken place, is made possible only by the prior conquest of political power and by deliberate political decisions as to how that power is to be used.

Revolution in the postwar era has been almost exclusively – with the rather doubtful exception of the satellite states of eastern Europe and the more plausible one of Yugoslavia – a third world phenomenon. The industrial states have so far at least proved effective at maintaining their existing political structures against revolutionary uprising, though at times – as in Hungary in 1956 – they have needed external intervention in order to do so. In the third world, a small number of states – China, Vietnam, Kampuchea, Cuba – have undergone a transformation which must by any criterion be classed as revolutionary, while there is a much larger set, including Ethiopia, Mozambique, the two Yemens and Libya, to which the term may plausibly be applied. In Iran and Nicaragua, it is still too early to say whether a potentially revolutionary political order has succeeded in establishing itself; in Grenada, a potentially revolutionary regime foundered from internal division followed by external intervention. But it is not simply these actual cases which make revolution a live issue in the politics of the third world, in a way that it is not in the politics of industrial states: it is, equally, the fluidity, ineffectiveness and weak institutional structure of a great many third world regimes, which on the one hand appear to increase its likelihood, and on the other enhance its attractions as a solution to the full range of interlocking third world problems. What revolution offers in this respect is a more effective institutional order. It does not promise any withering away of the centralised and bureaucratic third world state. On the contrary, it offers to make that state more efficient through a ruthless application of power, which is legitimised by a combination of nationalism and universalist ideals of equality and social justice; which, if successful, will make the state more independent in its external relations as well as more effective internally.

An assessment of revolution in third world politics then requires answers to three main questions. First, why do they take place? Secondly, how do they take place? Thirdly, what difference do they make? The remainder of this chapter will look at each in turn.

Why Do Revolutions Take Place?

Though modern revolutions are largely a third world phenomenon, even there they are unusual. Taking all those mentioned in the previous section, together with a few other states (most of them derived from nationalist guerrilla liberation movements) with some claim to be considered, we still emerge with no more than something in the region of twenty states, several of which have no more than contestable claims on revolutionary status. A recent survey of Marxist governments[1] — rather a different criterion, of course — lists fourteen in the third world, excluding some of the revolutionary states which I have referred to, but including others such as Benin and Congo in which no revolution could be said to have taken place. The revolutionary states are scattered here and there through the third world, only east and south-east Asia providing any substantial contiguous block, and though their number has been — and will doubtless continue to be — added to from time to time, it would be straining foresight to suggest that any massive upsurge of third world revolutions is about to take place.

In seeking to explain these revolutions, we are, therefore, looking at exceptional cases, with a view to discovering what distinguishes these from the non-revolutionary majority. None of the general theories of revolution derived largely from European experience is likely to be much use to us. There is in most cases no proletariat worth the name, and even where there is, as in China, its role is a secondary one. More importantly, no 'economic' theory of revolution, nor any theory which seeks to place revolutions at any particular stage of social evolution, appears to apply at all plausibly to the range of cases involved. While the exploitative conditions under which peasant agriculture was incorporated into the global economy may certainly help to explain the eastern Asian revolutions, they can scarcely apply to Ethiopia (where incorporation fell far short of the Asian stage), to Cuba (where it had already been established for centuries), or to oil-rich Libya. Incorporation certainly influences the form which the revolution takes, and the options open to the post-revolutionary regime, but cannot account for the revolution itself. It is much more profitable, in keeping with the emphasis suggested in the last section, to concentrate on the political causes of revolution. From this point of view, what we are looking for is a 'revolutionary situation', which requires both an existing political order which is in danger of collapse, coupled with the forces required to build a new revolutionary order in its place. Collapse in itself is not enough. Uganda after Amin was not a revolutionary situation; it was just a mess.

By far the most promising combination is an oligarchical regime which is unable either to establish effective links with the countryside, or to provide political opportunities for the urban intelligentsia. In identifying these as the key constituents of revolution, Huntington is basically right.[2] If the oligarchical regime is in addition closely associated with some external power which is intrusive enough to arouse resentment, but at the same time not strong or determined enough to maintain the regime in power, then the revolutionaries will have the additional advantage of nationalism. The two classic conditions from which this situation arises are first, a decaying traditional monarchy, and secondly, a colonial power which refuses to decolonise; but equivalent conditions can occur under a landowning oligarchy (especially when this is ethnically differentiated from its subjects) or some forms of 'impasse' military regime. In each case, a revolutionary modernising elite is able to gain access to a source of support which both sustains it (when necessary) during the struggle to overthrow the old regime, and also helps to ensure, after the takeover has been achieved, that the new regime does not simply degenerate into a neo-patrimonial urban coalition.

The astonishingly high proportion of successful revolutions which takes place in decaying traditional monarchies is much too great to be dismissed as coincidence. The revolution does not always, as in Ethiopia, overthrow the monarchy itself. It may, as in Russia or China, overthrow a government of the urban bourgeoisie which has directly succeeded the monarchy. The basic reasons for the success of revolution must none the less lie in the legacy of traditional monarchy: its weakness as a source of political mobilisation, but also its strength (when appropriately transformed) as a source of centralised national government. Some of the characteristic dilemmas of political change in traditional monarchies have been discussed in an earlier chapter. The process of modernisation normally involves the centralisation of power in a monarch, who heads an administrative apparatus which in many respects resembles the state structure elsewhere established by colonial governments. One of the ways in which this apparatus resembles the colonial structure is indeed in its failure to make provision for political representation, except through traditionalist mechanisms which find their equivalent in the colonialist use of indirect rule. But whereas the new educated nationalist group can usually achieve their goals through the organisation of nationalist movements against colonial powers, the same outlet is not available in states which are already independent. The easiest alternative is simply to take over the central government, but the new regime will then inherit the political weakness of its predecessor — further enfeebled by the destruction of what remained of monarchical legitimacy — and will either have to mobilise a broader base of political suppport, or will fall to someone else who does. It is not impossible for this support to be raised, as in Thailand, in a non-revolutionary way, but the possibilities of revolutionary mobilisation, either by the new regime or against it, are clearly open.

A second way in which traditional monarchy aids revolution is by combining a deeply entrenched sense of nationality with a tradition of central government. The continuities in this respect between pre- and post-revolutionary regimes which Tocqueville noted in France are equally marked in more modern revolutions. The sense of nationality, though it may be most articulately expressed by the new urban elite, goes well beyond the 'nationalism' of their equivalents in colonial territories, and furnishes a link between them and a much wider, especially rural, constituency. It will be all the greater if the monarchical regime, through its ineffectiveness, corruption or obvious subordination to an external power, has 'betrayed' the national tradition. One way in which this nationalist element is most strikingly expressed is through the revolutionaries' inheritance of the 'imperialist' tradition of the old regime: in Ethiopia and China, no less than in France or Russia, they are determined to reassert the 'historic boundaries' of the state, even when this involves the forcible reincorporation of peoples who are ethnically distinct from the core national culture and see the revolution as an opportunity to seek their own separate independence.

Unlike other third world revolutions, those directed against traditional monarchies frequently do not require any recourse to rural guerrilla warfare. The revolution may, as in Iran or Ethiopia, follow what Huntington terms the 'western' pattern (in contrast to the 'eastern' or Chinese model), where the revolutionaries first seize power at the centre and only afterwards go out to organise the countryside.[3] This is simply because the regime is feeble enough, in terms of its failure to control its own cities, to be overthrown at the centre by a 'breakthrough' coup or an urban mob. Where, as in China, the monarchy has already been replaced by a fairly effective urban government, the retreat to the countryside becomes the only possibility, and the mobilisation of the peasantry gains a critical importance. One strategy which has never yet worked is that of urban guerrilla warfare. If the regime is sufficiently well entrenched in the cities to be proof against the mob, then all that is needed to deal with urban guerrillas is a degree of pitiless repression which, in a counter-revolutionary situation, is likely to be forthcoming. The same is true in this respect of anti-colonial movements, as the French demonstrated during the battle of Algiers, and of the various movements directed against indigenous governments in Uruguay, Argentina and elsewhere in Latin America.

Wars of national liberation are the almost inevitable result of a refusal to decolonise (inevitable, that is to say, save in colonies like Gibraltar which do not wish to be decolonised anyway, and ones like Cape Verde which present intense problems of guerrilla organisation). Such wars provide the clearest possible basis for a nationalist alliance between the urban intelligentsia and an often exploited peasantry, and may even take place in territories such as Portuguese Guinea where the peasantry are not greatly exploited in any case.[4] The question that arises is whether they should count as revolutions, and the only sensible answer is that some do and some don't. Guerrilla warfare does not automatically produce a revolution. What it does produce is a much more powerful organisation linking the peasantry and the nationalist leadership than is found in states where parties have only had to be strong enough to fight elections. This organisation may be used to create a revolutionary transformation of society both in the base areas during the liberation war, or nationally after the seizure of power at the centre; but it need not. Whether it does depends partly on the historical condition of the peasantry and the intensity of the transformation required to fight the war, partly on the circumstances in which the guerrilla movement eventually takes over central power, and the decisions it makes when it does so. There is the sharpest distinction in this respect between the Khmer Rouge in Kampuchea, which on conquering Phnom Penh instantly evacuated the city and destroyed the urban groups on which the central state administration was based, and the Patriotic Front in Zimbabwe, which eventually gained power through a negotiated settlement under which it took over, lock, stock and barrel, the Rhodesian state apparatus against which it had previously been fighting. Most ex-guerrilla regimes take an intermediate course, which raises considerable tensions between the origins of the regime in a rurally-based armed struggle and the imposition of policies through a centralised state machinery; these problems will be considered in the discussion of revolutionary organisation in the next section.

The clearest examples of third world revolution outside the rather specialised conditions of decayed traditional monarchy and delayed decolonisation come from Central America and the Caribbean basin, most evidently in the cases of Cuba and Nicaragua, more doubtfully that of Grenada. In both Cuba and Nicaragua, the ousted regime was a personalist despotism which had alienated support both internally and internationally, Nicaragua in particular being a dynastic state marked by what even for Central America was an astonishing degree of exploitation and repression. Eric Gairy's Grenada is perhaps best described as the case of a former 'charismatic' leader decayed into moody autocrat. These cases are important in that they provide the only guide to the possibility of revolution as a general strategy for social and political change, divorced from specific historical conditions which by their nature apply only to a minority of third world states. At the same time, they point to conditions for revolution, derived from social and economic structure rather than simply political institutions, which in some degree they have in common with other revolutionary states.

What appears to be critical here is the relationship between peasantry and would-be revolutionary leadership. The comparatively easy success of the Cuban guerrilla movement, which took scarcely more than two years from the initial landing to the capture of central state power, encouraged a view of this relationship which proved to be entirely delusory: the 'foco' theory, which surmised that a group of revolutionaries, parachuted into an exploited peasantry, would generate its own revolutionary momentum, collapsed in the death of Che Guevara in Bolivia in 1967.[5] The most important pre-conditions for success lie among the peasantry itself, rather than being introduced by the revolutionaries. These involve more than misery and exploitation: most peasants everywhere in the third world are miserable and exploited, without much sign of revolution resulting from it. What matters is the destruction of the moral and organisational links between the peasantry and its patrons, and the ability of the revolutionaries to present themselves as alternative patrons instead. Scott has examined the process by which, in Southeast Asia, landlords shift from being local leaders with some moral authority based on reciprocal obligations with their peasantry, to being the absentee extractors of the surplus gained from cash crop cultivation.[6] The increasing uncertainty of peasant farming, due to population increase as well as commercialisation, combines with the disappearance of the mechanisms, however feeble, through which uncertainty could be mitigated. In monarchical systems, the patronage network is often almost deliberately destroyed by a monarch who, suspicious of any rurally-based source of political power, both weakens local leadership and turns it, Versailles-like, towards the introverted politics of the court. In colonial systems, the authority of local leadership is weakened by its association with the regime, which becomes all the more repressive when the government has to rely on chiefs or headmen as its local agents in suppressing opposition. The greatest resistance to revolution occurs where local leadership is left intact, as in the Fula areas of Guinea-Bissau, where the PAIGC never gained the support which it achieved in regions in which the Portuguese 'indirect rule' system was less effective,[7] or the Tigre region of Ethiopia, where an initial resistance led by local notables gave way eventually to a localist guerrilla revolutionary movement likewise directed against the central regime. The first priority of the guerrilla movement is, therefore, to kill or drive out anyone who might provide a link between the indigenous population and the government.

Whether the revolutionaries can succeed in establishing themselves as an alternative local leadership again depends to a large extent on peasant perceptions of the possible dangers and benefits of the extremely high-risk strategy of rebellion. Most peasant rebellions have historically been suppressed, with high loss of peasant lives and the imposition of a still more repressive system. The unfamiliar idea of a revolution, leading not simply to the rectification of abuses but to the entire restructuring of society, is one which peasants may well be justified in treating with the proverbial suspicion born of a long experience of finding themselves on the receiving end. Practical students of guerrilla warfare, such as Amilcar Cabral in Guinea-Bissau, constantly emphasise the need for revolutionaries to adapt themselves to the viewpoint of the peasantry, and to speak to them, both literally and figuratively, in a language they understand. Where these conditions can be achieved, however, the 'lesson' of Cuba and Nicaragua is that revolution is not inevitably restricted to those monarchical or colonial systems in which most third world revolutions have hitherto taken place. What is special about these systems is that they provide the easiest or most likely breeding ground for an increase in repression or exploitation, a decay of local level political leadership, and an alienation of urban intellectual elites; these conditions may, however, be replicated elsewhere.

Answering the question of why revolutions do take place also requires some attention to the question of why they don't; and in addition to the absence of the conditions making for revolution, or tactical mistakes on the part of the revolutionaries, this notably raises the issue of the amount of force available to either side, especially from external sources. Revolutions characteristically involve a challenge to the existing structure of the international system, no less than to the domestic. That is why, as in France, Russia or Vietnam, they often give rise to a high level of international conflict. The American 'domino theory' of the war in Vietnam, however ridiculed at the time, did at least embody a perception of the international dimensions of the conflict which was fully shared by their opponents. External aid is available to revolutionaries, as to their opponents, but the conventions or 'rules' of the present-day international system give a distinct advantage in access to outside aid to officially recognised national governments. Revolutionary regimes which, as in Ethiopia, seize power at the centre can benefit from these conventions to protect themselves with outside allies. The United States, having failed to take Castro sufficiently seriously during his guerrilla phase, found itself badly hampered in trying to overthrow him – as most embarrassingly demonstrated by the 1961 Bay of Pigs fiasco – once he was established in Havana. Revolutionaries, however, are more often in opposition than in government. The United States, in reaction to Cuba, stepped up its aid to counter-revolutionary regimes to a degree which made subsequent revolutions less likely and much more expensive; Cuba, in this respect, was the exception that produced the rule. Nor has counter-revolutionary aid been a monopoly of the United States, or even of the west. Two of the most effective Marxist guerrilla movements anywhere in the third world, the Khmer Rouge and the Eritrean People's Liberation Front, have been defeated (though not destroyed) by regimes, (Vietnam and Ethiopia), which are very heavily supported by the Soviet Union. Likewise the opposition to the Soviet-maintained regime in Afghanistan, though not in a full sense revolutionary, could certainly be classed as a war of national liberation. In an internationalised world, revolution and counter-revolution are internationalised as well.

How Do Revolutions Take Place?

The question of how revolutions take place is not one of how to organise successful guerrilla warfare or a radical central putsch. It is a question of how to organise an actual transformation of politics and society, following the seizure of power by a group which has (or subsequently develops) revolutionary aims. Any revolution goes through such a key period of organisation, during which choices have to be made which determine the subsequent pattern of development. These choices, moreover, may have to be made extremely early on. The decision by the Khmer Rouge to evacuate the cities on the morrow of their capture of Phnom Penh in April 1975, or the Derg's decision in Ethiopia to despatch troops to Eritrea in November 1974, in each case irreversibly set the critical priorities for the regime. It is at this stage, too, that some regimes, which in their origins seem not essentially different from their fellows, opt for paths which cannot properly be described as revolutionary, but are instead reformist or even sometimes conservative. The leaders of guerrilla national liberation movements, in particular, face a moment of truth in choosing between their initially reformist inclinations, not essentially different from those of leaders who gained power through a constitutionalist route, and the revolutionary implications of the route to power into which they were forced by the intransigence of their colonial regimes. It is this choice that Amilcar Cabral in Guinea-Bissau had in mind when he referred to the need for 'class suicide' by the petty bourgeoisie, in order to throw in its lot with the interests of the peasants and workers.[8] However nonsensical such a notion may be within a Marxist conception of class behaviour, it may none the less represent a real choice for a small group of important people at a critical moment. Cabral himself, assassinated shortly before independence, never lived to make it, and his successors made it in a way of which he would almost certainly have disapproved.

The immediate priority on seizing power, whether by central coup or guerrilla warfare, is the consolidation of control. Decisions like those in Kampuchea or Ethiopia noted in the last paragraph may be taken quite as much for tactical as for strategic reasons. Many revolutionary regimes come to power under an intense sense of threat, born both of their ideological view of the world and of their immediate political experience, which in many cases proves to be perfectly justified. The source of the threat is usually both internal and external — a domestic opposition group with support from a major foreign power — dealing with which involves both domestic repression and international realignment. The less secure the revolutionaries, the greater the degree of repression. In Kampuchea under the Khmer Rouge, it involved the mass extermination of almost the entire urban educated class. In neighbouring South Vietnam, where the new regime represented the well-established North Vietnamese Marxist-Leninist state, with all the self-confidence derived from the triumphal culmination of a long period of successful warfare against a major global power, the much larger equivalent social groups could simply be sent off to 're-education' camps. In some cases, such as Cuba or in some degree with the 'boat-people' in Vietnam, the potential opposition takes itself — or is driven — into exile, where it is converted into an external threat which presents much less of a danger, again as witness the Bay of Pigs, than it would do internally.

A related initial problem concerns the danger of fragmentation within the revolutionary group itself. Guerrilla liberation armies are potentially the least affected, since they should at any rate already have developed the strength of organisation and unity of command structure needed to pursue the war. Even here, however, major sources of division may arise. One is between the political leadership of the movement, which may have spent much of the war period engaged in external diplomatic activity (or even, as with Ben Bella in Algeria, in jail), and the local military leadership of the fighters on the ground. The most striking demonstration of Robert Mugabe's political skills in Zimbabwe lay in his success in the late 1970s in gaining control of the Zanla army in the field,[9] while Amilcar Cabral took care to ensure that he never lost operational control over the PAIGC in Guinea-Bissau. By contrast, the Eritrean liberation movements have been plagued by exile/fighter divisions, and both Ben Bella in Algeria, and Cabral's brother and successor Luis in Guinea, were overthrown by former guerrilla commanders who retained the loyalty of the troops. A second division occurs when the liberation movement has never been properly united in the first place, as in the inadequate alliance of Zanu and Zapu which formed the Patriotic Front in Zimbabwe, or the still deeper divisions between three rival movements in Angola. Finally, there is the division between those who formed part of the liberation movement before it took over, and groups in the 'enemy-controlled' areas, especially the capital city, who claim a place in it afterwards. The clearest example of this is the role of the old Cuban Communist Party (PSP), which took a negligible part in opposing the Batista regime but demanded a substantial share in Castro's victorious government.

Where the revolution derives from a central coup, there may be a long period of internal conflict before a clear winner emerges, or indeed before the regime irreversibly defines itself as revolutionary at all. The best modern example is Ethiopia, which none the less has quite a number of points in common with both France after 1789 and Russia after 1917. The initial surge of strikes, mutinies and demonstrations early in 1974 did not immediately lead to the overthrow of the monarchy, but produced a characteristic attempt to paper over the cracks with a constitutionalist regime, analogous in its way to that of Madero in Mexico after 1910 or Kerensky in Russia in 1917. The military took over directly in September 1974, but in the form of a broad coalition of radical soldiers whose membership was refined by personal conflicts and policy choices, almost always involving the killing of the losers, over the next three years. Civilian political groups, all weakly organised cliques with no pre-revolutionary experience of party formation, likewise threw themselves into the fray, adopting varying postures of alliance with, or opposition to, the military rulers. Not until the most dangerous of these, the Ethiopian People's Revolutionary Party (EPRP) had opted for the fatal tactics of urban guerrilla warfare, and been mercilessly crushed by the military during the Red Terror of 1977-8, was Mengistu Haile-Mariam's control over the central government secure.

Even after securing themselves in the capital, centralist revolutionaries — much more than guerrilla forces which have already conquered the countryside on their way to power — face problems of rural control, initially against 'white' or traditionalist forces, later against groups whose mobilisation has been prompted by the revolution, but has taken a form opposed to the central government. Both are likely to be supported by external opponents of the regime, and will require the regime to seek its own external allies, on whom it will have to take care not to become too dependent. In one vitally important respect, however, externally-aided regional revolts, or even direct external invasion, serve as an enormous boon to the revolutionaries. They force the newly-established and still uncertain regime to promote programmes of mass mobilisation in the core areas of the nation, in which the survival of the regime is linked to popular feelings of national integrity and defence. This is the most dramatic way in which the monarchical national tradition is turned to revolutionary purposes, and enables the regime, through the Islamic Guards after the Iraqi invasion of Iran, or the mass Ethiopian peasant armies formed to fight the Somalis and Eritreans, to expand beyond its initial often rather limited political support.

This leads to the key problem which faces the regime once basic control has been assured: that of creating institutions through which some kind of new social, political and economic order can be established and maintained. There is no guarantee that this problem will be solved at all. If events in Bolivia from 1952 onwards are classed as 'revolutionary' — and certainly they have many of the marks of it — they demonstrate that there is nothing inevitable about the progress from the initial revolution to the creation of the new order; by 1967 indeed, Che Guevara felt (mistakenly, as it happened) that the whole process was ready to be repeated. This again is essentially a *political* problem, demanding deliberate efforts by rulers working in crisis-ridden situations, and the most distinctive element in the process is usually the creation of a political party. Even where a revolutionary party already exists, and has organised the takeover of power, its transformation into a party of government amounts almost to the creation of a new institution. An oppositional orientation has to be turned into a largely conformist governmental one; guerrilla leaders, many of whom prove utterly unsuited to the business of running a government, have to be replaced by effective administrators, disappointing in the process the expectations of those who have carried the burden of the liberation war, and who look to the personal perquisites of government as their well-earned reward; most of all, the readily identified enemy has disappeared, and the creative tasks of peacetime, however necessary they are recognised to be, are difficult to carry out with the same sense of urgency and common purpose as wartime operations. The new government's tendency to rely on 'moral incentives', which from its viewpoint are not only glorious but also cheap, has to give way (as in Cuba in the late 1960s and early 1970s) to material reward.

Creating a new party is a still more difficult problem, and some of the most interesting revolutions are those in which this has to be done. Sometimes it is done in a manner which is purely cosmetic (or, as one might put it, fraudulent), as with the Somali Revolutionary Socialist Party which, when formed in 1976, had a Politburo identical in membership to the outgoing military council; such cases provide a strong indication that no real 'revolution' has taken place. Two less disputable cases of a revolutionary regime coming to power without a party, and subsequently having to create one, are Cuba and Ethiopia — in Ethiopia because the army seized power directly at the centre, in Cuba because a fairly small and self-contained guerrilla band proved able to take over fairly quickly and without widespread political organisation. The process in each case was rather similar. The first attempt was made by creating a composite party out of the various political groups which supported the revolution. In Cuba, this was the Integrated Revolutionary Organisations (ORI), composed of the Communists, the Student Revolutionary Directorate and Castro's own 26 July Movement, in Ethiopia, the Union of Marxist-Leninist Organisations (Imalered) consisted of various civilian left-wing groups with some military participation. Neither organisation was able to resist the pull of its constituent parts, especially since these included groups engaged in covert competition for power with the revolutionary leadership. Both were disbanded and replaced by new parties formed on the basis of individual membership. In Cuba, this eventually emerged as the new Cuban Communist Party (PCC), though this long remained extremely weak, and its first Congress was not held until 1975, ten years after its formation. The Commission for Organising the Party of the Working People of Ethiopia (COPWE) was established in 1979, but the party itself had still not formally been inaugurated four years later. In both countries, the process of institutionalisation implicit in party-formation threatened to restrict the freedom of action of the leader, and in Ethiopia also of the army as a whole.

The point of having a party is not so much to mobilise the population — a goal that is likely to have been achieved, willy-nilly, by the traumas of the revolution itself — as to bureaucratise it. It replaces the 'anything goes' ethos of revolution with a stable pattern of expectations in which, in particular, any ambitious individual has a clearly marked out route which associates his or her personal advancement with the interests of the regime. This process has a deadening effect quite at variance with the *élan* of revolutionary warfare, and at the same time turns the leader into the manager of an administrative machine which imposes its own constraints on what he can do with it. Both Castro and (most dramatically) Mao Tse Tung at the time of the Cultural Revolution have chafed under the restrictions on their sense of heroic revolutionary leadership; for Mengistu Haile-Mariam in Ethiopia, a man of very limited charisma but a strong sense of personal survival, the main drawback of the party is that it may come under the control either of domestic rivals or of his external backers in the Soviet Union. For the population, bureaucratisation may well have something to be said for it, after the dangers of the revolution and the subsequent period of 'guerrilla administration' by haphazard and enthusiastic appointees of the new regime; simple weariness is as good a base as any on which to build the new order.

This account of revolution has so far said virtually nothing about ideology, which is often regarded as the essential element of the revolutionary experience. Revolution is, in this view, a matter of changing the way people think, in order to change the way they behave. For committed revolutionaries, this is indeed the case: only a very deeply held belief in their ability to change the world in accordance with their own ideas could induce men such as Guevara in Cuba and Bolivia or Khieu Samphan in Kampuchea to undertake the extreme danger and discomfort of guerrilla warfare. The way in which, for revolutionaries, ideas are seen as determining action accounts for the bitter (and to the outsider often almost incomprehensible) disputes which take place between them as to the proper ideological line. But for most of the population, it is not like that at all. It is behaviour within a given social context which (in accordance with Marx's own explanatory rationale) determines ideas. While the change in ideas which accompanies revolution may be real enough, it follows from (rather than precedes) the new regime's success in altering the conditions of life, and especially those conditions which establish what constitutes 'rational action' in any given context. Even then, human beings' obstinate commitment to rational behaviour as they see it limits what can be done, a point most clearly made by the persistent failure of 'moral incentives' (i.e. ideologically determined regime goals running counter to individual conceptions of personal advantage) as a means of constructing the new social order.[11]

The most immediately beneficial way in which the new regime alters the conditions of life is through the removal of an exploitative regime, especially when this is directly colonial or foreign-dominated. As the euphoria of liberation dies away, however (and this is often severely restricted by the effects of political and economic disruption), it is up to the revolution to deliver the goods. So far as direct government services are concerned, this can often be rapidly achieved, the two commonest and most immediate benefits of revolution being increases in the level of education and health care, especially in the rural areas. Economic production is much more of a problem. Guerrilla warfare is in itself highly destructive, especially of communications. Landlords or settlers, in societies where control of commercial agricultural production was concentrated in their hands, are likely to have fled. The distribution network, in the hands of unpopular 'pariah entrepreneurs', may well have broken down. Multinational companies, even where they have not been nationalised, will be reluctant to invest. And for reasons not altogether clear to me, newly established revolutionary governments appear to suffer more than their just share of floods, droughts, earthquakes and other natural disasters.

In seeking to rebuild the economy, the revolutionary regime must make decisions, necessarily interlinked, about three key structures: those of production, exchange and control. The principal control over the economy inevitably rests with the state. This is not simply because the great majority of modern revolutionary governments espouse some form of Marxism. It may be quite as much the other way round; one of the great attractions of Marxism is as an ideology of state control. But at all events, a regime bent on reconstructing the social order will have to ensure that it directs the economy, regardless of formal ideological affiliation. Day-to-day management may none the less vary to a significant degree, in response both to political factors and to the practical inadequacies of a state bureaucracy (and especially an underdeveloped one emerging from a period of revolutionary upheaval) as an agency for economic management. One possibility is to hand over management to another and possibly more efficient branch of the state, such as the army in Cuba in 1968-70, in the hope that it could instil some military discipline into the workers.[12] Petty trading, often a target for state management because in pre-revolutionary times it was managed by politically exposed, small capitalist communities accused of exploitation, proves particularly difficult to run through a state bureaucracy. President Samora Machel of Mozambique announced in exasperation in 1978 that 'our state cannot waste energy selling needles and razor blades or running tea-rooms and barbers' shops', and arrangements were made to return at least some of the 'people's shops' to private management.[13] There are two other areas where economic control has directly political as well as practical implications. One is the management of major extractive industries, such as Gulf Oil in Angola, which may remain in the hands of foreign multinationals for essentially technical reasons, but involves in the process the maintenance of links with the developed capitalist economies; this in turn is closely linked to the structure of distribution. The second and in many ways more important is the control of agricultural land, where the choice rests essentially between the state on the one hand, and the peasants on the other. The most important single impetus for peasant participation in the revolution, at any rate in societies with estate or plantation agriculture or severe exploitation by landlords, will have been the promise of gaining control over their own land. Unregulated peasant production, however, is likely to be heavily oriented towards subsistence, and in the absence of any mechanism for extracting a surplus from them, peasants will consume the greater part of it themselves. This may lead not simply to a drop in export revenues, but to a critical fall in food stocks in the cities, such as occurred within two years of the revolution in both Ethiopia and Mozambique.[14] Some system of collectivisation or state farming then becomes essential, in order to enable the regime to maintain its urban base and balance of payments, state farms being the usual solution for efficiently organised large capitalist units of agricultural production (whether previously owned by indigenous landowners, settlers or multinationals) where the existing workforce is taken over by the state with very little change in their condition. State farms in turn suffer from problems of bureaucratic mismanagement, which may lead to a swing back towards the peasantry, as happened in Mozambique after the 1983 FRELIMO party congress.

The structures of production and exchange are for most purposes two sides of the same coin. What do you make? Who do you sell it to? What do you buy in exchange? The key choices are between a 'balanced' and an 'unbalanced' structure of production, and between a structure of exchange geared to external markets and one geared to domestic needs. Both choices turn on the possibility of changing an inherited structure of highly unbalanced production geared largely to external markets. The most thoroughgoing attempt to reorient the structure of exchange by cutting off the economy from the outside world was that pursued by the Khmer Rouge regime in Kampuchea, where it was aided by the existing concentration of agricultural production on the staple food crop, rice; the same option would scarcely have been open to an economy such as Cuba, though in any event the Kampuchean experiment was aborted by the 1978-9 Vietnamese invasion. Cuba, however, provides the best example of an attempt to reorient the structure of production by diversifying into a balanced economy which would lessen dependence on monocrop sugar cultivation. As Boorstein notes, the rationale behind this was simple: find out what imperialism had been doing, and then do the opposite.[15] This meant rapid industrialisation and growing domestically marketable crops in place of sugar. Within five years both programmes had been abandoned in the face of the drop in export earnings caused by declining sugar production, and by 1970 the target had switched to the opposite extreme: the subordination of all other economic tasks to the priority of producing ten million tons of sugar. This was equally disastrous. In contrast the 'pragmatic' economic policies of the 1970s, geared largely to market conditions and material incentives, proved extremely effective in raising annual GDP growth from 1.1 per cent in the 1960s to 6.0 per cent in the 1970s.[16]

A more specific structure of exchange is the trading bloc of which a state forms a part. Only two of the third world revolutionary states belong to the CMEA (or Comecon), these being Cuba which joined in 1972, and Vietnam in 1978. This is not entirely from choice, since both Laos and Mozambique applied to join in the late 1970s but were rejected, evidently because Eastern European states feared that membership would require them to subsidise poor third world economies, in a way that has evidently happened with Cuba.[17] Cuba undertook some 70 per cent of its overseas trade with the CMEA by 1972,[18] and Vietnam probably a similar percentage by 1978, though it remains open to the advantages of trade outside the bloc.[19] Membership also has implications in terms of dependence both on the Soviet Union and on a bureaucratic structure of domestic economic management. Other third world revolutionary states have conducted very little trade with the CMEA (the highest being Ethiopia, 7 per cent of whose exports went to the CMEA by 1979, the equivalent figures for Mozambique being 1 per cent and for Angola zero),[20] and have in consequence remained closely integrated economically with the capitalist industrial states. Ethiopia, along with a number of self-proclaimed Marxist-Leninist states such as Benin and Congo, is associated through the Lomé Conventions with the European Community, while Angola and Mozambique have also expressed an intention to join when the Convention is renegotiated in 1984. This affiliation does not necessarily negate the revolutionary credentials of the states concerned. What it does do, since revolution in the third world is often seen as a means of escape from external economic dependence as much as from domestic exploitation, is to raise in sharp form the question of just what difference a revolution makes.

What Difference Does Revolution Make?

In assessing the amount of hope — or threat — which revolution has to offer third world states and peoples, it is essential to start with two warnings. The first is that systematic comparative data with any high degree of reliability is extremely hard to come by. So far as statistical data goes, third world figures are in any event often unreliable, and the greatest gaps occur in just those revolutionary states which most interest us. Statistical services may be disrupted, and in a key state such as Kampuchea, especially after 1975, the degree of chaos is such that no figures of any kind are available beyond the biased claims of highly interested parties. Revolutionary regimes especially may withhold figures (whether because of paranoia or because they are potentially discreditable) and may well falsify them. Then again, a fairly long view is needed to assess the effects of revolution, particularly if the immediate aftermath is one of violence and economic decline, and many third world revolutionary regimes are too recently established to give much guidance; only North Korea, Cuba and Vietnam are more than a quarter of a century old, and in Vietnam's case war and unification with South Vietnam in 1975 exclude it from long-term assessment. Nor are revolutionary regimes validly lumped together as a single category: Cuba, Kampuchea and Ethiopia may all 'count' as revolutions, but one cannot, so to speak, add them all together and divide by three to discover what a revolution does. The degree of variation is certainly no less than is found, say, with military regimes, and in many respects may be more. Secondly, however, it would be a great mistake to recoil from the hazards of comparison to the easy cynicism of 'plus ça change, plus c'est la même chose'. Some things change, some things don't, but anything that can plausibly be described as a revolution will certainly have made, for better or worse, dramatic differences to the lives of many of the people living under it.

The area in which the clearest case can be made for the effects of revolution concerns the distribution of social benefits. Many revolutionary regimes, for example, have made enormous and very successful efforts in the field of literacy and education. Cuba had by 1976 an adult literacy rate of 96 per cent, exceeded only by Romania among sixty-four middle- and low-income countries, though several capitalist states (including Trinidad as the most directly comparable) come close.[21] Somalia's astonishing increase from 2 per cent to 60 per cent between 1960 and 1976 is due to its Marxist period after1969, though I am uncertain whether this should be classed as a revolution. Similar efforts have been made in Mozambique and Ethiopia. Health is harder to assess, but it cannot be coincidental that Vietnam and China are (with Sri Lanka) among the three states with a GNP *per capita* income under \$500 in 1979 and a life expectancy over 60, while Cuba (along with Romania and Albania, but also neighbouring Jamaica) was among six states with income under \$2,000 and life expectancy over 70.[22]

Income distribution figures are too fragmentary to be of any value: it is much easier to postulate that nobody is very rich in revolutionary states than that nobody is very poor, but a good case has been made that Cuba has achieved an even level of distribution of social services and basic needs, without any significant increase in national income.[23] There is indeed no evidence at all that third world revolutionary states have achieved any higher rate of economic growth than their capitalist counterparts, and the balance of evidence goes the other way.[24] The fact that the most successful, North Korea, has been exceeded by South Korea shows how careful one must be in separating the criterion of revolution from other factors.

The fact that revolutions produce, on the whole, states more ruthless and efficient than their predecessors may well be a mixed blessing for those who live under them, even though the actual apparatus is often much more ramshackle than any idealised model of it would suggest. Most revolutionary states have, not surprisingly, a bad record in terms of any western liberal conception of 'human rights', and are adamantly opposed to testing their claims for popular support through any contested election, even in those rare cases (such as Grenada) where conditions are peaceful and the population familiar with electoral procedures. It is indeed central to the idea of a revolution that it should be irreversible, and this implies the denial of any means by which the people could, if they wished, reverse it. Revolutionary or liberation wars may involve a high level of destruction of human life, but by no means all revolutionary regimes go through any large-scale terror after they have seized power; the chief exceptions here are the extermination campaigns of the Khmer Rouge, and the Red Terror (combined with a high loss of life in the various secessionist wars) in Ethiopia. Revolutions do frequently, however, result in a large-scale exodus of refugees, going well beyond the simple flight of the privileged strata of the old social order. The centralising nationalism of many revolutions often leads to a rejection (save on terms they will not accept) of ethnic or regional minorities, such as the Somalis and Eritreans in Ethiopia or the Chinese community in Vietnam, but this cannot account, say, for the level of refugee emigration from Cuba. Political imprisonment sometimes reaches high levels, especially in the form (as in Mozambique and Vietnam) of compulsory re-education camps. The conscription of the workforce for military or economic purposes generally far exceeds that in non-revolutionary states.

At a different level of concern is the question of whether revolution affects the nature of the third world state itself. I have already suggested that what revolution offers is the intensification of a concept of statehood common to almost all third world leaders. What most impressed Afro-Asian leaders during their almost obligatory visits to China during the later years of Chairman Mao was, I have heard it suggested, the sheer scale of organisation and power represented by mass gymnastic displays. What is not so clear is whether this increased level of power is the result of some qualitative change in the way the state is run, or whether it is just the result of greater ruthlessness (applied, in the case of the Chinese gymnasts, to a people whose cultural characteristics are so different from those of the people whom admiring African visitors have to govern that it is hard to sort out what is due to revolution at all). The rulers of a revolutionary state are not vastly different from their non-revolutionary counterparts; it is a government of the same educated elite, though of its initially more excluded, embittered and ideologically oriented members. There is, however, a more readily recognisable and enforceable ethos of public behaviour, which at least helps to limit the grosser forms of personal exploitation of subjects by rulers, and in so far as this works and is accepted, it points to the real difference that revolution may make: it may create the basis for a *public* ethic of behaviour which limits, and perhaps replaces, the essentially private ethos of the neo-patrimonial state, and thus makes possible the formation of legitimate institutions. I emphasise the 'may'; there is nothing magic about it. Revolutionary states are often filled with exhortations to officials (as well as the rest of the people) to behave in the prescribed manner, which may indicate the enforcement of public norms, but also show that these are being flouted. Blatant cases of personalist behaviour by leaders such as Kim Il Sung in North Korea scarcely pass much sense of public goals to people lower down. But the possibility is there, reinforced by the sense of nationalism which revolution often intensifies, of constructing a state on the basis of shared sets of responsibilities between rulers and people, and thus sustaining a government which is stable internally, and assured and autonomous in its dealings with the outside world.

This raises one of the most important problems of revolution. If third world states are dependent parts of a global system which they can do nothing to control, what difference can be made by changing the internal structure of their individual governments? In many respects, revolution does little to reduce dependence, and may even increase it by intensifying economic and strategic difficulties which call for rescue from outside. The Ethiopian revolutionary regime of Mengistu Haile-Mariam has in part (though by no means only) survived because of external military help, while the Khmer Rouge regime in Kampuchea was (again at least in part) overthrown because it had cut itself off from outside patrons. Economically, the United States' severance of relations with Cuba forced Castro to look for alternative markets (and a scarcely less dependent relationship) with Comecon and the Soviet Union, while the Angolans (since the Americans have not been so foolish as to repeat their Cuban mistake) continue to depend on revenues generated by an American multinational despite their sharp differences with the United States government. An island such as Grenada, which meets the severest standards of global economic insignificance, has no prospect whatever of achieving any process of autonomous economic development. The logical corollary of the view that exploitation and under-development are inevitable consequences of the structure of the world economic system, is that only global revolution can do anything to remove them.

And yet there is some evidence of autonomy. Strategic assistance to third world revolutionary regimes is a matter more often of protecting them against external enemies than of enabling oppressive regimes to impose themselves on their own people – the two great exceptions in this respect, if either can be classed as revolutionary, being the governments of Heng Samrin in Kampuchea and Babrak Karmal in Afghanistan. The Cuban and Vietnamese governments have been secure enough to be able to engage in large-scale foreign military intervention on their own accounts. And the economic ups and downs of revolutionary governments, as most clearly indicated by Cuba, are the result of their own decisions quite as much as of international economic forces. Their generally rather weak developmental record cannot simply be ascribed to a lack of control over their own economies. The promise which revolution offers third world leaders and peoples of securing control over their own destinies, is one which can only be realised at the cost of a great deal of stress and suffering, and through a shrewd combination of determination and initiative with a recognition of the limitations imposed, both internally and externally, by the structure of the world in which they operate; but it is not altogether false.

Notes

1. B. Szajkowski, *Marxist Governments: A World Survey* (Macmillan, 1981).
2. S.P. Huntington, *Political Order in Changing Societies* (Yale University Press, 1968), Chapter 5.
3. Ibid., pp. 266-8.

4. P. Chabal, *Amilcar Cabral: Revolutionary Leadership and People's War* (Cambridge University Press, 1983), pp. 24-5, 175-6.

5. G. Chaliand, *Revolution in the Third World* (Harvester, 1977), pp. 39-50.

6. J.C. Scott, *The Moral Economy of the Peasant: Rebellion and Subsistence in Southeast Asia* (Yale University Press, 1976); J.C. Scott and B. Kerkvliet, 'How Traditional Rural Patrons Lose Legitimacy: A Theory with Special Reference to Southeast Asia' in S.W. Schmidt *et al., Friends, Followers and Factions: A Reader in Political Clientelism* (University of California Press, 1977).

7. Chabal, *Amilcar Cabral*, p. 79.

8. Ibid., p. 177 *et seq.*

9. X. Smiley, 'Zimbabwe, Southern Africa, and the Rise of Robert Mugabe', *Foreign Affairs*, vol. 58, no. 5 (1980), pp. 1060-83.

10. W. Leogrande, 'Republic of Cuba' in Szajkowski, *Marxist Governments: A World Survey*, vol. 2, pp. 240-2.

11. See ibid., p. 243.

12. Ibid., pp. 243-4.

13. B. Munslow, 'Peasants, Politics and Production: The Case of Mozambique', *Political Studies Association of the U.K.* (Exeter, 1980), p. 15; see also *The Annual Register 1980* (Longman, 1981), p. 249.

14. Munslow, ibid., p. 11; *The Annual Register 1976*, p. 214.

15. E. Boorstein, *The Economic Transformation of Cuba* (Monthly Review, 1968), p. 182.

16. World Bank, *World Development Report 1981* (Oxford University Press, 1981), Table 2; E. Mesa-Lago, *Cuba in the 1970s* (University of New Mexico, 1978), Chapter 2.

17. See P. Wiles (ed.), *The New Communist Third World* (Croom Helm, 1982), p. 364.

18. Mesa-Lago, *Cuba in the 1970s*, p. 18.

19. See Wiles, *The New Communist Third World*, pp. 348-9.

20. *World Development Report 1981*, Table 11.

21. Ibid., Table 23.

22. Ibid., Table 1.

23. J.I. Dominguez, *Cuba: Order and Revolution* (Harvard University Press, 1978).

24. C. Young, *Ideology and Development in Africa* (Yale University Press, 1982), Table 6.5; the final chapter of this book provides an excellent appraisal of the effects of different forms of government on development in Africa.

9 CONCLUSION

Politics, in the third world as elsewhere, is very largely concerned with the immediate problems of management and survival. In concentrating on the state, and the dilemmas of those who run it, I have therefore tried to show how third world politics works. In the process, I have ignored many of the wider questions which themselves go unasked in the day-to-day business of government. The most basic of these questions is: what does this politics actually *do* for the people whose lives are shaped by it? And whatever allowance is made for variations between states, it is hard to regard the politics of the third world, from the viewpoint of those at the receiving end, as anything but deeply unsatisfactory. The moral purposes for which political institutions exist may ultimately be reduced to two. The first and most important is security: to keep people safe from violence, and to provide them with reasonable opportunities to enjoy whatever benefits the resources of the world in which they live can make available to them. The second is the opportunity to express their own aspirations in the way in which that world is organised, at least in so far as these aspirations can be reconciled with those of others. In neither respect is the record of the third world state a good one.

The third world state's failure to provide the most basic requirement of physical safety should not be exaggerated. The one thing which it *does* on the whole impose is a framework of order, the breakdown of which is the exception, not the rule. This framework is none the less appreciably less effective than in other parts of the world. The state *is* fragile, and on occasion, as in Lebanon or Chad, proves quite unable to control the conflicts which arise within it. Sometimes, as in Uganda, it may break apart beneath the pressure of its own mismanagement. But as the Ugandan case helps to demonstrate, the state is not just the solution to the problem of ensuring physical safety: it is also part of the problem. The rulers of weak and artificial states, only too aware of the feebleness of the instrument on which they have to rely, are all the more determined to suppress any expression of opposition; while in Afghanistan, Kampuchea and Salvador, the state itself, heavily backed by foreign force, becomes the primary instrument of violence directed against many of its own people. The failure of the state is most sharply illuminated by the growth in the numbers of refugees, people for whom their own state has so utterly failed to provide the basic necessities of existence that they prefer to leave it altogether for a wretched existence beyond its frontiers. Sometimes, as for the famished people struggling over the border from Mozambique into Zimbabwe in early 1984, the failure is an economic one, though exacerbated by political turmoil. More often, it is directly political: the result of an attempt by central government to impose a state of a kind which (whether for ethnic or more explicitly ideological reasons) is unacceptable to many of those who would be forced to live under it: Vietnam, Kampuchea, Afghanistan, Palestine, Namibia, Ethiopia, Equatorial Guinea. The problem is most intense in Africa, where states are for the most part smaller, boundaries more artificial and more easily crossed, than in Asia. Africa has by far the largest number of refugees in relation to its population of any part of the world. But the misery created by enforcing state control onto a reluctant population is much more widely spread.

Inefficiency and exploitation are less dramatic than violence, but more common. Again, the variation in the extent to which states are concerned to achieve a better life for their people needs to be emphasised. But the extractive role of the state, the degree to which it extorts revenues from its people in order to provide benefits for a privileged group of government employees and hangers-on, is very much more evident than in industrial capitalist or even socialist countries. In any society, one of the functions of the state is to divert resources (perhaps entirely laudably) from producers to consumers, and from those with less to those with more political influence. Where third world states are in some degree distinctive is the small and self-perpetuating nature of the group of beneficiaries. Resources tend to be redistributed from the countryside to the towns, away from the food and cash-crop producing sector of the economy towards that sector most dependent on imported goods, and within the towns towards a group most conveniently described as the bureaucratic bourgeoisie. Inefficiency and exploitation are both expressed through a neo-patrimonial pattern of social relationships, and most evidently through corruption, which simultaneously benefits those with political influence and distorts the application of any universalist criteria for running an organisation or allocating its benefits. While the external economy and especially the multinational corporation are often treated as the villains of the piece, their role is often just to act as the mechanism through which domestic elites extract a surplus from their own economy, and establish a clientelist relationship with the external world. The role of the corporation ceases to be a 'problem' once the state itself becomes efficient and accountable.

As a vehicle for expressing the aspirations of its people, the third world state has one great success to its credit: the achievement of national independence. Colonialism failed, and has almost entirely disappeared from the earth, because it had no means of combatting its subjects' desire to be ruled by a government drawn from their own kind, which could command an allegiance which an alien regime could not. Colonial regimes could go peacefully, or they could try to cling on by force, but sooner or later they had to go. This was, of course, a process in which many aspects of colonial government and economic management were carried over into the independent state, and shaped the extent to which popular aspirations could actually be realised. It was also one in which the aspirations of the mass of colonised peoples were shared and led by their educated elites, and in which the benefits accruing to those who took over the formerly colonial administration were substantially greater than those accruing to the mass. Expressing aspirations against an indigenous ruling group has been a much more difficult business. In the few third world states which escaped formal colonialism, where power remained in the hands of a local monarch or oligarchy, equivalent demands for participation have often arisen, on which the younger educated elite could draw in order to overthrow a system which they regarded as anachronistic, sometimes to such an extent as to lead to revolutionary change (as in Ethiopia) rather than just constitutional reform (as in Thailand). An entrenched state structure controlled by a united and established elite group has, however, proved extremely hard to dislodge, and the great majority of regimes forced to cede power in response to popular pressure have been military governments with peculiar difficulties of political organisation, and sometimes an enfeebling doubt about their own legitimacy. Only a very small number of states have maintained competitive electoral and party systems which ensure a periodic accountability of the government to the electorate. Elsewhere, competitive elections have usually been held by military regimes seeking to hand over to an acceptable successor and have not led to the creation of any stable multi-party democracy; usually, they have been followed within a few years by further military intervention. The revolutionary state claims at least to provide another mechanism through which the aspirations of its people can be achieved. In some degree it may succeed, though at the cost of restricting these aspirations to ones that can be realised through an intensely mobilised and ruthless state, and of killing, subjecting or driving into exile those who fail to share them. Revolutionary regimes are scarcely less prone than military ones to blame all current problems simplistically on a group of readily identifiable enemies — the bourgeoisie, the international capitalist system — whose removal lays the foundation for a better life, even though the engineering required to create that better life is of a much more thoroughgoing kind than the constitutional tinkering that the military are prone to indulge in.

The maintenance of the state, and thus its ability to achieve its goals in so far as it can do so at all, depends on its access to the outside world, both for military and for economic help. The more artificial and threatened it is, the greater the need for external support. This support comes both from the industrial states and from fellow third world ones, all of which have a general interest in maintaining the global state structure, even though particular states may have specific local interests in undermining parts of it. In the case of the African states, which are the most artificial and threatened of all, the Organisation of African Unity has found it necessary to articulate explicit rules of respect for state boundaries and non-intervention in the internal affairs of other states; these rules, in turn, can only be policed by the industrial states, either through arms supplies to indigenous governments or in extreme cases through direct military intervention. Intervention, which is easily condemned as a derogation of the sovereign independence of third world states, may ultimately be the only means through which the state system can be maintained in the face of the weakness of third world states themselves. The more pressing danger is then not that external intervention may make a mockery of the state's independence, true enough though that may be, but that it may offer no benefit sufficient to induce external states to run the risk of intervening at all. Politically as well as economically, the weaker third world states may be endangered not so much by the industrial world's exploitation as by its neglect. Propping up the Chadian state, like propping up the Ghanaian economy, could scarcely be regarded by any industrial state as a cost-effective exercise.

Though deep-seated social and economic problems underlie many of the failures of the third world state, these failures themselves are in key respects *political* ones, for which political solutions must be found before there is much chance of improvement in economy or social structure. And even though the nature of the state is in many respects the source of the problem, there is still no alternative to the state as a mechanism for trying to achieve solutions. The revolutionary *götterdämmerung* which seeks to destroy the entire state structure as the source of exploitation has nothing to put in its place but another state structure, perhaps more attuned to local aspirations but in key respects little different from the old one, which it hopes will rise from the ashes. The short-term costs of destroying the state are all too evident, the possible long-term benefits of replacing it very much less so.

If the state is accepted as the inevitable framework for political action, then the way out of the vicious circle of irresponsibility, illegitimacy and ineffectiveness lies in the incorporation of the governing elites into a set of shared values which acknowledge their accountability to the governed. Since accountability in itself implies the acceptance of universal values of honesty and efficiency in place of the particularistic values of the neo-patrimonial state, it may be taken to imply the creation of more effective institutions capable of achieving goals such as economic development and gaining, ultimately, the accolade of popular legitimacy. The problem is not where you should be trying to go, but how you should get there. And the most evident tragedy of third world states lies in the fact that many of those comparatively few states which have seemed to be in a position to build effective institutions on the basis of shared values have dramatically failed to do so. Chile (for long apparently the home of the most effective liberal democratic political structure in South America) and Argentina are the most striking examples. In these cases the most evident source of the problem, expressed in the concept of bureaucratic authoritarianism, has been the refusal of those elites which control the state to accept the diminution in their position of privilege which accountability would imply, and their willingness to resort to repression in order to protect it. Something of the same difficulty may be seen in Pakistan, though there the nature of any civilian political order is much more problematical; while in Turkey the problem appears to lie in the structure of civilian political leadership and organisation, quite as much as in the military or civil bureaucracy. The Philippines is another state where an acceptable political order appears to be possible but is none the less some way from achievement. In Mexico, the great transition appears to have been achieved; in India, in its perpetually perplexing way, partially so. But there are a great many third world states, especially in Africa, where no stable and effective political order is remotely in prospect, and where the best hope is for reasonably skilful and honest government of an inevitably personalist kind. It would be straining optimism to suggest that they will get it.

BIBLIOGRAPHICAL NOTE

The following list of books, arranged very broadly according to the chapters in this book to which they most closely correspond, is simply intended to provide some ideas for further reading about third world politics. I have for the most part excluded books concerned with a particular country or region of the third world, and apologise to all those authors whose works I have omitted. The possible candidates for inclusion are endless, and my own reading largely determines what I have picked.

Chapter 1: Politics and the Third World

The only two brief introductions to third world politics of which I am aware are both now about a decade old: G.A. Heeger, *The Politics of Underdevelopment* (Macmillan, 1974) is shorter and more straightforwardly political; R.E. Gamer, *The Developing Nations: A Comparative Perspective* (Allyn & Bacon, 1976) includes material on pre-colonial political systems, and social and economic change. Paul Harrison, *Inside the Third World* (Penguin, 1981) provides a readable and committed survey, and also includes a useful list of further readings. The most convenient ready source of comparative statistics about third world and other states is the *World Development Report* (annual, Oxford University Press for The World Bank), though the *United Nations Statistical Yearbook* (annual, UN) is also useful. M. Kidron and R. Segal, *The State of the World Atlas* (Pan, 1981) provides a fascinating collection of politically relevant maps.

On theoretical approaches, G.A. Almond and G.B. Powell, *Comparative Politics: A Developmental Approach* (Little, Brown, 1966) is an interesting example of a now outmoded genre, while S.P. Huntington, *Political Order in Changing Societies* (Yale University Press, 1968) has survived very much better. Among Marxist-oriented studies, I. Wallerstein, *The Capitalist World-Economy* (Cambridge University Press, 1979) outlines the currently most fashionable perspective, while B. Warren, *Imperialism: Pioneer of Capitalism* (Verso, 1980) is belligerently revisionist. The range of writings in this field is enormous, and I. Roxborough, *Theories of Underdevelopment* provides a useful though disappointingly brief introduction.

Chapter 2: The Colonial State and its Demise

The best general history of colonialism is D.K. Fieldhouse, *The Colonial Empires: A Comparative Survey From the Eighteenth Century* (Macmillan, 1982); V.G. Kiernan, *The European Empires from Conquest to Collapse, 1815-1960* (Leicester University Press, 1982) is also useful but excludes the Americas. L.H. Gann and P. Duignan, *Burden of Empire* (Pall Mall, 1968) provides a generally favourable overview of colonialism in tropical Africa. P. Gifford and W.R. Louis, *The Transfer of Power in Africa* (Yale University Press, 1982) looks at decolonisation mostly from the standpoint of colonial policy, while E. Kedourie, *Nationalism in Asia and Africa* (Weidenfeld, 1971) does so more from that of the colonised.

This may also be the point at which to mention a number of useful comparative volumes on the history and politics of different regions: J. Pluvier, *South-East Asia from Colonialism to Independence* (Oxford University Press, 1974); J.J. McAlister, *Southeast Asia: The Politics of National Integration* (Random House, 1973); J. Dunn, *West African States: Failure and Promise* (Cambridge University Press, 1978); R.H. Chilcote and J.C. Edelstein, *Latin America: The Struggle with Dependency and Beyond* (Wiley, 1974); F. Ambursley and R. Cohen, *Crisis in the Caribbean* (Heinemann, 1983).

Chapter 3: The Third World State

There is no general study of the third world state, but the chapters by Alavi and Saul in H. Goulbourne, *Politics and State in the Third World* (Macmillan, 1979) are helpful. There are several collections of comparative studies on neo-patrimonialism, clientelism and corruption, including S.W. Schmidt *et al.*, *Friends, Followers and Factions: A Reader in Political Clientelism* (University of California Press, 1977); C. Clapham, *Private Patronage and Public Power: Political Clientelism in the Modern State* (Pinter, 1982); S.N. Eisenstadt and R. Lemarchand, *Political Clientelism, Patronage and Development* (Sage, 1981); and A.J. Heidenheimer, *Political Corruption* (Holt, Rinehart, 1970). J.C. Scott, *The Moral Economy of the Peasant: Rebellion and Subsistence in Southeast Asia* (Yale University Press, 1976) is the outstanding introduction to the peasant view of politics.

Chapter 4: Managing the State

R.H. Jackson and C.G. Rosberg, *Personal Rule in Black Africa* (University of California Press, 1982) provides an interesting though uenven discussion of political leadership. Several useful though now dated studies of bureaucracy appear in J. Lapalombara, *Bureaucracy and Political Development* (Princeton University Press, 1963), and of parties in J. Lapalombara and M. Weiner, *Political Parties and Political Development* (Princeton University Press, 1966). Three books concerned, with the relationship between government and the 'ordinary' population are: J.M. Nelson, *Access to Power: Politics and the Urban Poor in Developing Nations* (Princeton University Press, 1979); N. Kasfir, *The Shrinking Political Arena* (University of California Press, 1976); and H.R. Tinker, *Ballot Box and Bayonet: People and Government in Emergent Asian Countries* (Oxford University Press, 1964).

Chapter 5: Managing the Economy

Books about third world economies are generally more concerned with what governments ought to do than with why they don't do it, and with international rather than domestic problems of economic management. The two Brandt Commission volumes, *North-South: A Programme for Survival* (Pan, 1980) and *Common Crisis: Co-operation for World Recovery* (Pan, 1983) are extreme examples. Two books which are rather more useful on the political problems of international economic relations are D. Seers and L. Joy, *Development in a Divided World* (Penguin, 1971) and D.H. Blake and R.S. Walters, *The Politics of Global Economic Relations* (Prentice-Hall, 1976). C. Elliott, *Patterns of Poverty in the Third World* (Praeger, 1975) is particularly useful on the effects of internal class structures and M. Lipton, *Why Poor People Stay Poor: Urban Bias in World Development* (Temple Smith, 1977) on the rural-urban gap. Crawford Young, *Ideology and Development in Africa* (Yale University Press, 1982) is an excellent analysis of the differences that government policies may make to the economy, and a useful antidote to studies which tend to assume that the structure of the global economy removes all effective choice from third world regimes.

Chapter 6: Managing the External Political Arena

C. Clapham, *Foreign Policy Making in Developing States* (Saxon House, 1977) provides a series of regional introductions to the role of foreign policy, while O. Aluko, *The Foreign Policies of African States* (Hodder, 1977) consists of individual country studies, M. Ayoob, *Conflict and Intervention in the Third World* (Croom Helm, 1980) also consists of regional case studies. J.J. Stremlau, *The Foreign Policy Priorities of Third World States* (Westview, 1982) is mostly concerned with the economics of foreign relations. R.A. Mortimer, *The Third World Coalition in International Politics* (Praeger, 1980) discusses the Non-Aligned Movement, the United Nations Conference on Trade and Development and the New International Economic Order. K.P. Sauvant, *Changing Priorities on the International Agenda* (Pergamon, 1982) is also useful.

Chapter 7: Soldier and State

S.P. Huntington, *The Soldier and the State* (Belknap, 1957) and S.E. Finer, *The Man on Horseback* (Pall Mall, 1962) are the classic studies of the role of the military in politics, often disagreed with but still a basis for reference. E. Feit, *The Armed Bureaucrats* (Houghton Mifflin, 1973) emphasises the role of the military within the state apparatus, while C.H. Enloe, *Ethnic Soldiers: State Security in Divided Societies* (Penguin, 1980) examines the potential clash between ethnicity and the military's role as guardian of the state. C. Clapham *et al.*, *The Political Dilemmas of Military Regimes* (Croom Helm, 1984) is concerned with the relationship between military governments and domestic political organisation. There are several studies of the military in particular regions of the third world, especially Africa and Latin America.

Chapter 8: The Revolutionary State

G. Chaliand, *Revolution in the Third World* (Harvester, 1977) provides a general overview, while J.W. Lewis, *Peasant Rebellion and Communist Revolution in Asia* (Stanford University Press, 1974) is concerned with the rural roots of revolution. B. Szajkowski, *Marxist Governments: A World Survey* (Macmillan, 1981) and P. Wiles, *The New Communist Third World* (Croom Helm, 1982) discuss regimes which often, though not always, have revolutionary origins. For further enlightenment, it may be best to read about individual third world revolutions and the regimes which follow from them, especially Vietnam, Cuba and Ethiopia.

INDEX

192